THE VIRTUAL OFFICE SURVIVAL HANDBOOK

What Telecommuters and Entrepreneurs Need to Succeed in Today's Nontraditional Workplace

ALICE BREDIN

John Wiley & Sons, Inc.

NewYork ▶ Chichester ▶ Brisbane ▶ Toronto ▶ Singapore

To my mother and father

Copyright © 1996 by Alice Bredin.
Published by John Wiley & Sons, Inc.

Library of Congress Cataloging-in-Publication Data

Bredin, Alice.
    The virtual office survival handbook : what telecommuters and entrepreneurs need to succeed in today's nontraditional workplace / Alice Bredin.
        p.   cm.
    Includes index.
    ISBN 0-471-12061-8 (alk. paper). — ISBN 0-471-12059-6 (pbk. : alk. paper)
    1. Home labor.   2. Home-based businesses.   3. Telecommuting.
4. Telecommuting centers.   I. Title.
HD2333.B74   1996
658'.041—dc20
                                                                                96-1327

Printed in the United States of America

10 9 8 7 6 5 4 3 2 1

CONTENTS

PART THREE   SETTING UP YOUR VIRTUAL OFFICE

Chapter 8   *Nuts and Bolts*   **112**

PART FOUR   LIFE IN THE VIRTUAL OFFICE

Chapter 9   *Structuring Your Unstructured Work Environment*   **155**

PREFACE

Before I started writing about the virtual office and running a home-based business, I worked as a freelance magazine and newspaper writer in my Greenwich Village apartment. I covered health and fitness and occasionally wrote articles for business or trade magazines. Things were going pretty well. I had variety in my work, made a decent living, and could take a nap every afternoon.

I noticed that whenever I told people that I worked at home, they were very intrigued. "What's it like to work at home?" they asked. "How do you get started?" "Aren't you tempted to watch TV?" They wanted to know what it was like to work outside of a traditional work environment, and I liked talking about it. When I met other people who worked at home, I always asked about their survival techniques. I became more interested in my work than I ever had been before. I had found a subject that really fascinated me!

At about the same time, an old friend called to see how my life was going and we talked about my growing interest in nontraditional work arrangements. He is the kind of person who has a knack for knowing the right thing to do, and said, scrap the health and fitness . . . go with the home office.

I started by interviewing 100 people who work at home, as preliminary research for what I thought would be my first book. The book never materialized, but the database of information I gathered provided the foundation for my work in this area. In my interviews, I asked dozens of questions about working in a home office to learn about people's work habits, marketing, how they resist distractions, how they set limits on work, and what they wear at home. As I became more immersed in the topic, I expanded my research to include people who worked at home as corporate telecommuters, on the road in mobile offices, or in telecommuting centers. Every variation of nontraditional work I investigated appealed to me because each enabled people to pursue professional goals without having to sacrifice personal objectives completely. When they work in a virtual office, parents spend more time with their kids, people find more satisfaction with their work and have more time to pursue hobbies, and they have the potential to reduce stress.

It gradually became clear that there are certain techniques and skills that are needed to thrive in a virtual office, and that most people learn these skills by trial and error. The successful people I spoke with had developed survival skills over time, but most said they wish they'd known more, sooner. I also realized that even people who had already mastered these skills needed ongoing support. My newspaper column, "Working At Home," and my public radio commentaries grew out of that realization.

This book is a product of what I have learned in my years researching and living this topic. If you are just starting out in a virtual office, *The Virtual Office Survival Handbook* will be a shortcut to learning the skills you'll need to know. If you are a veteran, use this book as a support tool and a means to maintain your edge.

If you would like to share any experiences from your virtual office, please contact me at BredinA@aol.com, AliceBredin_MSN, or at Tribune Media Services, 435 North Michigan Avenue, Suite 1500, Chicago, IL 60611. I am not able to respond to all my mail, but please know that I enjoy hearing from you.

Good luck!

ACKNOWLEDGMENTS

This book would not have been possible without the help of many people. I would like to thank: my husband, Stu, for his patience and support, and for his editing help; my sister, Siobhan, for her encouragement; my mother for her encouragement and professional consultation for the psychology sections of this book; Eve Tahmincioglu and Brooke Loening for helping me shape the book; my editor, P. J. Dempsey, for her enthusiasm and great ideas about how to organize and present the material; my agent, Jane Dystel, for getting this project off the ground and for her expert counsel on this book and other projects. I am grateful to the following people for their input and assistance: Chris Boyd, Nancy Cohen, Kirsten Lagatree, and Nan Warwick.

I would also like to thank all of the people who answered my questions and who were so generous with their time, including the telecommuters and entrepreneurs who shared their experiences with me. Each of you added to the value of this book.

Part One

THE EVOLUTION OF THE VIRTUAL OFFICE

WHAT IS A
VIRTUAL OFFICE?

1

DEFINING THE VIRTUAL OFFICE

A *virtual office* is any worksite outside of the traditional office in which people still do the work associated with a traditional office. People who work in a virtual office can be either *telecommuters*, who work outside of a corporate office for an employer, or *entrepreneurs*, who are self-employed. The *virtual* in the term *virtual office* implies the use of technology. Virtual offices are typically equipped with some combination of technology that enables information workers to re-create the support services of the traditional office. But there are exceptions. Some virtual offices operate with just a phone and a pad of paper.

I work in a virtual office. Technology that was either unavailable or prohibitively expensive just a few years ago is now accessible and enables me to write and run my business from home. I meet with people when I need to, but I don't have to leave my office to complete my work.

Corporate employees who work at home a few days a week work in virtual offices too. They complete most of the same tasks they would in their regular offices, except they sit at desks in their dens, spare bedrooms, garages, or other home office spaces.

Salespeople who work on the road with cellular phones, portable computers, and all kinds of other technology are also virtual office workers. These "road warriors" do as much work in their virtual offices as possible so they don't have to waste valuable time going into the office.

The exciting part of the virtual office is what it can do for people's personal lives. The virtual office has the potential to enable you to achieve professional goals without sacrificing personal objectives. Working at least part-time away from a traditional work site means you can complete your work efficiently and still have some time left over. It means you can drop your kids off a little later at day care and pick them up a little earlier. You can finally find time to stay in shape because you aren't giv-

4

ing a couple of hours a day to a commute. It means you can do the quality of work you know you are capable of because you have interruption-free time. It means you may be able to better manage all of your personal and professional responsibilities.

WHERE THE VIRTUAL OFFICE CAME FROM

One reason there are so many virtual offices today is that America has shifted from a manufacturing economy to a service- and information-based economy in which employees no longer must report to a central site to perform their jobs. The increase in the number of virtual offices has been fueled by the increasing power and affordability of office technology. The price of desktop computers dropped by roughly 40 percent in the early part of this decade, and today's personal computers are about 80 times faster than the original IBM PC. Ongoing technological developments like widespread use of the Internet, video conferencing, groupware, and digital phone technology will make the virtual office even more popular. Link Resources, a New York City–based research firm, estimates that at the end of 1995 there will be slightly more than 40 million people working at home full- or part-time. By the end of 1998, Link predicts, that number will jump to 60 million, an increase of 36 percent from 1994.

Baby boomers' demands for more flexible work arrangements have also contributed to the popularity of the virtual office. Baby boomers are increasingly dissatisfied with daily double-digit hours in the office and long commutes. The pressure of caring for children and aging parents also prompts baby boomers to look for a better way to integrate home and work life. In a 1994 Hilton Hotels survey of 1,000 professionals, 77 percent said their top priority for the next decade was spending time with family and friends. Money and prestige came in second. A 1995 survey by AT&T Home Business Resources found that wanting to be near family was one of the primary motivators in people's decision to work at home. While corporate downsizing has made many people fearful for their jobs, companies are still willing to make concessions to keep valued employees. These companies have realized that well-designed telecommuting programs can retain high performers and boost company morale.

The massive downsizing in corporate America has also contributed to the increasing popularity of the virtual office in two ways. First, employees who have left corporate jobs are starting businesses in record numbers. Second, the overworked employees left behind in corporate offices are looking for ways to improve productivity. In some cases, these workers and their managers have agreed that one way to stay on top of the workload is to do more work outside of the office, either by spending more time with clients or in home offices where there are fewer interruptions. Their conclusions are confirmed by a Booz, Allen & Hamilton study, which showed that about 25 percent of managers' time in the office is unproductive; for employees, the percentage is even higher. Telecommuters report a minimum of a 15 to 20 percent increase in productivity when they work outside of the office, a figure that their managers corroborate.

WHAT THIS BOOK WILL DO FOR YOU

So why this book? Well, for one thing, people all across the country are wondering how they can become part of this workplace revolution, or if they are already involved, how they can maximize their productivity and manage the change. People who aren't working in virtual offices yet need to know how to make a case for telecommuting to their managers or how to evaluate the various entrepreneurial opportunities.

People who currently work in virtual offices need help managing the psychological components of their work arrangement. Working outside of the traditional corporate environment has the potential to reduce work-related stress, but it can also *create* stress if not handled properly. There is increased stress from things like technological glitches that are difficult to resolve without a computer-services department nearby, and setbacks with no coworkers and managers around to commiserate with. Working in a virtual office also can become addictive. It begins with a drive for success and is fueled by the adrenaline high that can come from working under pressure and the gratification that is part of professional accomplishment. This book contains strategies for managing stress and maintaining a work/life balance in the virtual office.

The Virtual Office Survival Handbook shows you how to take charge of your schedule. Working according to your own clock and deadlines may sound ideal, but the reality is sometimes different. It is not unusual for people to have trouble managing this freedom, especially initially. After all, most of us have very little experience with it. We've spent most of our lives in the structured environment of a school or a company. The challenge of designing and controlling a schedule can generate stress in itself.

This survival guide will also teach you how to manage the technology you use to stay in touch with customers, coworkers, and managers. Most of us use technology for important communications every day and are judged constantly on how we present ourselves. Therefore, it is ironic that very few people are trained in communicating effectively via the phone, fax, e-mail, conference calls, and newer technologies.

WHO WORKS IN THE VIRTUAL OFFICE?

The term *virtual office worker* encompasses entrepreneurs and telecommuters. Virtual office workers, whether they work for themselves or someone else, share many concerns and problems and may find certain sections of this book relevant. But the two groups also have different concerns. Entrepreneurs, for example, probably don't need to read "Negotiating a Telecommuting Position" in chapter 3. Likewise, corporate telecommuters may not be concerned with the sections that discuss pricing and marketing a product. Throughout this book, when necessary, I will address entrepreneurs and corporate telecommuters separately.

TYPES OF VIRTUAL OFFICES

The most common types of virtual office work setups are home offices, telecommuting centers, mobile offices and hoteling. This section defines each and discusses its benefits and drawbacks.

Home Offices
A home office can be a room, a portion of a room, a hallway, a garage, or any other space you choose to work in. See chapter 8 for the details on what kind of office qualifies for home-office tax deductions.

The primary advantage of working at home is that it makes it easier for people to run their lives. Those who have to drop children off at school or take care of a sick parent can juggle their personal and professional responsibilities better if they aren't rushing to the office every day on a fixed schedule. Dropping the daily commute may also free up time for other activities such as time with a spouse or children, exercise, or hobbies.

Working at home also means fewer meetings and interruptions. Not surprisingly, this often translates into productivity gains. The study by AT&T Home Business Resources found that 80 percent of work-at-home entrepreneurs say they are more productive at home than they were in a traditional office. An overall increase in control over scheduling can improve your sense of satisfaction and can lead to a higher quality of work. This increased feeling of control over your work and your life cuts down significantly on stress levels.

The downside of working at home is that it can be lonely and stressful. You may find yourself missing water-cooler conversation and looking for substitutes for the interaction you had in the office. (I now know my neighbors, and can tell you all the details of my UPS delivery man's recent wedding.) Juggling a variety of responsibilities without the support of a traditional office can also prove stressful. You may feel the temptation to provide instantaneous responses to the information and requests that pour in via faxes, pagers, voice mail, and electronic mail. Also, while it's nice to be able to enjoy family life and take care of personal tasks with more flexibility, increased exposure to your personal life can create stress. Without a commute to start your day, for example, it may be hard to define when getting ready for work ends and the work day begins. Or your neighbors may be tempted to use you as the local package delivery drop.

A telecommuting center is a site where employees work, usually part-time, outside of a central corporate office. These centers are either used by employees from one company or shared by employees from several different employers.

Telecommuting Centers

The federal government and companies like NYNEX and GTE run centers for their employees. These centers differ from branch offices in that workers are grouped based on where they live, not what function they perform for the company.

Multi-employer centers are a variant of this idea and at the printing of this book are used by Kaiser Permanente, Healthnet, the Army Corps of Engineers, and AT&T. Many multi-employer centers have had difficulty finding tenants for their centers, and some have closed because of a lack of interest. Some of the centers that *are* making it at this point are in a "demonstration phase" and are being subsidized by federal, state, or local governments. Others are targeting small and home-based businesses. The Landmark Executive Offices and Telework Center in Anaheim, California, for example, has almost filled its space with entrepreneurs; only 15 percent of its space is used by corporate telecommuters.

Telecommuting centers can offer many of the advantages of working in a home office without some of the disadvantages. Centers present fewer distractions than a home office and more opportunity for social and professional interaction. They also can provide access to computer networks, secretarial services, conference rooms, and copiers, which are not always available at home. In addition, some supervisors feel more comfortable with employees working at another office site rather than in the home.

In *Telecommuting Centers and Related Concepts*, Michael Bagley, Jill Mannering, and Patricia Mokhtarian at the University of California, Davis, Institute of Transportation Studies report that centers can benefit people who otherwise might not have the opportunity to work at home. "Affluent professional workers are likely to have adequate space in the home, and to be able to afford their own personal computer and other costs associated with home-based telecommuting. But it is desirable to extend the personal and societal advantages of telecommuting to a broader segment of the workforce, and telecommuting centers may be able to do that." Telecommuting centers also may give support staff and administrative workers an opportunity to telecommute in the future.

The major barrier to widespread use of telecommuting centers is their cost. For obvious reasons, home offices are much less expensive.

Mobile Offices

The term *mobile office* describes a car, or sometimes even a briefcase, used by people who spend a lot of time on the road. These "road warriors" have all the technology and other tools they need in their mobile office to complete their work without returning to the central office. They complete their work in their mobile office, at a client site, or in a home office, and go to the corporate office only for meetings, to pick up mail, or for support services that are not available elsewhere.

Enabling mobile workers to spend more time with their clients through technology is appealing to employers. The same technology that allows mobile workers to keep in touch enables them to improve productivity and spend more time with clients. At the client's location, mobile workers use computers to access inventory information, process orders, and provide quick turnaround for all kinds of services. Employers also save on real estate costs by having mobile workers do the bulk of their desk work outside of the company office.

AT&T reports that mobile offices have increased by 15 to 20 percent the amount of time salespeople spend with customers. Mobile workers who are available in their home offices before 9 A.M. and after 5 P.M. also make global business easier to conduct.

IBM's Andre'a Chetam, manager of the national mobility project office, says IBM's decision to move its marketing and service sales force out into the field has had the desired effect. Chetam says these highly paid professionals are spending more time with customers and showed productivity improvements of up to 10 percent in 1994.

The personal effect of mobile work varies. Some mobile workers say they are glad they do not have to return to the office because it saves time and energy. Keeping in touch with work teams via voice mail, e-mail, fax, and other technology works well for these people. But some people are not so satisfied with the new mobility. They enjoyed trips to the office as a break from the sometimes lonely life of a consultant or salesperson. For them, being moved out of the main office and keeping in contact primarily via technology is stressful and isolating.

Hoteling

Although technically not an office, *hoteling* is a catch-all term for work arrangements in which corporate employees use desks on an as-needed basis. This concept has many names, but *hoteling*, the term coined by Ernst

& Young, LLP, for its program, is my favorite because it sounds like what it is: when you need a desk, you reserve one.

Employees in hoteling arrangements do not have assigned offices on a long-term basis. Armed with portable computers and other technology, these employees visit clients and perform administrative tasks on the road or from offices at home. They return to the corporate office for meetings or when they need other support services.

Thousands of IBM salespeople no longer have offices. In the New York–New Jersey area, for example, IBM has closed a number of sales offices. It now requires 700 employees to report to a warehouse in Cranford, New Jersey, when they need a desk. In this facility, there are no private offices—just desks in a 100,000-square-foot building with exposed heating and air-conditioning ducts painted in bright colors.

When salespeople arrive at the facility, they are assigned a cubicle with a telephone, electrical outlets, and some office supplies. Incoming phone calls are automatically routed to that cubicle's extension. Each salesperson is assigned two file drawers in the cabinets that line the halls.

At Ernst & Young, auditors also use hoteling. They call ahead to a hoteling coordinator when they need office space. By the time they arrive in the office, support staff have stocked an office with supplies, hooked up computers, and brought in files and personal effects (family pictures and so on) from the hoteler's storage space. The hoteling coordinator has a database on each hoteler and adds any requests the hoteler has to the list of things to be moved into the office.

The coordinator who assigns an auditor to an office enters the office location into a computerized system so that anyone can find the hoteler by typing the name on a touch-sensitive computer screen in the elevator lobby on each floor. As with IBM's system in Cranford, the employee's direct-dial number is also routed to the temporary office space.

Managers are motivated to offer hoteling primarily because it has been shown to increase the amount of time employees spend at client locations. It is also a way for employers to save money on real estate. According to Cornell University's International Facility Management Program (IFMP), a consortium of private- and public-sector organizations studying the effectiveness of alternative work arrangements, desk space often is unused in traditional offices. IFMP case studies found that field salespeople, management consultants, project managers, and customer service people are at their desks only 25 to 30 percent of the time. Ernst and Young has experienced a 15 to 20 percent real estate savings, despite an increased head count. IBM consolidated its New York–New Jersey sales force from 400,000 square feet of office space spread around the area to a single 100,000-square-foot warehouse.

Other names for similar but not identical concepts include *unassigned offices*; *free-address, nonterritorial offices*; *Just In Time* (a term coined by Anderson Consulting); and *hotdesking* (a slightly pejorative term with origins in the Navy's bunk-sharing by sailors on different shifts). At the far end of the continuum is the virtual office, a term that encompasses all of these concepts. It was pioneered by Chiat-Day, where most individual offices have been abolished. Employees keep personal items in lockers, sign out portable phones and computers at a concierge desk when they arrive for work, and work in project rooms.

Is the Virtual Office Right for You?

Assessing Your Skills and Work Habits

To work successfully on your own as an entrepreneur or a telecommuter, you need to know your strengths and weaknesses. Understanding these tendencies will allow you to capitalize on what you do well and compensate for your weak areas. With this knowledge, you will be better able to manage your work and your personal life in your virtual office.

The Quick Home Office Readiness Survey that begins on page 12 will assess your ability to manage time, deal with challenges, resist distractions, obtain motivation, and create and maintain work/life balance. A quiz at the end of the chapter will test your tendency toward overachievement or underachievement.

ALICE BREDIN'S QUICK HOME OFFICE READINESS SURVEY

The content of this survey was created in conjunction with Katherine Crowley, a New York City–based psychotherapist and consultant to entrepreneurs. The survey was created by The Potomac Group, Inc., a Cambridge, Massachusetts–based company that provides business and technology evaluation, advisement, and education. This survey is excerpted from a software package titled *Alice Bredin's Home Office Advisor*. For information on buying a copy, call The Potomac Group at (617) 577-1067.

Quick Home Office Readiness Survey

This survey provides a quick evaluation and pointers to recommendations in five of the key areas that you need to manage well in order to be most effective as a home office worker. These are:

The ability to manage time

The ability to deal with challenges

The ability to deal with distractions

The ability to manage business support relationships

The ability to balance business with the rest of your life

Instructions:

1. For each statement, circle the number in either the "yes" or the "no" column. If you cannot tell which to choose, circle the numbers in both columns.

2. Total the circled numbers in each column.

3. Refer to the advisory paragraphs corresponding to your evaluation score.

Time Management

	A (yes)	B (no)
I am reluctant to give myself a concrete schedule for completing daily work tasks.	1	
		1
The beginning and ending point of my work day varies greatly, depending on my work.	1	
		1
At the beginning of the day, I do not usually have a clear idea of what I want to accomplish by day's end.	1	
		1
When I am faced with many responsibilities, I have difficulty determining what to do first.	1	
		1
I often work very hard and later realize I have not accomplished some of my most important tasks.	1	
		1
Column Totals		

If Column A Totals 3 or More:

If you are not currently using time management techniques, it may be because you are concerned that a schedule and other routines will rob you of spontaneity. You may also have been unsuccessful in implementing traditional time management techniques in the past and question if they can ever work for you. But structure with room for flexibility will better serve you to complete your work with a minimum of stress and maximum efficiency. Time management can also reduce the amount of time and energy you devote to work. The key to successful time management is determining what techniques will work based on your personality and your work.

Refer to sections that cover time management, creating structure, and goal setting.

If Column B Totals 3 or More:

You are probably good at budgeting your time, prioritizing your goals, and keeping yourself on track. In fact, you may have yourself so carefully scheduled that you cannot tolerate any deviation from your plan. When things do not go according to schedule, you probably become overly frustrated. An important lesson for you to learn is that interruptions, diversions, and delays from the path you have laid out are part of life. You also need to realize that although you are now more independent, you do not have to go overboard in controlling your schedule. You need to leave some unscheduled time in your life for spontaneous activity, be willing to adjust your schedule when opportunities arise, and not be too rigid with others when scheduling. Keep in mind that planning does not have to rule out spontaneity.

Refer to sections that cover stress, enjoying your freedom, and overachiever syndrome.

Ability to deal with Challenges

	A (yes)	B (no)
When I am faced with an unfamiliar task, concern about failing causes me to postpone embarking on it.	1	1
I tend to procrastinate when faced with an unappealing task.	1	1
When I experience rejection or failure, I have a difficult time getting back on track.	1	1
When people around me do not believe in what I am doing I question my objectives.	1	1
When I encounter roadblocks, I lose my motivation and question my goals.	1	1
Column Totals		

(Continued)

If Column A Totals 3 or More:

You are probably easily derailed or delayed by rejection, failure, setbacks, negative comments, and other roadblocks. Without the support network of an office to keep you on track, you are likely to waste valuable time and energy in your independent work arrangement recovering from these situations. To avoid this pitfall, you need to learn to anticipate setbacks, better manage them when they occur, and minimize the amount of havoc they wreak after the fact. This will help you maintain your productivity and will minimize the ups and downs you experience working on your own. It is important for you to seek out the company of others when you have experienced a setback. You should also keep in mind that setbacks are part of any pursuit and that very successful people have failed many times. Lincoln was defeated in nine races for public office before being elected president!

Refer to sections that cover rejection, failure, naysayers, and goal setting.

If Column B Totals 3 or More:

You are probably unstoppable. What you need to watch for is taking your unwillingness to be derailed too far. You may be so impervious to input that you think you always know best. You may also be so difficult to dissuade that you barge ahead on projects without stopping to think a project through. Just because you move ahead without hesitation does not mean that you are always doing things in the most efficient manner. Working alone will provide you with ample opportunity to go astray, so your task is to continually examine what you are doing to make sure you are on track. When you are questioned or given input, at least consider what has been said. Put together a group of advisors you trust and with whom you can periodically check your progress.

Refer to sections that cover goal setting, time management, marketing plans, vision, and delegation.

Dealing with Distractions

	A (yes)	B (no)
When people ask me to do things during the day, it is difficult for me to say no, and I usually agree to their requests.	1	1
I often get a later start in the morning than I had planned.	1	1
When family and friends call during the day, I feel that I should make time to talk to them no matter how busy I am.	1	1
Because I have a flexible schedule, I assume the bulk of household responsibilities.	1	1
When I am bored or am faced with a difficult task I go to the refrigerator.	1	1
Column Totals		

If Column A Totals 3 or More:

Each of us has distractions that we are particularly vulnerable to. The key to managing them is to determine what is most likely to take you away from your work, and then develop a strategy for coping with them. If responses to requests from family and friends eat up your day, you may have to train them to take your work arrangement seriously. Household chores are best handled by hiring someone to clean, tidying up before you start work, or creating a clear separation of labor among household members.

Refer to sections that cover creating structure, resisting distractions, creating boundaries for family and friends, and common distractions.

If Column B Totals 3 or More:

You may be shutting out all parts of your personal life in your flexible work arrangement to the extent that you are not taking advantage of its freedom. If this is the case, you need to learn to enjoy your freedom. For some people, this means taking care of personal business when stores aren't crowded. For others, it involves taking a break for hobbies during the day. If you ignore everything except your work responsibilities, you are not reaping the benefits of your work situation and you run the risk of overwork.

Refer to sections that cover learning to enjoy your freedom, taking vacations, isolation, and depression.

Internally Motivated versus Externally Oriented

	A (yes)	B (no)
I prefer to get input from other people before proceeding with projects.	1	1
I believe other people can do parts of a job as well as, or better than, I can.	1	1
I feel comfortable asking for support and guidance.	1	1
I enjoy work which involves constant interaction with others.	1	1
I am more focused on the world around me than on my own thoughts.	1	1
Column Totals		

(Continued)

15

If Column A Totals 3 or More:

You need and enjoy input, guidance, and collaboration. This doesn't mean that you cannot work independently, but it does mean that you must continue to find the input you require to do your best work. Over time, you should also try to learn to provide yourself with some of the feedback and support you require. You should also encourage yourself to make more decisions on your own by trusting your judgment. In the meantime, find the support you need. You may also have a tendency to cut corners because you are not interested in the details of a project. If this is the case, find someone to handle these details for you so that you can concentrate on the tasks you perform best.

If Column B Totals 3 or More:

You are likely to want to do everything yourself and you will have no trouble working independently. Your task will be to learn to share your burden with others by delegating and asking for input. You are probably the type of person who jumps into a project without asking for a lot of help or guidance. This can often mean wasted energy and a tendency to do more than is asked of you. You probably also make things more complicated than they need to be. If you find yourself getting bogged down with details, take a break, focus on the eventual goal, and refocus your orientation. When you begin a project, sit back and contemplate the best way to complete it before jumping in.

Work/Life Balance

	A (yes)	B (no)
My family and friends consistently do things without me because I am working.	1	1
I am almost always reachable for work calls, including after work hours and on weekends.	1	1
I am not able to take time off from work without feeling anxious.	1	1
When I am setting weekly, monthly, or yearly goals, I exclude personal objectives and create work objectives only.	1	1
At the end of the day, all I can think about is what I have yet to accomplish rather than what I have already completed.	1	1
Column Totals		

If Column A Totals 3 or More:

You have succumbed to one of the greatest perils of working independently: overwork. Chances are you have been unable to create bounds for your work. You may have abandoned activities that used to bring you pleasure because you do not have time. You probably rarely feel a sense of accomplishment and spend a lot of time worried about your responsibilities. The irony of your situation may be that your conscious priority may not be to devote so much of your energy to work, but your unconscious priority has led you there. The first thing you need to do is examine how you would like to change your life and then create a plan for making small, gradual adjustments until you regain balance.

Refer to sections that cover creating work/life balance, dealing with stress, keep- ing in touch with family when you're on the road, time management, and acknowledging accomplishments.

If Column B Totals 3 or More:

You have maintained balance in your life despite the temptation to let work with no bounds worm its way into your personal life. As long as you are satisfied with the amount of work you are accomplishing, you may not have to make many changes. What you will want to do is examine how it is that you are maintaining balance now and make sure that you take steps to stave off overwork.

Refer to sections that cover staving off overwork, maintaining work/life balance, and creating a vision.

ARE YOU AN OVERACHIEVER OR AN UNDERACHIEVER?

Understanding your tendency to overachieve or underachieve will enable you to better apply the recommendations in this book to managing your work, integrating your work life and personal life, and maintaining your business relationships.

You may be surprised at the results of the Overachiever/Under-achiever Quiz, but do not be upset by them. Overachievers and under-achievers are equally able to attain the goals they set for themselves as long as they learn how to manage their tendencies. For example, I'm an overachiever. I jump into projects without hesitation and eagerly take on new work. While this may seem like a recipe for no-fail success, I have to moderate my tendency to take on too much and to start projects without thinking them through. On the other hand, the underachievers I know, although they are more likely to put off starting a project, have the knack for carefully determining what is worthy of their time and for foreseeing problems that would broadside an overachiever.

The following quiz will help you determine your *tendencies* in regard to overachievement and underachievement.

The Overachiever/Underachiever Quiz

Read each of the following statements and decide which response (**a** or **b**) best fits your personality. Very few people are completely overachievers or underachievers, and you will most likely find yourself relating to the characteristics of both types. Circle the answer that you believe represents how you *usually* act or feel. At the end of the quiz, tally your responses. References to sections of this book that you may find helpful are listed after each set of recommendations.

1. When someone asks me to try something new, my immediate response is usually:

   a. yes
   b. no

2. In school, my teachers described me as:

   a. a conscientious student who completed all of my assignments
   b. a bright student who did not apply myself fully

3. I was the kind of student who:

   a. worked hard in all of my classes
   b. worked hard only in the classes that interested me

4. I am the kind of person who:

   a. tackles problems quickly by taking immediate action
   b. ignores problems until they require immediate action

5. When someone criticizes my work, I usually:

   a. assume the criticism is valid and work harder next time
   b. feel offended and decide to stop trying

6. I like my days to be:

   a. fully booked with many activities
   b. loosely planned with lots of options

7. In my relationships, I normally:

   a. jump in and see what I can offer the other person
   b. step back and see what the other person has to offer me

8. When it comes to deadlines:

   a. I usually meet them
   b. I usually extend them

9. When I have an idea:

   a. I usually take action on it immediately
   b. I usually think about it a lot, but rarely take action

10. When I am not sure what to do next:

    a. I look at my to-do list and begin work on the next item
    b. I watch television, or find some other form of distraction

11. I periodically work myself into a state of exhaustion by taking on too much.

    a. yes
    b. no

12. My family and friends frequently complain that my work takes precedence over them.

    a. yes
    b. no

Total responses of **a.**____
Total responses of **b.**____

If you scored 5 or more in the **a** category, read the following advice for overachiever personalities. If you scored 5 or more in the **b** category, read the advice for underachievers.

Overachievers

Overachievers are driven by the motto, "If I don't do it, no one else will, and no one can do it better than I can anyway." When they're busy doing it all, overachievers feel like they should do even more. They jump in without worrying or spending a lot of time planning, and thrive on juggling a lot of work.

The downside of being an overachiever is burnout. Working all the time zaps their creativity and takes a toll on the quality of work they produce. Overachievers also work so quickly and so hard that they don't always stop to figure out the best way to do a job. The following recommendations provide techniques that will help you rein in your overachiever tendencies.

Recommendations

1. Build breaks into your day by scheduling activities, and take at least one day off a week.
2. Designate specific time in your schedule for examining the big picture of your work and the direction you want to go in.
3. When presented with a new project, take time to map out what that project will do to your schedule. Then evaluate those consequences before agreeing to it.
4. Incorporate personal goals (time with family, things for yourself, etc.) into your work planning to prevent work from taking up all of your time.
5. If possible, do your goal setting and accomplishment evaluation with someone else who can help you combat the feeling of never having done enough.
6. Hone your vision for your work and your life and put it down on paper. Use this vision to help you choose assignments that are in sync with your financial and career goals.
7. Don't confuse working hard with getting ahead. Continually evaluate the tasks you are engaged in to determine if you are using your time wisely.
8. Teach yourself to let go of responsibility by delegating small tasks. Start by hiring someone to do minor jobs like cleaning your house or handling payroll.

See chapter 9 for help with work/life balance, stress, and overwork.

Underachievers

Underachievers have good intentions but they sometimes have such high ideals of what they want to accomplish that they prevent them from doing something until they think they can do it perfectly. If you are an underachiever you probably have a lot of good ideas you never act on and people may frequently tell you you have a lot of potential. You may also find ways to procrastinate and avoid doing projects you care about. Consequently, you most likely feel as though your skills and intelligence are underutilized. See the following recommendations to learn how to get more accomplished.

(Continued)

Recommendations

1. When you experience rejection, find support to help you stop yourself from taking it personally. Share your experiences with other people.

2. When goal setting, concentrate on setting attainable goals.

3. For one week, add up the time you waste procrastinating. Motivate yourself by thinking about some things you enjoy that you could use that time for if you stopped procrastinating.

4. Break big ideas down into small, concrete goals; take daily steps to reach your goals.

5. Join a peer support group or find a mentor for support and accountability.

6. Try to realize that it is okay to make mistakes.

See chapters 9 and 10 for help with creating structure and dealing with setbacks.

Source: The Overachiever/Underachiever Quiz was created by Katherine Crowley, a New York City–based psychotherapist and consultant to entrepreneurs.

Part Two

BECOMING PART OF THE VIRTUAL OFFICE

Working for a Corporation ◄

Working for Yourself ◄

Managing Your Family and Other Personal ◄
Relationships

WORKING FOR A CORPORATION

As an employee, you may be able to initiate a telecommuting program, but making a case to management will require you to dispel some myths and make a strong case for the benefits, using the success of other companies to sell the concept. This chapter will tell you how to make a case for telecommuting at your company. It provides information to help you create a convincing argument and negotiate the arrangement effectively. The chapter also includes the statistics, testimonials, and success stories you'll need to build your case.

SELLING TELECOMMUTING TO MANAGEMENT

A telecommuting program, no matter how small, usually requires an okay from top management. Management is worried about the bottom line, so when you make your case be sure to stress the cost savings and productivity increases documented here. You can also stress the benefits of complying with Clean Air Act regulations, which in some cases require a reduction in the number of vehicles traveling to the office, if this is relevant.

Middle managers have their own concerns with telecommuting. The greatest is usually how their department or group will complete its work if people are scattered outside of the office. To sway them, it is crucial to let them know that telecommuters will still spend some time in the office, will adhere to strict deadlines and guidelines for performance, and will keep in close contact with the office when they are out. Involve these managers in designing the program and emphasize that they may terminate their involvement whenever they choose to. You do not need the support of every single manager before launching a pilot telecommuting program. If one or a few managers are very resistant to the idea, leave them out of the pilot and let the success of telecommuting in other departments win them over.

To help you build a case for a pilot program in your company, the following section lists the most common objections to telecommuting and responses to them. It also includes testimonials on the benefits to companies that have already implemented programs, and negotiating tactics from the author of the best-selling negotiation book *Getting to Yes.*

COMMON TELECOMMUTING MISCONCEPTIONS

I did not realize how misunderstood telecommuting was until I spoke about it with my brother-in-law. He reads a lot but had put together an idea of telecommuting that was pretty far off base. Unfortunately, I do not think he is alone. These misconceptions are a major barrier to starting telecommuting programs. Following is a list of some of the most common misconceptions about telecommuting and your responses to correct them.

Perception: Telecommuting is a fad.

Reality: Telecommuting shows no signs of fading. It is growing at a rate of 15 percent annually, according to Link Resources, a New York City market research and consulting firm. Several factors suggest that this growth rate will continue and probably increase. Link Resources reports that, during 1993, nearly 8 million Americans worked in their homes as telecommuters, and estimates that that number will more than triple—to 30 million—by the end of 1996.

There are several reasons for telecommuting's popularity. First, as the requirements of an aging population change, professionals who must care for children and aging parents demand more flexibility in the workplace. While downsizing has made many people fearful for their jobs, companies are still willing to make concessions to keep valued employees.

Second, the constantly growing workload that employees are expected to manage in the workplace has prompted some employees and managers to realize that the only way to stay on top of all this work is to spend part of the time outside of the office meeting with clients or working in an environment that has fewer interruptions than the office.

Third, the 1990 Federal Clean Air Act mandates that some companies with 100 or more employees at one work site in areas of the country where the air is particularly polluted must reduce the pollution their employees generate getting to work. These employers must create "employee trip reduction" plans to curtail work-related vehicle miles traveled by their employees. Carpooling, increased use of public transportation, and more telecommuting are all options for achieving this goal. You'll find a list of telecommuting companies and case studies later in this chapter.

Perception: Telecommuters work full-time at home.

Reality: Most telecommuters work at home from one to three days a week. This is because most jobs require that employees spend at least some of their time in the corporate office for meetings and other tasks that can be done only at the work site. It is also because of the human need for interaction with coworkers and a desire for face-to-face meetings.

Perception: Employees who telecommute waste time.

Reality: Most telecommuters experience significant increases in productivity. Fewer interruptions and more time and energy from not having to commute, among other things, usually lead to significant productivity increases. In his book, *Making Telecommuting Happen: A Guide for Telemanagers and Telecommuters* (New York: Van Nostrand Reinhold, 1994), Jack Nilles, who coined the term *telecommuting*, stated that in a survey of 300 telecommuters and their managers, effectiveness levels increased an average of 30 percent. Most telecommuters also improve their organizational skills. This improvement is directly related to the increased responsibility and autonomy that comes with the new work arrangement.

Perception: Telecommuting is always expensive.

Reality: Telecommuting is a business solution designed to increase productivity and flexibility and to improve the bottom line. Sometimes this requires a significant investment, but some programs have been instituted at little or no cost. Some telecommuters work at home reading reports or working with a pen and pencil. Lots of other telecommuters work on their personal computers; employers pay only phone expenses. United Airlines, for example, instituted its telecommuting program at no cost to the company. Look for details on this in the case studies section later in this chapter.

Telecommuting can work in a number of ways, some of which do not require a significant investment. Even if your company does decide to provide technology, telecommuting does not require a personal computer on every home office desk and an extra phone line for each telecommuter. Many telecommuters share laptops with other employees to keep costs down.

Perception: Managers can't manage people they can't see.

Reality: Looking over an employee's shoulder is probably the least productive management style. Management by objectives is not the norm in many offices, but removing managers' ability to look over employees' shoulders should not prevent starting a telecommuting program. If managers do not trust employees to complete their tasks in the office, they will not trust them to complete tasks at home. Not every employee is fit to be a telecommuter, nor is every manager right to manage telecommuters. There must be mutual trust. Low-performing employees can be coached in the office and motivated with the promise of telecommuting based on improved output. By the same token, mistrustful managers can learn from the success of telecommuting programs in other parts of the company.

Perception: If a few people telecommute, then everyone will want to.

Reality: A well-designed telecommuting program has a set of very specific criteria for selecting telecommuters. These guidelines make it possible for the powers that be to explain why some people can telecommute and others cannot.

Furthermore, not every employee wants to telecommute. Organizers of telecommuting programs are sometimes surprised at the lower-than-anticipated level of employee interest when a program is announced. Many workers fear the isolation or do not have an appropriate home arrangement.

Perception: Telecommuting leads to chaos.

Reality: Telecommuting can cause chaos if not implemented properly. But many company programs have increased productivity and savings in employee training, recruitment, overhead, and other areas.

Companies that experience chaos are those that begin without planning. Making telecommuting a success requires more than sending employees out of the office. A successful program requires proper design, planning, training, and follow-up. Designing a program is beyond the scope of this book. For a step-by-step guide to setting up a program, read Jack Nilles' book, *Making Telecommuting Happen*.

Perception: Telecommuters are overlooked at raise and promotion time.

Reality: Because telecommuting employees are usually more productive at home than in the office, they are frequently rewarded in their performance reviews or when a job opens up. Also, a well-designed telecommuting program includes a mechanism that makes it easy for telecommuters to apprise managers and coworkers of what they accomplish at home. Meetings, memos, voice mail, and e-mail are the tools telecommuters use to make sure that they get credit for what they do at home.

Perception: Telecommuters will not be around for meetings.

Reality: While it is true that telecommuters are not available for spur-of-the-moment meetings, they are more available than they may initially appear. Many telecommuting agreements (documents that set out conditions for telecommuting) require that employees telecommute only when there are no meetings planned. Telecommuting is postponed or canceled when a telecommuter is needed in the office. See chapter 8 for details on what should be included in these agreements.

In emergencies, telecommuters can come in to the office for last-minute meetings if they are given some notice; at other times they can attend via a telephone conference call.

Perception: Few jobs are telecommutable.

Reality: Many jobs' responsibilities can be clustered so that part-time telecommuting is possible. By scheduling meetings and other face-to-face contact for the days a telecommuter is in the office and clustering reading, writing, computer work, or phone work, part-time telecommuting is possible for many employees. See chapter 12 for tips on how to organize your work for the days you spend out of the office.

Perception: Telecommuting is perfect.

Reality: Telecommuting requires flexibility on the part of telecommuters, managers, and management.

COSTS AND BENEFITS OF TELECOMMUTING

In order to make a case for telecommuting, you will need to provide some data on costs and benefits. The following statistics are from research conducted for and reported in the book *Making Telecommuting Happen* by Jack Nilles.

This data is based on a multi-year program involving 300 telecommuters from a large urban organization. Telecommuters, traditional office workers, and supervisors from the organization were surveyed every nine months. In addition, Nilles examined departmental cost records and conducted interviews with participants. Nilles states that the data this study produced is consistent with what he has observed in his twenty years of work in telecommuting consulting.

Research: An Independent Study

Costs

Additional Training per Employee: $150

Telecommunications: The employer in the study did not supply any telecommunications equipment. Nilles reports that telecommuters' home phone costs increased by an average $48 per year, with a corresponding $48 increase in calls from the office to the telecommuter. The numbers will be higher for telephone-intensive work.

Administration: These costs include evaluation of the pilot project, changes in the administrative system to support the program, duplication of supplies or effort caused by telecommuting, and system integration and coordination. These costs also include part of the salaries of project managers and department coordinators and consulting costs outside of training. Total: $700 per employee.

Benefits

Increased Employee Effectiveness: This figure was derived by averaging supervisors' and employees' estimates of changes in effectiveness (including output and quantity) and multiplying that by individual telecommuters' salaries. Using this approach, Nilles calculated a monthly effectiveness change benefit of $642 at the end of the pilot program.

Decreased Sick Leave: Telecommuters in this program took two fewer sick days per year than in-office employees. Savings totaled 1 percent of telecommuters' salaries.

Increased Organization Effectiveness: Approximately 0.5 percent of telecommuters' salaries. Nontelecommuters also attested to a slight increase in their productivity because of the increased effectiveness of the telecommuters.

Decreased Turnover: Eighteen percent of the telecommuters in the pilot said they had seriously considered leaving the company, and telecommuting had kept them from doing so. Nilles estimated that replacing these employees would have cost 25 percent of their salaries.

For more detailed information about the costs and benefits of telecommuting, refer to *Making Telecommuting Happen: A Guide for Telemanagers and Telecommuters.*

Research: New York City The New York Metropolitan Transportation Council, New York Telephone, the New York City Department of Telecommunications and Energy, and the New York City Department of Transportation conducted a study of telecommuting from March 1992 through January 1993. The study involved employees from Banker's Trust Company, Merrill Lynch, New York Telephone, and the New York City Department of Transportation, and was based on 62 telecommuters, 48 nontelecommuters, and 46 supervisors. The findings below are based on telecommuters who worked at home 3.7 days per month.

Transportation

Telecommuting reduced the number of vehicle miles traveled by an average of 189 miles per month per person. This included all modes of transportation, including subway, bus, and car.

Other Cost Savings or Increases

Telecommuters saved an average of $44.10 per month because of lower costs for food, gasoline, subway fares, dry cleaning, and other daily costs associated with work. These savings were offset to some degree by increased costs for energy. The telecommuters in the study indicated that the cost of air conditioning and lighting in summer months raised their electric bills by an average of $11 per month. Heat and lighting costs in winter months increased by $7.95.

Work Patterns

Telecommuters said they were able to keep work and home responsibilities separate when they were telecommuting. Most telecommuting occurred mid-week, not on Monday or Friday. Many telecommuters also said they preferred not to have a designated telecommuting day. The day of the week changed from week to week or month to month. While many people worked the same schedule at home as in the office, others indicated that they started their work day earlier and ended it earlier.

Effects and Attitudes

Telecommuters said they were more productive working at home. Many supervisors of the telecommuters also noted improvement in productivity, although their perceptions were not as strong as those of the telecommuters themselves. Telecommuters also indicated that telecommuting helped them to better manage their time and work at personal peak times, and improved their morale, attitudes about their jobs, and attitudes about their employer.

CREATING YOUR OWN COST/BENEFIT ANALYSIS

Lots of people ask me how they can put together a financial case for telecommuting of some kind. But while there are great potential savings associated with telecommuting, usually along with some kind of investment, cost varies widely depending on the investment, the size of the program, the size of the company, and the type of business.

An analysis of the state of California's telecommuting program (done by Commuter Transportation Services, Inc., a Los Angeles–based, private, nonprofit research institute), broke the savings down this way:

Real savings in terms of increased productivity: 8.81 percent of the average telecommuter's annual salary.

Avoided costs: as much as 5 percent savings on office space; 0.5 percent average salary savings due to decreased use of sick leave; and 50 percent average salary savings on turnover, i.e., recruitment, training, and other costs associated with replacing staff.

Use the following worksheets to calculate costs and benefits in your business. These worksheets are reprinted with permission from Pacific Bell.

Telecommuting

Cost/Benefit Analysis Worksheet

Telecommuter works at home 2 days per week.

Productivity increase	$____	1
Absenteeism	____	2
Office space	____	3
Parking	____	4
Annual total saving per employee	$____	5

Assumptions:

Figures based on annual salary of $____, productivity increase of 10%, parking @ $____/year reduced by 40%, and use of central office facilities of 150 square feet @ $____/square foot rent per year reduced by 40%.

Instructions:

1. **Productivity increase:** Determine average annual salary at your company. Multiply it by 10% (expected productivity increase) and write the answer in space 1.

2. **Absenteeism savings:** Divide average annual salary by 242 (number of workdays per year) and multiply by 2 (expected number of sick days not taken by telecommuter). Write the answer in space 2.

3. **Office space:** Determine cost per square foot for office space (include rent, utilities, furnishings, etc.). Multiply it by 40% (expected reduction in office space needed). Write the answer in space 3.

4. **Parking:** Determine cost per employee parking space. Multiply it by 40% (expected reduction in parking spaces needed). Write the answer in space 4.

5. Add the four figures together and write the total in space 5.

Cost/Benefit Analysis

Fleming Ltd., telecommuting advisers to the State of California and other employers, has compiled the following figures:

Telecommuter works at home 2 days per week.

Personnel factors	Benefit-savings
Productivity (quantity)	$3,000
Productivity (quality)	1,000
Recruiting/training/retention	1,000
Absenteeism	1,000
Facilities	
Office space	$1,800
Parking	200
Annual total per employee	$8,000
$8,000 × 100 telecommuters	$80,000

Assumptions:

Figures based on annual salary of $20,000, productivity increase of 20%, reduced personnel costs of 10%, parking @ $500 per year reduced by 40% and use of central office facilities of 150 square feet @ $30 per square foot rent per year reduced by 40%. Source: Schepp, *The Telecommuter's Handbook.* (New York: Pharos Books, 1990).

(Continued)

31

Sample Cost/Benefit Analysis

Telecommuter works at home 2 days per week.

Productivity increase	$2,500
Absenteeism	206
Office space	3,600
Parking	240

Annual total saving per employee	$6,546

Assumptions:

Figures based on annual salary of $25,000, productivity increase of 10%, parking @ $600/year reduced by 40%, and use of central office facilities of 150 square feet @ $60/square foot rent per year reduced by 40%.

Sample Start-Up Cost

IBM-compatible or Macintosh Classic w/40MB hard disk	$1,500
Letter-quality printer	270
VoiceMail ($7 installation; $5/month) or answering machine (minimum $70)	67 /1st year
Fax machine	480
2-line telephone	100
Call waiting	20 /year
Personal copier	530
Integrated application software package (spreadsheet, word processing, communications)	300

Total	$3,267

Nice Plus:

Fax-line manager, a voice/data switch that plugs into your telephone and determines whether the incoming call is a fax message, modem transmission, or voice call.

Cost:	$230
Modem (if you need it)	200
Communications software	150

Negotiating a Telecommuting Position

If your company does not have a telecommuting program, one of the first steps in convincing your management to allow you to telecommute is to understand exactly what is at the root of their resistance. You will then be more able to shape a case to meet their concerns. You may know several management concerns just from working in the company. To dig deeper, talk to the human resources department or ask for input from several managers. Ideally, you can enlist the support of coworkers and have them ask their managers as well.

Convincing your boss to let you work at home is a negotiation, so I talked to a negotiation expert about what you should do to increase your chances of success. Roger Fisher is director of the Harvard Negotiation Project and co-author, with William Ury, of *Getting To Yes* (2nd ed., New York: Penguin, 1992), the best-selling book on negotiation strategy. This is his advice for the negotiation.

Put yourself in the other person's shoes. Think about how your manager will be better off if she accepts your proposal to telecommute. Will you get more done because of fewer interruptions? Will you have more energy because you will no longer have a daily commute?

When you are constructing your case, take your manager's concerns into account. To be sure you do this, try the following exercise: Imagine that your boss has to explain to her boss that you are being allowed to telecommute. How can your manager justify this decision as something that is in the best interests of the company? Your boss cannot simply explain that it was agreed to because you wanted it! Write out a short memo as though you are your manager explaining the decision and why it is good for you, the boss, and the company.

Be clear about what you are asking for. Are you interested in leaving the office and never coming back? Do you want to work at home two days a week, or once every other Friday? Often, when managers hear the word *telecommuting*, they think of employees who work outside of the office five days a week. This is probably not your intent, so clearly lay out for your manager the work situation you are proposing.

Indicate what you are committing to in exchange. In order to convince your manager to let you work at home, you need to promise to do more than give up your commute. You must demonstrate what you are willing to commit to as well. For example, you could provide suggestions for how you will demonstrate that you are doing enough at home. (This can be done easily by filling out a daily work plan with your manager for the days you telecommute.) You may want to promise to come in to the office for last-minute meetings, or commit to returning to the office after an agreed-upon time, without complaint, if your manager is not happy with the situation. "Do not waste your time telling a manager or executive that you promise to work hard outside of the office," says Fisher. "If, like most telecommuters, you do not do piece work, you will have to have a mechanism in place to measure your productivity."

Know your alternatives. If the discussion does not result in agreement, are you willing to leave your job? Are there other possibilities available to you besides the job you have? Would you be difficult to replace if the company lost you? Knowing the answers to questions like these will help you determine how tough you can be in the negotiation and may help build your confidence. Do not threaten to quit unless you are prepared to follow through. On the other hand, if you have done some looking around and you have other options for telecommuting, you may want to make this known during the negotiation. This is what Fisher calls BATNA: Best Alternative to a Negotiated Agreement. It is what you will do if the negotiation does not produce the result you desire.

COMMON OBJECTIONS TO TELECOMMUTING

Following are answers you can give to responses you may get when you are trying to convince your boss to let you work at home. Sometimes these concerns are genuine, but in many cases they are a smoke screen for other concerns about telecommuting. Either way, you will need to be prepared with replies to these common objections so that you can make your case successfully or move beyond them to the real areas of concern.

1. **"It is not our policy."** You must demonstrate why it is in the company's interest. You can do this by presenting research on companies currently offering telecommuting and the benefits they have reaped (see the testimonial and case studies following). It may help to present the situation as an experiment, rather than a policy change (most telecommuting starts this way). Agree to try the arrangement and see what problems and benefits arise from it.

2. **"If I let you do it everyone will want to do it."** If there are only a few people who complete their work in the same manner as you do, state this. If your responsibilities cannot be distinguished from oth-

ers', make the point that if the arrangement works well the company will want to expand it; if it does not, it can be terminated. Also, tell your boss that many companies are surprised to find that not all employees want to telecommute. Furthermore, a good telecommuting program has specific criteria for choosing telecommuters that make clear why some employees are allowed to telecommute and others are not.

3. **"What if we need you and you are not here?"** Your telecommuting agreement should stipulate that you will telecommute only when there are no meetings scheduled in the office. Reassuring your boss that you will be available for impromptu meetings will be part of your conversation about what commitment you are making to the situation. Perhaps you can commit to come in as long as you have a few hours' notice.

Common Negotiating Pitfalls

There is a lot at stake when you are negotiating to telecommute. Not only must you state your case clearly and be able to back up your promises, but you also must negotiate as a professional who is capable of self-management and able to work without close supervision. This negotiation can also serve as an "interview," so be sure to avoid making the following negotiating mistakes:

✔ **Not listening.** Listen to and paraphrase your boss's or employer's concerns. Don't say, "That is not a problem." If your supervisor thinks something is a problem, it is a problem. Listen and then address the concerns; do not dismiss them.

✔ **Simply announcing your position.** Do not just say, "I want to work at home." State your reasons for wanting to do something and be honest.

✔ **Not thinking about what they get out of it.** You should think about what you are offering that makes this a good deal for you *and* your employer.

One Woman's Story

A few years ago, Leslie Seabrook's husband got a new job that required him to relocate from Washington state to Maryland. Seabrook's boss joked to her asking when the divorce would take place, but because she was happily married Seabrook knew she needed another option. She thought about telecommuting, but since no one at Univar Corporation, the multinational chemical distribution company, was telecommuting, she needed to make a case for her suggestion. As a manager of insurance and risk services, she manages two employees, works with insurance brokers and third-party claims administrators and advises them of their responsibilities, and keeps them on track and accountable.

To prepare for her conversation with her boss and the senior vice president to whom she would need to sell the concept, Seabrook researched what it would cost for her to work outside of the office. She

A Selected List of Some Companies That Telecommute

Many businesses allow employees to telecommute, and the number is growing. Some companies have formal programs; others have been allowing employees to work at home for years without ever formally creating a program of any kind. The number of companies that should be included on this list changes every day. If you know of any companies that should be added to this list, write to me at Tribune Media Services, 435 North Michigan Avenue, Suite 1500, Chicago, IL 60611 or online at BredinA@aol.com.

Allstate Insurance, American Express, Apple Computer, AT&T, Bankers Trust, Baxter Health Care, Bell Atlantic, Bergen Brunswig, Best Western International, Inc., Blue Cross/Blue Shield, Compaq, Chiat-Day, Citibank, City and County of Los Angeles, Continental Cable, Control Data Corporation, Detroit *Free Press*, Digital Equipment Corporation, Dun & Bradstreet, Federal Express, the federal government (almost all agencies), First Chicago Corporation, Gannett, GTE, Harris Trust and Savings Bank, Healthnet, Hewlett-Packard Corporation, Hughes Aircraft, IBM, Jet Propulsion Laboratory, John Hancock Mutual Life Insurance Company, Link Resources Corporation, Los Angeles *Times*, New York Department of Transportation, New York Life Insurance, NYNEX, Orange County *Register*, Pacific Bell, The RAND Corporation, Rockwell International, Sears, 3Com., Seattle *Times*, Time, Inc., Travelers Corporation, United Airlines, US West, Wendy's International, Inc., Weyerhaeuser, Worldwide Church of God, W. W. Norton & Company, Xerox.

went to office furniture stores and determined what it would cost for technology, phone lines, and supplies. Her presentation was verbal to her boss and higher-ups, but in it she made the case that if the company let her go it would have to hire someone to take her place. The company would probably have to pay more to get someone new, Seabrook argued, because since she moved up from within, she felt she was paid less than market rate. It would also cost the company money to hire and retrain someone.

She also knew that the company was short on office space, and reminded her boss and the senior vice president that her solution helped address that problem as well. All the work that she performed in the office could be done just as well in a home office. The senior vice president was more concerned with her output than where she worked, so they all agreed to a six-month trial. The company's initial idea was to set Seabrook up in an office in Maryland, but she requested that she be given the opportunity to try working from her home. During the six months, they would evaluate output and see what increased costs the work arrangement generated.

It has now been two years. Seabrook's output increased when she began working outside of the office, and increased costs were manageable from the company's perspective. Other people at Univar now telecommute. Costs include Federal Express and trips to Univar (Seabrook travels there every other month for five days to conduct meetings). She originally traveled to Univar once a quarter, but she determined that she needed to be there more frequently so that she could run meetings.

THREE TELECOMMUTING CASE STUDIES

These three case studies demonstrate the different ways that companies can implement telecommuting programs, along with some of the benefits these companies have reaped.

Between June 1993 and April 1994 Hughes ran a telecommuting pilot project at its El Segundo facility. A total of fifty employees and ten managers participated. All of the Hughes telemanagers who participated in the survey found that the telecommuting program resulted in improved employee morale. Nearly 40 percent felt that productivity had increased, and about the same number felt the quality of work had improved among the telecommuters they supervised. Twenty-five percent said they spent less time managing telecommuting staff.

Case Study 1: Hughes Aircraft

Notably, only a few managers reported any negative effects to the program and none reported that productivity had decreased. The majority of Hughes telemanagers indicated that they would be willing to subsidize employees with software and hardware purchased for telecommuting. Of the managers, 92 percent felt that the telecommuting program should continue beyond the pilot program. All said they would recommend telecommuting to others at Hughes.

Of the telecommuters who participated in the pilot survey, 80 percent had never telecommuted before. Prior to telecommuting, almost half of the survey respondents were concerned that they would not be able to maintain ties with their coworkers if they telecommuted; however, less than 16 percent of the telecommuters felt that this was a problem after they had participated in the program.

Many of the employees (36 percent) had also been concerned that they would lose visibility within the company if they telecommuted; however, only 5 percent of the telecommuters said that the program had caused them to lose visibility. None of the telecommuters believed that distractions at home had a negative impact on telecommuting.

After the program was in place, the telecommuters indicated that their productivity, autonomy, and work quality had improved. Their supervisors also indicated that the telecommuters had improved performance in all of these areas. The telecommuters also felt that the program was beneficial to their personal and professional lives. Furthermore, neither group envisioned that the program would result in any major short- or long-term problems.

Case Study 2:
United Airlines

United Airlines launched its telecommuting pilot project in 1992 with ten employees and ten managers. The pilot program was highly structured and very strict. The goal was to reduce the number of trips to the work site, especially during peak driving times. Initial skepticism among upper-level managers was considerable.

In response to this, United declared this imperative for the program: that it would cost the company *absolutely nothing.* No hardware or software was purchased. No expenses for extra phone lines or other equipment were reimbursed. (A toll-free line was installed for employees who lived a distance from the facility and spent significant phone time hooked into the mainframe computer. Monthly cost for that line is minimal.)

Despite the strict no-reimbursement policy, finding people for the program was easy because there was a great deal of interest in telecommuting among employees and United was highly selective in choosing participants. Employees were permitted only one telecommuting day per week. Prior to that day, employees had 5-minute meetings with managers in which they presented a written statement of what they intended to accomplish during the day away from the office. After each telecommuting day, employees met with their managers again to demonstrate and quantify their accomplishments.

Telecommuters were required to call in for voice-mail messages at least three times a day. They were instructed to keep the telecommuting program invisible to outside customers and vendors. A formal "buddy system" was instituted so that each telecommuter had an office colleague to count on for assistance. Usually, the office colleague was a fellow telecommuter.

Telecommuting was permitted only on Tuesday, Wednesday, and Thursday. This was to prevent possible jealousy about "long weekends" for telecommuters. The policy was accompanied by a company-wide directive that all meetings were to be held on Monday or Friday, when all employees would be present.

Productivity increased 20 to 30 percent among telecommuting employees. All managers said they had better communication and better work relationships with their telecommuting employees than with non-telecommuters.

The downside to the program was overwork and burnout among some telecommuters who had a difficult time knowing when to stop working on days away from the office. The solution was to hold periodic meetings for all telecommuters, in which they heard a technical presentation but also had time to talk with one another, exchange experiences, and build camaraderie.

United is now in the process of opening up its telecommuting program to all 8,000 employees in its Southern California facilities. It will permit no more than 10 percent of the workforce to be away on any given day.

Case Study 3:
Pacific Bell

Pacific Bell has had a telecommuting program in Los Angeles since 1984. The goal of the initial program was to help ease traffic congestion from that summer's Olympic Games. The pilot program included approximately 100 people. By July 1989, the number of telecommuting employees was over 600. Today at least 1,500 professional and management personnel telecommute at least one day a week. That number still represents only about 15 percent of management, but the company plans to keep the number of telecommuters continually expanding. Depending on the outcome of bargaining talks this year, the program may expand to include nonmanagement workers.

Current reasons for telecommuting focus mainly on productivity. Pacific Bell found an average increase in output of 10 to 20 percent among telecommuting employees. Two-thirds of managers said they believed the reason for that increase was improved morale. Pacific Bell management also believes that organizational skills are enhanced by the program. In contrast to the United Airlines approach, Pacific Bell installed phone lines, purchased laptop computers and fax machines, and generally subsidized the purchase of any necessary telecommuting equipment.

Telecommuters themselves reported fewer distractions and increased autonomy. Some disadvantages mentioned by a minority of participants were lack of support tools (such as clerical help), missed interaction with other employees, and burnout from working too many hours when at home. However, the telecommuting coordinator stated that he believes the company's competitive advantage is enhanced by telecommuting.

FINDING A WORK-AT-HOME JOB

At this point in time, you will most likely have difficulty entering a firm and being able to telecommute right off the bat. With some exceptions, most employers are still allowing only employees with proven track records to telecommute. Time and again, telecommuters and their managers have said that a foundation at a workplace is an essential component to successful telecommuting. This may change over time, but it is the current reality. Having said all that, I provide the following advice for people who want to try to land a telecommuting job and for those of you who are interested in doing contract work from a home office.

Telecommuting Jobs

If you want to telecommute, you should target companies with telecommuting programs (assuming you have a strong enough background to be an appropriate candidate for employment with them) and then discuss telecommuting during the interview process. A good place to start is with the list of these companies in this chapter. Because companies are realizing the importance of recruiting and keeping good employees, you may be able to negotiate for telecommuting if the company wants you. If you are negotiating for telecommuting, keep in mind that telecommuters are entitled to all of the benefits of nontelecommuting employees. Therefore, you should not have to sacrifice compensation for a chance to telecommute.

Contract Work

If you want to work at home doing project work for an employer, such as data entry or typing, you will have to use a different approach. This is technically not telecommuting; it is contract work. Jobs like these are highly coveted for obvious reasons and therefore you will not usually see them advertised. Word of mouth fills most of these positions before an employer ever considers placing a classified ad. For that reason you will have to pound the pavement to find one.

When you are evaluating an ad for work at home, be very suspicious of any company which advertises for employees and then wants money to "train" you. The BBB representative I talked to put it this way: "The last time I checked, someone who is hiring you should not be asking you for money." Look for more on the subject of avoiding work-at-home scams in chapter 4.

Finding Contract Work

✔ **Evaluate your skills and eligibility.** Do you have a computer, or access to one? Do you have strong typing skills or computer skills? These are the tools and skills that are usually necessary to do work at home.

✔ **Talk to people.** Ask everyone you know if the company they work for ever hires people to complete work at home. Good bets are companies that need large documents typed or require data entry.

✔ **Pound the pavement.** Market research firms and insurance companies are two types of employers that sometimes hire home-based employees to do computer work.

✔ **Avoid scams.** There are lots of ads promising work from home. Often these ads are just schemes to fleece people. According to the Better Business Bureau, some popular scams are: assembling crafts or stuffed animals, reading books, taking videos, stuffing envelopes, tending vending machines, tracing unclaimed government funds, and photographing people for photo IDs.

WORKING FOR YOURSELF

Evaluating the Options

If you want to work at home for yourself, you can start a business, buy into a business opportunity, purchase a business outright, invest in a home-based franchise, or become part of a multilevel marketing organization. To determine your best option you need to research the possibilities and then match one of them to your personality, your work experience, and your personal life. This chapter walks you through the field of options and shows you how to begin this process.

FINDING A BUSINESS IDEA

There are two basic steps involved in finding a business idea.

Looking inward: determining your skills, interests, and inclinations.

Looking outward: discovering an unfulfilled need that you can meet with your product or service.

Don't worry if you lack an idea right now. It's okay to decide you want to work for yourself first, and then choose a business idea.

Make a list of at least ten things you are good at. This is not the time to be modest! Everyone is good at something; many skills can be the foundation for a business. You might be naturally organized or have a knack for fixing things. My friend Sharon is natural at hooking people up with what they need. She finds apartments for people, arranges blind dates, and refers job seekers to jobs. She has always done her matching without thinking and didn't even consider it a skill until she started thinking about what she is good at.

    Assemble this list by observing yourself for a few weeks, keeping an eye out for your aptitudes, and asking people who know you

Looking Inward to Determine Your Skills

Discovering Your Vision

To capture *your* vision, try this exercise. Close your eyes for about two minutes and conjure up a detailed image of how you would like your life to be. Create an image of what you want your life to look like in five years. Where do you live? How do you spend your days? What kind of work do you do? Do you work alone or with other people? Who are you surrounded by? What do you do when you aren't working? Be as specific as possible.

This activity will help you determine whether you want to travel, work alone, spend a lot of time out of the office, do heavy phone work, sit at the computer, live in a city or live on a farm. It is best if you can do this exercise with someone else and then share your vision. If you cannot, write your vision down to make it more concrete. Once you have this vision, you'll have a foundation for choosing a business and for making business decisions.

well for their impressions of what you excel at. You should also write down all of the work responsibilities you've had, to jog your memory about the varied tasks you know how to complete.

Make another list of things you like to do. This may not be as easy as it sounds. This list should also have at least ten items on it and should stretch beyond your hobbies and interests that spring to mind immediately. If you are stymied, ask people who have known you for a long time—particularly people who knew you as a kid—what they have seen you doing when you are most content.

Decide what you want out of life. When I give seminars on starting a home-based business, we do a vision exercise that helps participants crystallize how they want their life to be. I learned this exercise from Katherine Crowley, a New York City therapist who specializes in working with entrepreneurs. Your vision should include your work and personal life and provide a clear idea of what you want to attain. Once you have this idea, it will be easier for you to make decisions and set goals.

Looking Outward to Find an Unfulfilled Need

There are plenty of lists out there with titles like "Top 10 Businesses" and "Hot New Businesses." These lists may stimulate some ideas, but the best business ideas will come from you and will be based on who you are and what the market is looking for. So while you are doing the list-making and soul-searching described in the preceding section, put up your home business antenna. This means read the paper, talk to people, and watch TV, all with an eye out for opportunities. Once you start doing this, you'll be surprised at how many ideas you come up with.

It's important not to be judgmental during this period. Don't be afraid to contemplate the most outlandish ideas and don't be discouraged if the first few ideas you generate have flaws. Be willing to put them aside and keep searching. When you're going through this process be careful who you share your business ideas with. Some people will lack vision and may shoot down good business ideas because the ideas are unconventional. See chapter 11 for more on naysayers.

Although I'm not a fan of "Top Ten" lists because I feel that a business idea isn't a good one unless it lights your fire, it won't hurt to look in some obvious places for good opportunities if they fit your talents, background, and preferences. Businesses that fill gaps left by corporate downsizing are a good bet. These include consulting, referral services, graphic design, desktop publishing, staffing services, and computer maintenance. Import-export work and child care also have potential. A November 1995 article in *Home Office Computing* magazine, "35 Hot New Businesses for the year 2000," provides home business ideas based on interviews with futurists about what they see as potential future businesses. The list includes neighborhood concierge, educational consultant to help kids understand technology and supplement what they learn in school, personal chef, personal trainer, on-site computer repair for home business owners, blue-collar career counselor, customer service expert, and agent for home-based caregivers. When you are contemplating business possibilities, keep in mind that you don't have to stay in the business you start forever. You can run a business for a few years until you come up with an offshoot of your idea or are in a position to start a more capital-intensive business.

Remember to think during this period about what people need. Is there something that everybody hates to do that you can do for them? Or is there a product that would make life easier for people you know? Questions like this will help you come up with a product or service that has a market.

Whatever you do, *do not* start more than one business at a time. This is a recipe for trouble because customers want to patronize an expert. Even if you are talented in several areas, it may be difficult to convince potential customers of it. Think about it. Would you want to do business with someone who is a carpenter, a chef, *and* a dentist? No! You would want to do business with the person who is the *best* carpenter, the *best* chef, or the *best* dentist.

RESEARCHING YOUR BUSINESS IDEA

Once you have determined what you are good at, and you believe you have found something for which there is a market, it is time to do some market research. This may sound obvious, but many entrepreneurs who start businesses like an idea but have no idea how many other people feel the same way.

Researching the market for your potential business is pretty simple. It is something you can easily do yourself as long as you are willing to roll up your sleeves and ask a lot of questions. The only tricky part about researching a business idea is that you have to remain open-minded during the process so that you will be able to recognize signs that your business has no market. This is not always easy because when you are excited about an idea there is a tendency to ignore any evidence that your business is not as viable as you originally thought. To avoid this trap, gather lots of information using the steps below and then discuss your findings with several people whose judgment you trust.

Check out your competition. Look in the yellow pages, in trade magazines, and on the Internet for businesses related to the one you want to start and determine whether there is room for you in the market. You can often do something cheaper, faster, or better than existing competition. If there are no businesses currently offering the service or product you want to sell, that can be good and bad. You may have hit upon a great untapped idea, but then again there may be a reason why it's not being done. Research will tell you which is the case.

Talk to your potential customers. Identify who you would be selling to and contact some of these people. Ask them if they would be interested in a service or product like yours, what they would be willing to pay for it, and what services they currently use. If they are currently buying what you plan to sell, ask them how they would like to see the product or service improved.

Seek assistance from people who are already successful in the business you want to start. This is by far the most expedient way to learn the nuances and pitfalls of running a particular business. I have a friend who runs a successful beer-brewing store who has hired himself out to help people get started in the business. He has helped people find suppliers and storefront space, and he even set someone up with a mock interview with his banker the day before her appointment to make a pitch for a loan.

To find someone in your business to help you, contact five or ten people who are excelling in the business you want to start or in a related business. Write to people to tell them you admire what they have done (this will not be flattery, since presumably you do admire someone who is succeeding at what you want to do), and ask them if you can have a few hours of their time to discuss the ropes and pitfalls of the business. For obvious reasons, it is preferable to contact people who work in a different area, or who have a slightly different target audience than your business. But in some cases even direct competitors may help you.

Some people you contact will say no; that's why you should write to ten people. If all the people you contact balk at volunteering their time to help you, offer to pay them for a few hours as consultants.

Go to a business library. Talk to a research librarian about what industry publications you should look at and how to find industry sales figures and other data that will help you evaluate your business idea.

Go to industry association meetings and talk to people in the business to research trends. You will want to make sure there is no pending legislation or other imminent change in an industry you are considering entering. You can find a list of associations in a book called *The Gale Encyclopedia of Business and Professional Associations* found in the reference section of the library.

Talk to everyone you meet. To gauge interest, talk to friends, people you meet at parties, your bank teller, and anyone else you come in contact with about your idea. You may want to ask them questions in a roundabout way in order to keep your idea secure.

WHAT YOU CAN EXPECT: TWO HOME BUSINESS SURVEYS

The following surveys shed light on the reality of running a business at home.

The California Business Challenge Survey was conducted from September 1994 to January 1995 by the Home Office and Business Opportunities Association of California in Irvine, California, a tax-exempt, nonprofit, statewide organization with national membership devoted to supporting, promoting, and protecting home-based business owners and telecommuters. The HOBO Association surveyed 200 people. Ninety percent of the respondents were full-time or part-time home-based business owners. Ten percent were telecommuters, moonlighters, or prospective home-based business owners. The vast majority of the respondents lived and worked in California. Some of the results of the surveys follow. The number one response is the one chosen most often. Two responses on one line indicates that the answers tied for that spot.

The California Business Challenge Survey

What are the top challenges or obstacles in starting?

1. Fear of starting something new; lack of confidence in the California economy (tied for first place)
2. Lack of capital to get started
3. Afraid to fail and a lack of knowledge and expertise and a lack of support to get started

Other choices included: don't know what to do; need a business idea; need help with legal, tax, and insurance issues; and do not want to work from home.

What are top challenges you face in growing?

1. Not enough new customers
2. Lack of cash flow; lack of capital (tied for second place)
3. Increased competition for customers in what you do
4. Increased cost of doing business

Other choices included: lack of programs to support home-based businesses; lack of skills; and family issues.

AT&T Work At Home Survey
The AT&T Home Business Resources Work At Home survey (September 1995), a national survey of 1,005 full- and part-time business owners, found the following:

▶ Eighty percent of respondents say they are more productive in a home office than they were in a traditional office.

▶ Three-quarters of business owners say that distractions are not a problem.

▶ Eight out of ten people shower or bathe before heading to work in the home office.

▶ Two-thirds say they exercise regularly.

▶ Sixty-one percent say they feel as though they get sick less often now that they work at home.

▶ The average work week for full-time work-at-homers is 53 hours.

OTHER OPTIONS FOR HOME-BASED WORK

If you want to work at home but you don't want to start from scratch with your own business, you may want to buy a business opportunity, buy a franchise, or get involved with multilevel marketing. While these options can represent great opportunity, they are fraught with potential for fraud. The following sections will help you navigate in your search for a worthwhile opportunity in these areas.

BUSINESS OPPORTUNITIES

When I was working as the Business From Home advisor on the Prodigy online service, I received a lot of messages from people who had bought into business opportunities. Some people had had great results, but I also heard my share of sad stories from people who had invested a lot of money in opportunities that couldn't possibly pay off. One woman bought into a mail order business. Not only was there no profit margin, but the merchandise took so long to get to her that she lost all her sales. A man wrote to me to say he had sucked his savings account dry trying to make personalized children's books on his computer. He paid a bundle for the business because it was supposed to include support from experts, but every time he called for help, the experts were in a meeting. Time and again, I heard from people who had assembled crafts at home, only to be told by the company that was supposed to buy the completed crafts back from them that the quality was not up to snuff. These people were stuck because they had already paid for the materials they used to put the crafts together.

Ads for home-based business opportunities are advertised on everything from TV to matchbooks. Some of these ads are more legitimate than others; you need to carefully examine all of them before you spend any money on them. There are many, many scam artists out there who prey on people's desire to work from their homes. Following are some tips that may help you to separate the good from the bad.

Do's

Do's and Don't's for Business Opportunities

▷ **Ask yourself the following question: Am I buying worthwhile components that I couldn't pull together for less money myself?** Worthwhile components include marketing support, training, proprietary software, advice from people who are real experts in the business, or help finding customers once you're ready to go. Putting a business opportunity to this test will help prevent you from falling prey to companies selling overpriced books, recycled mailing lists, and tapes you can find at the library.

▷ **Be careful of advertising flyers with no address.** Plenty of flyers have only a sales pitch and details of where and when to go to learn about a great home-business opportunity. Consequently, there is no way of investigating these ads because there's no address.

▷ **Ask for references.** You should talk to ten or twenty people involved in a home-business opportunity you're considering buying into. Companies have been known to hire a few people to act as references for a bogus opportunity, but most companies can't hire twenty actors.

▷ **Check for complaints.** Call the Better Business Bureau, the state attorney general's office, and the consumer affairs office.

▷ **Check with the state to see if the principals in the business have any other businesses in the state.** This may identify those people who open businesses and shut them down regularly.

Don't's

▲ **Don't give any money to people selling business opportunities at a small-business or home-business seminar until you have verified their legitimacy with a lot of other people.** And beware of any price that is available for only a short period of time—such as fifteen minutes during a hard-sell seminar at a home-business conference. It's probably bad news.

▲ **Don't take the word of references over the phone.** Regardless of how many references you speak to over the phone, insist that a company also provide references near you. If possible, follow these people through a day of work to verify that what they say about the business is true. If a company says they can't give you any names because of privacy laws, be suspicious. All a company has to do to comply with the law is to ask permission of references before giving out their names. To find references beyond what is provided, ask the company where people in the business advertise (pennysavers, trade magazines, etc.), then contact these people on your own. Another good method for locating reputable references is to post a note on a home-office bulletin board on one of the online services. You'll get input from people all across the country and you can arrange to meet those who live near you.

▲ **Don't be lulled into a false sense of security because a company has a booth at a trade show.** It's not the responsibility of show organizers to screen vendors. When it comes to getting involved in a business opportunity or a home-based business, it's your responsibility to make sure your investment is sound.

Who Gets Scammed by a Business Opportunity? Everyone is a potential scam victim, but because of today's demographics and corporate downsizing trends, Call for Action, a nonprofit group that provides free mediation services to people who have been defrauded, says the typical profile of someone who gets taken in by a business opportunity scam is a white male between ages 45 and 55 who has been out of a job for close to a year. Typically this person has been forced to retire early or has left a company with a lump-sum settlement during downsizing. This man has usually not been able to find a job and is looking for ways to work. He sees a business opportunity as a way to take the place of the job he cannot find. The average loss for this person is tens of thousands of dollars.

Following is a list of some frequently advertised opportunities and what you should know about them.

Common Work-at-Home Scams

Medical Transcription. This can be a legitimate opportunity, but you have to be careful about companies wanting a lot of money to help you start up. If you're signing up for training, check out the school by talking to its students and calling other schools to make sure the program is competitively priced. If you already have medical transcription skills, you should be able to start up on your own without spending money with one of these companies. Be on the lookout for opportunities that are no more than an overpriced computer, some videos, and a reprint of a directory of doctors. Make sure you're paying for real education and/or help finding clients at the end of your training.

No-Money-Down Real Estate. Procuring distressed real estate and negotiating a seller-financed contract is one of the ways no-money-down real estate works. And it does make money for a small number of people. However, it takes a lot of time (it's not a sideline) and you need a good set of contacts and a source of information on distressed property to succeed. Beware of paying a lot of money for the promise of expert hand-holding with these packages. The real experts in the company are often not available, and calls are handled by neophytes who may not know much more than you do about the business.

Computer Businesses. There are legitimate companies out there selling computers, customized software, mailing lists, and other supplies needed to start a variety of specialized businesses. When you buy from these companies, make sure they are selling you something you couldn't get yourself. In other words, I wouldn't buy a kit made up of a computer I could get myself, software available at Egghead, and a mailing list from the library. On the other hand, a customized software package you cannot get anywhere else or expertise it would take a long time to acquire is worth paying for.

Bogus Advertisements. Call for Action says it frequently hears from people who have been contacted by scam artists who claim they have publications that will help them reach their target markets. A man who started a home-based security business and wanted to reach new homeowners got a call from someone who claimed to have a directory that would be delivered to real estate offices. The man spent $1,500 for an ad in a directory that doesn't exist. When he tried to reach the company, they were gone.

The Vending Machine Business. Locators promise multiple good locations for vending machines selling anything from bubble gum and soda to "Your Weight and Fortune." To avoid this scam, when a locator promises locations, ask for exactly what they will be, including street addresses and store or shopping center names. If they can't tell you, don't give them any money. If they give you a list of locations, visit the sites, talk to the store or mall managers, and check to see if in fact they will allow you to place your display there. Otherwise you may be stuck with a bunch of vending machines and nowhere to put them.

Post-Incorporation Scams. After you incorporate, prepare for an onslaught of scammers. Bottom feeders looking for a way to make a fraudulent buck call newly incorporated businesses hawking counterfeit brand-name copying equipment, community directories, and a whole range of bogus products. So heads up after you make your business official.

Other Scams. Assembling crafts or stuffed animals, reading books, taking videos, tracing unclaimed government funds, and photographing people for photo identifications are also scams to watch for, according to the Better Business Bureau.

HOME-BASED FRANCHISES

The word *franchise* brings to mind McDonald's and Dunkin' Donuts, so many people don't think of franchising as a home-business option. But it is. The most popular home-business franchises include bookkeeping and tax services, home inspection, pest control, lead testing, leak detection, home decoration, lawn care, upholstery and carpet cleaning, house cleaning, nanny referral service, computer classes for children and other children's services, and house and pet sitting.

How Franchises Work

A franchising arrangement works in the following way: you (the *franchisee*) lease the right to create a business that is identical to all other businesses being run under the same name. In order to be able to do this you may have to buy things such as products, tools, advertising assistance, and training from the company that owns the rights to the business (the *franchisor*).

Franchising is not necessarily cheap, nor is it always easy. Be aware that the benefits of name recognition and training have costs that can range from reasonable to exorbitant. Also keep in mind that buying name recognition and assistance in setting up a business doesn't mean you are going to be successful. Franchise terms and conditions vary widely; be sure you understand all the details before you commit.

The investment for a home-based franchise varies widely, but according to Ellen Schubart, editor of *Franchise Buyer*, you can usually *buy into* a home business franchise for anywhere from $1,000 to $35,000. *Buying into* a franchise means purchasing the right to use the company's name for your business. This is called a *franchise fee* or *initial fee*. But your *total investment* is the sum you need to evaluate to determine if you can afford a franchise. Your total investment is the franchise fee plus other costs of launching your franchise. As a home-based franchise, you probably won't have up-front costs such as rent for a business space or purchase of a building, but in most cases you may need to purchase services, supplies, and equipment. You'll also need money for business expenses, for local advertising, and to keep you going for at least a year until your business is off the ground.

Your Investment

You typically will also have at least two other responsibilities as a franchisee. One is a monthly *royalty fee*, which is a percentage of gross sales that you pay to the franchisor. Fees vary widely, from as low as 4 percent to as high as 20 percent. You will also be required to pay a percentage of your gross income into an advertising pool that the franchisor uses to promote the business.

What do you get for your investment? Along with the right to use a franchisor's name, the money you pay a franchisor will typically get you some or all of the following: help with obtaining financing, assistance in selecting and procuring equipment, guidance in opening your business, ready-made ads and other advertising materials, and economies of scale for purchasing of supplies. Some franchisors will even provide field support in the form of visits is sales are slow.

If you like the sound of a home-based franchise, but don't know anything about the businesses I mentioned earlier, it may not matter. The best franchisors will train you in their business because they understand that their success is dependent on yours. Be sure that any franchise you consider provides adequate training and support.

Step 1. Consider a phrase commonly used to describe franchising: "You're in business for yourself, not by yourself." This aptly describes the difference between franchising and entrepreneurism. It's important to remember that franchisors are selling a proven concept and are not looking for

Four Steps to Determining If They Are for You

people to come in with a lot of ideas for changing it. If you want to call all the shots, you may be better off starting your own business.

Step 2. Contemplate the daily reality of the particular business you are considering. If you're thinking about a house-cleaning business, be sure you would be comfortable cleaning other people's houses and spending a lot of time alone. If you've got your heart set on one of the child-oriented home-based franchises, imagine what it would be like to work with kids all day instead of adults. Some franchises may mean that you'll have calls coming in to your home office at all times of the day and night. If this would be the case, be certain you and your family could tolerate it.

Is Franchising for You?

✔ Do you understand the difference between a franchiser and entrepreneur?

✔ Have you chosen the right franchise for you?

✔ Are home businesses permitted in your neighborhood?

✔ Are you financially able to start a franchise?

Step 3. Determine if home businesses are permitted in your neighborhood. *Permitted*, when it comes to home-based businesses, may mean what you can get away with, because zoning rules often prohibit home offices. I'm not advocating breaking the law—I'm just quoting zoning officials who have told me that they sometimes look the other way if a business is quiet and neighbors don't complain. A business that will have high visibility in the neighborhood—because of use of a truck, for example, or increased traffic to your home—is a different story. In these cases, it may be essential to square the business with zoning officials, or at the very least, be sure your neighbors are in full support of it so they don't complain to the zoning board. You wouldn't want to be shut down after making a large up-front investment.

Step 4. Evaluate your financial suitability for franchising. You can determine the initial and monthly investment of a home-based franchise by talking to the franchisor and other franchisees. To find out what you can make from a franchise, you will have to talk to other franchisees, because most franchisors won't tell you. By law, they don't have to, and they are leery of making any promises. Keep in mind that you'll also need anywhere from six to eighteen months' worth of savings to keep you afloat while you build up your business.

Evaluating a Franchisor Once you've determined that you are suited to running a home-based franchise, and you've figured out what business you would enjoy running, it's time to evaluate franchisors. This will be a lengthy process during which you will determine if the franchisor you are considering is reputable, is in good financial health, and will make a good business partner. Do not rush this process. There are plenty of reputable franchisors out there, as well as lots of companies that collect hefty initial investments and then do nothing to help a franchisee succeed. Keep in mind that the failure rate of franchises is higher than the failure rate of entrepreneurial start-ups. Without a franchisor who will protect your interests and help you succeed, you won't have a chance of survival.

When you start having serious talks with a franchisor, they will give you a Uniform Franchise Offering Circular (UFOC). This document has the names, addresses, and phone numbers of current and former franchisees, as well as everything you need to know about a franchisor's financial situation. After you get this list you should contact lots of franchisees to ask them about their experiences. Visit about one dozen and make calls to more. It's also a good idea to call former franchisees to find out what happened.

When you visit the franchises, ask the owners if the franchisor delivers the service it promises, how much money you can expect to make, and what kind of training and support the franchisor has provided. Since your franchise will be home-based, you should also inquire about the impact of the business on the franchisee's home life.

During this time, you should also evaluate the franchisor as a business partner. Do you feel comfortable with the people you've been talking to? How responsive have they been in providing you with information and answering your questions? Do they appear capable? Do not be taken in by nice personalities.

The company should also provide you with audited financial statements. Evaluate these records and determine the financial health of the franchisor, including what level of capital it has. A franchise attorney or an accountant can help you with this evaluation.

The UFOC contains details about any ongoing litigation the franchisor is involved in. It's probably okay to see some litigation in the records, but if there are a lot of suits, investigate the nature of them.

Finally, look at management's background. Does it have experience in franchising as well as the business the franchise is in? Ideally, you want management that has worked in a franchise organization before.

If you like what you see and you're looking at a contract, ask about the following and have a franchise attorney check your contract for details about all the costs you will incur in setting up and running the franchise, how much you will pay for products, if you can sell the franchise, how disputes will be handled, and what restrictions the franchisor has on other franchisees in your area. If you don't have a lot of experience in the business you'll be running, make sure they provide extensive training and continued support. And remember, as with any business opportunity, everything is negotiable, so don't think you have to sign a contract as is! Red flags include a company that does not have a UFOC available, a franchisor with a lot of closings, or a company that derives its revenue primarily from fees and initial costs of joining. Be suspicious if the franchisor seems too eager to sign you up and get your money without evaluating you, or if the company used high-pressure sales to get you to buy. Check for complaints against the company by contacting the Better Business Bureau and the attorney general's office in the company's home state.

BUYING AN ESTABLISHED BUSINESS

A friend of mine poured his life savings and a good portion of his parents' money into the purchase of a business. Because the business belonged to his coworker's father, my friend sank his money into equipment and other expenses before thoroughly investigating the company's records. When his lawyer finally did some checking, he discovered six-figure IRS tax liens on the business. Now my friend has two choices: settle with the IRS to get the business on track or lose the money he has already invested.

When I heard his story I was struck by how easy it is for smart people to overlook the basic steps they should take when they are buying a business. After speaking to some attorneys, I discovered that my friend's experience is common. The biggest mistake people make when they buy a business is not doing enough research. In many cases, if a seller appears reliable, buyers become convinced that a business is a good bet after doing only minimal research.

To avoid this trap, first ask yourself why the owner is selling. It may be that she is just tired of running the business, but make sure that she isn't getting out because of factors such as a conflict with the neighborhood or suppliers, impending competition, tax liens, or a change in a law that adversely affects the business.

Next, determine the financial health of the business. Conduct preliminary research by examining revenues, expenses, and profits. Once you have determined that the company is at least a viable prospect, hire an attorney or accountant to conduct an in-depth study.

I'm a believer in doing as much as possible yourself, but when it comes to examining a business I recommend hiring a professional who specializes in evaluating businesses for sale. They know what questions to ask and how to recognize problems in financial records. The person you hire should do a close examination of five years of financial statements, income tax returns, sales tax returns, and employment withholding tax returns. All of these documents should then be cross-checked to be sure they jibe, according to Steven Gersz, a Rochester, New York–based attorney who concentrates in this area and lectures on the topic of buying a business. As my friend learned the hard way, a search for liens and lawsuits is also important.

Other matters to investigate include:

△ **Equipment.** Make sure it's not due for a major overhaul. Observe the operation of the business and make sure the equipment is being used. If the business is equipment-intensive, hire an engineer to inspect the equipment or include a guarantee of its efficacy in your buying agreement.

△ **Inventory.** Determine if the level of inventory is what the owner stated and if all inventory is in good condition.

△ **Permits and licenses.** Ensure that the business has all the necessary permits and that they are transferable (they often are not). This is important because authorities like to investigate new businesses.

△ **Competition.** Contact an industry association, talk to other local businesses, and read trade publications to find out about competition.

△ **Pending environmental legislation and current restrictions.**

One last piece of advice: Before you buy a business, ask yourself whether it wouldn't be cheaper, easier, or better for you to set up a business of your own.

MULTILEVEL MARKETING

MLM is an acronym for *multilevel marketing*, also called *network marketing* and *cooperative marketing*. Time-Life Books, Mary Kay Cosmetics, and Encyclopedia Britannica are a few of the most well-known MLM companies.

MLM is an alternative to traditional retailing in which products are sold through a chain of distributors instead of through stores. Distributors (people like you) make money by selling products and by recruiting new distributors; they also make a commission on their own sales as well as on the sales of anyone they sign up. In exchange, the recruiters provide training, supplies, and guidance in the business. The hierarchical structure created by this recruiting and commission arrangement is called a *downline*. The person who sponsors someone and brings him into a MLM company is that person's *upline*; the sponsoree or recruit is in the sponsor's *downline*. Each person makes money on the sales of the people in his downline. Because of this, it's to a distributor's advantage to sign on as many people as possible.

Training and support vary from company to company. Upline managers provide it, as well as newsletters, voice mail tips, and members of the *telephone tree* whom you can call with questions. Sponsors or uplines are usually responsible for training recruits they bring into the company. However, if you're getting involved in a company that sells something technical, such as long-distance phone service or alarm systems, training probably will be provided by the company. If you are planning to sell technical products, make sure the company will provide the training you'll need to succeed. *Commissions* (what you make on a sale) and *margins* (what the company lets you have the product for) may also vary depending on how high up you are in the distributor chain.

The MLM concept isn't bad; in fact, plenty of companies (and distributors) have done well in MLM setups with a significant investment of time and energy. Unfortunately, dishonest businesspeople frequently use the MLM concept to fleece distributors by closing a company down suddenly and taking distributors' money with them. In these cases, distributors are often left holding merchandise they bought to join an MLM company. It also takes about a year to start making money in an MLM company, so if a company shuts down soon after you join, you'll be in bad shape.

Another common problem with MLM is that companies make unrealistic promises about earning potential. If you're considering MLM, keep in mind that the lower you are on the chain of distributors, the more difficult it is to make money because the market gradually becomes saturated with distributors. People who make money in legitimate MLM put a lot of time and money into it. They also tend to be good salespeople. Before you join any MLM organization, ask yourself if you believe in the product you'll be selling and have a strategy for finding customers. "MLM is a business. If you treat it like a hobby, you aren't going to make any money," says Bill Morgan, editor of the MLM newsletter *I'M IN* and special contributor in the Network Marketing section of the Prodigy online service. "Regardless of what your sponsor tells you, MLM is a business like any other, and it takes work and investment to be successful."

MLM is also problematic when a company isn't really trying to sell products. Some companies are set up to make money simply on people joining (usually for a fee that includes purchase of the products), rather than on distributing products. In these cases, the MLM organization is more like a *pyramid scheme*. The Direct Selling Association defines a pyramid scheme as "an illegal scam in which large numbers of people at the bottom of the pyramid pay money to a few people at the top. Each new participant pays for the chance to advance to the top and profit from payments of others who might join later." The people at the top make lots of money, people in the middle make some, and a whole bunch of people at the bottom get stuck with nothing except a depleted bank account. Pyramid schemes are illegal; that's why bogus MLM schemes will always at least make a show of selling products.

When determining the legitimacy of an MLM company it's important to make sure that commissions are based on sales of products to customers, not just on bringing in new recruits. It is the commissions on sales of products to consumers that separates MLM from pyramid schemes.

▶ **Use diligence in investigating any company you are considering working with.** Just because someone is a friend, or looks like you could trust him, or has a movie star endorsing the company, does not mean you shouldn't check out the opportunity thoroughly.

▶ **Steer clear of any company that pressures you into buying substantial quantities of inventory to join or move up the ladder.** Many companies keep the price of joining low and will often let you borrow against future earnings for your sample kit. Because many states have laws that declare anything sold for over $100 or $500 as a business opportunity, lots of companies try to keep their prices under these two figures to avoid the increased bureaucracy that goes along with that classification.

▶ **Make sure the company will buy back inventory you cannot sell.** This is to prevent a practice called *inventory loading*, in which a company makes money from requiring you to purchase a lot of inventory that you may not be able to sell. Companies should buy back 90 percent of merchandise that you cannot sell. Make sure you ask about what time frame the buyback policy refers to; 90 days is the minimum. Businesses that are members of the Direct Selling Association (DSA), a trade group, buy back 90 percent of unsold marketable merchandise purchased in the last year.

Multilevel Marketing: What to Look For in a Company

You also need to ask about what merchandise the company buys back. DSA members buy back only *marketable* merchandise, which excludes things such as sale items that are discontinued, makeup that has been opened, and food products that have expired. Find what the return details are before you buy.

▷ **Avoid organizations that require a significant investment for the right to bring people into the organization.**

▷ **Don't get involved in MLM companies that don't really sell a**

Places to Find Help

✔ Chamber of Commerce
✔ Better Business Bureau
✔ Library
✔ Local business dealing with similar product
✔ Local district attorney's office, consumer fraud department
✔ State attorney general's office, consumer fraud division
✔ Federal Trade Commission, (202) 326-2222
✔ National Fraud Information Center, (800) 876-7060

product. The company's marketing plan will delineate on what basis you are paid. A legitimate company usually pays you on the basis of sales rather than on finder's fees or money given to you for the sake of recruiting someone. Evaluate how much emphasis is placed on selling the company's product or service. If you don't, you run the risk of getting involved in a pyramid scheme. Some pyramid organizers try to make their schemes look like multilevel marketing arrangements by taking on a line of products. New distributors are pushed to purchase large and expensive amounts of inventory when they sign up.

▷ **Make sure the product is a consumable product that people want and will pay for.** Evaluate how you will sell products before getting involved. Do you have a sales strategy? Is there a lot of competition in your geographical area? Do you have a means of generating customers beyond your immediate family and circle of friends? You may receive some assistance from the company, but market research and sales planning is your responsibility.

▷ **Watch for companies promising that you'll make thousands of dollars a month shortly after starting up.**

Managing Your Family and Other Personal Relationships

Family responsibilities are often the reason that people want to work in a virtual office. Ironically, managing family relationships can also be one of the most challenging aspects of working in a virtual office. It is not easy to keep your family from infringing on your work time when you are not shielded by the structure of a traditional office. Likewise, if you aren't careful, your work can threaten your family life. This chapter will tell you how to make sure your family does not get in the way of your work in a virtual office and your virtual office does not wreak havoc on your family life.

Selling the Idea of a Home Office to Your Family

In an ideal world, family members would support your dream of working and living under the same roof. But the mail I get from my readers and listeners suggests we're not living in Utopia. Spouses, children, and parents who have concerns about how a home office will affect them may try to discourage you from establishing a home office. Family worries are particularly likely if you are setting up your virtual office for entrepreneurial pursuits. But even if you will be working at home as a telecommuter, you may encounter some family resistance because the arrangement threatens the household's status quo.

It is important to take steps to generate family support for your virtual office because this support will make your adjustment easier and your work arrangement more pleasant. Try the following steps to make your case and gain family support.

1. Fully investigate the source of your family's concern. Ask your family members what they object to and listen to them without interrupting to defend your idea. To make sure you unearth everything they're thinking, ask them to describe their worst fears about your potential new work arrangement. Once you know their concerns, you'll be able to address them.

2. Do a sales presentation. Most of us reserve sales pitches for our customers, the bank, or potential business partners. But you may need to apply some of your sales techniques toward a pitch to your family if they are not sold on the idea of you working at home. In order to do this, spend some time assembling facts about what your new work arrangement will consist of and how you plan to make your virtual office fly. For example, if you're currently responsible for household chores and child rearing, explain how you plan to manage your family duties along with your new tasks. If you will be coming back into the house after many years of working in an office, reassure your family that you have a plan that will prevent your work from disrupting the household routine. Your family's fears may be based on a lack of understanding of what you plan to do and how you are going to go about it.

3. Establish some rules for your home office. If your family is concerned that your working at home will interfere with their lives, create structure for your hours or work habits that take this into account. Draw up guidelines stipulating when you'll take business calls in the home office, and where in the house you'll do your work. A list of suggestions for setting boundaries between your family and your work appears later in this chapter.

4. Talk about failure rates for home-based businesses. If you plan to work at home as an entrepreneur, educate your family. While not all home-based businesses make it, the widely publicized failure rates for small businesses don't always apply to ventures started at home. For one thing, many home businesses have minimal overhead since they're run out of the spare bedroom and don't have payroll to worry about. As a result, home-based business owners can stay afloat longer if customers or clients are slow in showing up. Low overhead also means you can skip to another business idea if the first one flops. All of these things give home businesses a little more lasting power than small businesses started outside the home.

5. Educate your family about entrepreneurs. Entrepreneurs have a reputation for being risk takers, and this may concern your family. But the reality is that most successful entrepreneurs I know do not take a lot of risk. Instead, they carefully examine projects and plan for how they will manage various outcomes. Two characteristics that successful entrepreneurs share are a belief in themselves and a willingness to persevere even when things look grim. Educating your family about this may help convince them that you aren't taking them over a precipice by starting a home-based business.

WORKING AT HOME WITH KIDS

A desire to spend more time with their kids and cut down on the stress of trying to find, pay for, and juggle day care often prompts parents to work at home. I used to believe that the only way to manage working at home with kids was to pay for child care. But as I investigated this subject, I discovered that child-care solutions are as varied as the businesses the parents of these children run. If you work at home as a corporate telecommuter, you will most likely be required to have some formal child-care arrangement. Otherwise, you can carve out a solution that fits your schedule, your budget, and your child's needs. (See chapter 9 on self-management and time management.) The child-care solutions I came across fall into three main categories:

1. Preschool children and no child care: These are parents who have decided to do it all and attempt to work at home with preschoolers underfoot. These parents are usually entrepreneurs, because most telecommuters' bosses do not allow this arrangement. Parents who work at home with their kids full-time squeeze work hours out of the day before the kids get up, while the kids nap, while their spouses are home in the evening, after the kids go to bed, and whenever they can find some way to occupy the kids during the day.

These parents do it all by accepting that a full work day for them will consist of a maximum of six hours of work. They also say they have lowered their standards about what constitutes a clean house and quiet time to concentrate. Two other techniques these parents have adopted are being upfront with clients about the fact that the kids are at home and being willing to tell people they need to call them back if the kids are acting up. This mode of operation is obviously not an option in all types of businesses, but some professionals say it works for them. These parents also hire child care when they need guaranteed uninterrupted time to complete a project.

2. Preschool children and child care: Even parents whose primary reason for wanting to work at home is a desire to spend more time with their children often opt for child care. These parents are able to spend more time with their kids than they did when they worked in an office, even if they have child care full-time. When child care is in the house, these parents have lunch and take breaks with their kids. If the children go to outside day care, parents still say they get more quality time with their kids than when they commuted to work because they can drop the kids off later and pick them up earlier than they used to.

Parents who have part-time child care say having someone to watch the kids enables them to give their full attention to work when they are working and to the kids when they are not.

3. School-age children: These parents take advantage of the concentrated work time when their children are in school to talk to clients, have meetings, and do work that requires uninterrupted time. When the kids get home from school, these parents tend to give them their full attention over a snack or lunch, and then run business errands with them or resume work that requires less than their full attention.

The ability to return to work after a child gets home from school obviously depends on how old the child is and how many children you have. Parents say unanimously that having a playmate for a child increases the likelihood of getting any work done.

Five Components of Child-Care Success

Regardless of what child-care option or combination of options you choose, there are a few steps you should take to increase the chances of making the arrangement run smoothly.

1. Do not consistently make yourself available to your kids physically without being available emotionally. It won't enhance your relationship with your kids if you are present in the house but always tied up on the phone or working on the computer. This kind of unavailability can make kids feel unimportant. Be sure there are times when you are completely available to your kids.

Home Office Childcare Tips

✔ Have a stop/go sign on your office door to control traffic.

✔ Instruct older kids not to interrupt when you are on the phone.

✔ Train kids not to touch the computer keyboard.

✔ Ask kids not to pick up your business phone. If your business and personal line are one in the same, teach your kids to take messages cordially.

---

2. If you have hired someone to care for your children in the house, explain to your children why you are not the one watching them even though you are at home. Liken your home office to a corporate office and tell them that you need to put in work hours like anyone who goes to an office.

3. Don't expect too much from your kids. Young children may not be able to understand the concept of not interrupting you when you are in the office.

4. Establish rules. If your kids are old enough to understand rules about the home office, establish some guidelines for when they can and cannot approach you there. Make yourself available for them at certain times and make it clear that you are not always available (unless it is an emergency). Spell out what an emergency is. If you are not available to your kids when they come into the home office, make sure that when you take a break you investigate what your kids wanted.

5. Expect to be tested. Older children will test the boundaries you have established for the home office. They may make noise and interrupt a lot. As long as the guidelines you have established for them approaching you while you work are fair, be firm with them.

What to Do If You Cannot Afford Child Care

Child care is expensive. Some parents I hear from are using home-based work as a way to generate income to cover basic expenses; hiring someone to look after their children is just not financially feasible.

Following are some low-cost or free ideas for managing your kids at home without spending a lot of money.

1. Create a co-op with other parents. Some mothers I talked to have created a neighborhood program in which they earn credit for watching other people's kids—credit that they can cash in when *they* need child care. It works this way: You watch someone's child on a Saturday afternoon for five hours when you're spending time with your own kids and you get a five-hour credit in your account. If you watch two children on Tuesday afternoon when your child comes home from school, you get credit for the time you spent watching them, times two. When you need uninterrupted work time, another parent watches your kids. Co-ops require a lot of organization and vigilant record keeping, and the person who sets it up and coordinates it usually receives credit for hours spent coordinating. For help setting up a co-op, read a booklet called *The Babysitting Co-op Guidebook*, by Patricia McManus. Send a check for $12.95 to 915 North Fourth Street, Philadelphia, PA 19123.

2. If a formal co-op sounds like too much, approach another parent and suggest setting up a reciprocal arrangement.

3. Enlist the help of your older children. In many of the letters I receive, parents talk about the responsibility of caring for younger kids and older kids at home. My advice to them is to put the older kids to work. It's good for older children to pitch in to make the household run smoothly, so feel free to request that they watch their younger siblings in the afternoons so you can get some work done. My mother got her master's degree and worked full-time when I was growing up, and my older sister picked up a lot of slack by watching me and keeping the house in order so that my mother could finish up her term papers.

4. Hire a younger babysitter. Obviously you want to entrust the welfare of your kids only to someone you trust, but since you will be in the house, you may be able to save money by hiring a slightly younger (and cheaper) babysitter than you would if you were going out for the day. It's a modern phenomenon for parents to expect all child care to be performed by adults with impressive credentials.

5. Work at night. Mothers and fathers I talk to often squeeze work hours in after dinner while their spouses get the kids ready for bed, or after the kids are asleep.

6. Use distraction techniques at critical times. Depending on the ages of your children and the work you do, you may be able to use the following technique: Keep a box of special toys near the phone to occupy the kids when you are on important work calls. Parents say the novelty of these toys sometimes keeps the kids quiet for a few minutes.

WORKING AT HOME WITH YOUR SPOUSE

Couples who work at home together have the potential to distract each other and get on each other's nerves. Following are some tips from couples who work at home successfully together for maintaining productivity and a healthy relationship.

You can cut down on conflicts by making a schedule. A couple I know in Massachusetts plans over breakfast. They discuss who's having clients visit the office and when each of them needs to use the one computer. It sounds formal, but they say it cuts down on disagreements in the heat of the business day.

Psychologists who work with couples suggest planning home duties too. It will eliminate last-minute strife over who can pick the kids up from ballet. Some couples even plan the minutiae. A New York City husband-and-wife design team decides ahead of time which one of them will sit at the head of the table during staff meetings, and who'll launch a client presentation. Experts from the Family Business Institute in Atlanta say couples should put egos aside and divvy up these jobs based on who's best at what.

A Long Island couple that works at home keeps the peace by helping each other as much as possible, even if it means doing a little extra. Their advice is, don't keep a scorecard. One of you may have to do all the tedious chores around the house for weeks while the other finishes a major project. To keep on track, think about the common goal of making the business and house run smoothly.

At the same time, you also need to be sure that the help and advice you give each other does not work against you. The Family Business Institute claims couples can become insulated and can reinforce each other's bad habits. To avoid this problem, get an outside advisor—someone who understands your business but can give you a fresh perspective. This can be someone in your industry or just a businessperson you admire. You can offer to pay her for her time, barter, or appeal to her desire to help.

If you want to cut down on inevitable wear and tear on a relationship, do something together that shakes up the way you relate. If one person usually runs the show, spend a weekend doing something the other person is good at; take turns being in charge.

CREATING BOUNDARIES FOR FAMILY AND FRIENDS

No matter how carefully structured your schedule is and how expertly you manage your work life, you may encounter a common problem: family and friends not taking your work seriously because you are not working in a traditional environment. My mother and I once had a struggle over the issue of having my cousin from Ireland stay in my apartment for more than a week while he was visiting New York. My mother stressed the importance of family and the distance he had traveled to get here. She even said she'd have to cover the cost of the hotel if I didn't let him sleep on my sofa. She persisted until I drew the analogy that having a guest sleeping on my sofa would be equivalent to her having someone living in the waiting room of the office where she works as a therapist.

This is a quintessential example of how tough it is to set up boundaries between yourself and your family when you work at home. Even after years of working at home, my family and friends occasionally treat me as if I'm not working just because my office is in my apartment. You may encounter the same kind of treatment. It can range from neighbors asking for errands and favors while you're "home" to friends feeling hurt when you can't spend an afternoon over lunch with them. The way to decrease the frequency of these disruptive episodes is to train your family and friends. Try the following steps to train the people in your life:

1. **Constantly reinforce the fact that you are working.** When friends call and you are on another call, make sure to say, "I'm on with a client." If you are busy when a family member calls with a non-urgent request, say, "I am finishing up a proposal—I will call you back later." These reminders set up boundaries that are automatically observed in an office.

2. **Let people know you have hours.** I sometimes request that people who call me socially call me back after 9 P.M.

3. **Always refer to the place where you work as your office.**

4. **Create a list of rules for family members regarding interruptions.** This can mean, for example, that your kids cannot interrupt you unless it is an emergency when you are on the phone (this works only for older kids, obviously). I also know a mother who posted her hours outside of her office so that her family knew when they could interrupt.

5. **Go to the door to answer neighbors' requests with a portable phone on your ear.** Talk into the phone with a business associate (whether there is one on the other end or not) whenever neighbors come to your door with a request. You can even mouth to them that you will get back to them in a few minutes and then take an hour to do so. Apologize for the delay, but say you do not have a minute to spare. They will get the message.

6. **Dress up.** Many people use dressing in professional clothes to send a message to the family that they are working. Look for more on dressing for work in this chapter.

7. **Answer all unwelcome requests on your time with specific reasons why you cannot participate.** Say, "I'd love to, but I'm finishing up a proposal Wednesday morning," or "I have a client meeting that day." This will send a clear message that your home office is a place of business, not a hobbyist's desk.

8. **Confront the problem head-on.** Sit people down and describe a busy day in your home office. It may be that your friends and family do not realize how hectic your day really is. Then work out some guidelines for when they can make some requests.

9. **Answer your phone with a professional greeting.**

10. **If your family makes requests on your time for during the day,** tell them you can take care of it after hours, just as they would.

11. **Create a formal division of labor among family members** so that the burden of chores does not automatically fall on you.

MAINTAINING TIES TO FAMILY WHEN YOU'RE ON THE ROAD

About 5 million workers in this country travel more than half the time. While they often share the isolation problems of home office workers, they have the added burden of having to find a way to keep in touch with family and friends they are not around to see.

According to Dr. Daniel Kuna, psychotherapist and leadership coach for business owners and upper management in Toledo, Ohio, it is normal for people who are frequently on the road to feel isolated. He stresses the importance of maintaining contact with people with whom you can be yourself and have close, personal interaction. Time spent during the day with clients, with whom there is an agenda aside from interacting, cannot take the place of contact with family and friends. The tips that follow may help you maintain this much-needed contact.

▲ **Use pictures to rekindle emotional ties.** Lots of people keep pictures of loved ones on their office desk or a dresser at home. If you are frequently away from these two places, carry pictures with you. You can set these pictures up in your hotel room and look at them at the beginning of the day to evoke feelings of love for your family. You are reminded of how you feel about them, and for a moment you are taken to the experience of being with them. You may also want to keep pictures of yourself in your kids' rooms.

▲ **Use pictures to add another dimension to phone calls.** When you call home to talk to your family, enhance the experience by looking at pictures of your kids or spouse while you are talking to them. "This provides you with two modes of input," says Kuna.

▲ **Recreate the rituals you have at home.** If you have young children, call at bedtime and do a "tuck-in" over the phone. Have your spouse bring the portable phone into the bedroom and talk to your children the way you would if you were there. Ask them if they have their teddy, tell them you love them, and tell them to sleep well, or whatever you normally do. You could even bring a short book with you on a trip and read them a story over the phone. This will be comforting to your children and is also a nice ritual for you to include in your day.

▲ **Call in the afternoon.** If you have some freedom in your schedule, call your kids when they get out of school and ask them how their day was.

▲ **Do not feel guilty.** Dr. Kuna says if you spend ten minutes talking to your children, even if it is over the phone, you are probably spending more quality time with them than the average parent who is at home in the evening.

▲ **Bring gifts sparingly.** If you always bring a gift home from a trip, Dr. Kuna says you may spoil a child and hurt yourself. If you hand over a gift each time you reunite with your child, you may begin to wonder if your child is happy to see you or just happy to get the trinket. The presentation of the gift moves the agenda from your relationship with your child to the gift, Kuna says. If your child asks for a gift, say, "Here I am!"

▲ **Do not forget older children.** Even kids in their teens may enjoy a call at bedtime. You may not want to tuck teenagers in, but you can call at the time you know they get ready for bed and talk to them about their day, and tell them you love them. Teenagers are in the process of going off on their own, but even if they do not admit it, they derive a lot of pleasure from knowing they are important to you. If your teenagers are noncommunicative when you call, ask them what is wrong. If they are not in the mood to talk you can offer to tell them about your day.

▲ **When the kids are older, consider taking them on a business trip with you.**

▲ **Have a different routine for keeping in touch with your spouse.** Conversations with your spouse may be better conducted in the morning. At the end of the day, you will probably both be too tired for a good talk. Instead, call in the morning and replicate your usual routine by talking about how you slept and what you each have planned for the day. This is also important for reminding each other that you support each other even though you may be hundreds or thousands of miles apart.

▲ **Bring along an object that reminds you of your spouse.** This can be anything from a picture to a gift that you received from your spouse when you first met, as long as it is something that has emotional importance and evokes feelings about your partner.

▲ **Share all your feelings, not just the bad ones.** It is easy to get into a habit of sharing the downside of your work or your travel experiences with your spouse. While this is important, it is also a good idea to remember to share victories or pleasant experiences of your traveling.

▲ **Have sexual conversations.** Dr. Kuna says it is healthy for partners to talk about missing each other physically and have sexual conversations if they choose to.

▲ **Keep in touch with only a few good friends.** When you are on the road all the time, it is even more difficult to keep in touch with friends. According to Dr. Kuna, this becomes particularly daunting if you believe you have to keep in touch with a dozen people. In reality, you may only be able to keep in touch with a few friends. Realizing your limits may make you more willing to make an effort to keep in touch.

Part Three

SETTING UP YOUR VIRTUAL OFFICE

Customizing Your Workplace ◀
for Efficiency and Comfort

Technology ◀

Nuts and Bolts ◀

CUSTOMIZING YOUR WORKPLACE FOR EFFICIENCY AND COMFORT

6

If you are setting up a virtual office, this may be the first time you've had the freedom to design an office the way you want it. As a telecommuter, you will probably receive some guidelines on where to place electrical cords and how to configure equipment, but beyond that you'll be free to set up your office as you choose. As an entrepreneur, you are totally on your own. While this may at first appear to be just the kind of freedom you have wanted, you may find yourself stymied when you have this latitude because for so long you've had an office set up *for* you. This chapter provides easy-to-apply advice on setting up a home or mobile office. It includes guidelines on office design, organization, and product selection. A section on ergonomics details how to avoid injury from repetitive work in your virtual office.

SETTING UP A HOME OFFICE

The first thing you should do when you set up a home office is forget traditional notions about what an office should look like. Design one that makes it easy for you to complete your work. The biggest mistake you can make is to design a home office that looks just like the corporate office you left behind.

I once interviewed the world-renowned chef Craig Claiborne. As you would imagine, he has a wonderful kitchen. It is big and bright and is set up to make his job—cooking—easy to do. He has three refrigerators, an island/table in the center of the kitchen that is about the size of two-and-a-half dining-room tables, about a dozen burners on the stove, and an entire room devoted to spices. Claiborne set up his home office so that it would be easy to do his work, and you should do the same thing when you are setting up *your* home office.

This doesn't have to be expensive. My big issue when I set up my home office was periodicals: how to keep in order all the newspapers and magazines I needed to read for my work. I found an inexpensive solution in a dozen wooden cubes that form a bookcase on my wall, with a cube for each periodical. Price: under $200. A friend of mine needs a lot of surface space to work in his home office. Since he couldn't find a desk big enough, he made one out of a door.

What it *will* take to design a home office for yourself is a willingness to put some time into determining how you spend your time in the home office and what configuration will best serve you. You will also need to forget a lot of the traditional notions you have about what constitutes an office and realize you may not find the answers to your problems in an office supply store.

To help yourself figure out what your office should have, examine your work patterns for a few days in the office and take note of what you spend the bulk of your time doing. Are you on the computer frequently? Do you have a lot of paper to keep track of? Do you need a large surface space to work on? Are you constantly reaching for reference books or manuals?

Every time you encounter a problem or an inconvenience, make a note of it. Then sit back and imagine what could be done to resolve it. You may not find the solution overnight. I discovered the wooden cubes that tidied up my periodicals mess after months of tripping over piles of magazines and newspapers on my office floor.

That's the general advice. You should also consider the following specifics when you are setting up your office and choosing a site for your home office in your house.

Establish your work space in a part of the house that has lots of light and air. Think about the year-round conditions in this spot, not just what it's like during the season when you are setting up your office.

Set up shop away from the busy areas of your home. Make sure your office is as far as possible from potential distractions such as the kitchen, the front door, family traffic, or a lot of noise. This is especially important if you have children and will have child care in the house during the day. If you can see or hear your children and they can see you, it will be both difficult for you to work and potentially problematic for your kids.

Turn your desk and chair away from the door. Now that you aren't in a corporate environment, you don't have to face the door anymore. Being shielded from the activity at the door will help you concentrate.

Hide supplies that you don't use every day. This is because piles of stationery, extra rolls of tape, and high stacks of envelopes look messy, no matter how neatly they are stored. Disorder can be distracting. If space permits, keep extra supplies in a closet or cupboard.

Keep a small cache of supplies at your desk or near enough that you can easily reach them. This will prevent you from having to get up and cross the room whenever you need something. Time savings like this may seem inconsequential, but small chunks of time add up.

Organize supplies so that they are not only easy to reach, but easy to grasp. For example, you shouldn't have to move two piles of paper and open a box to get your hands on a piece of your letterhead stationery.

Set up things so they function smoothly. I've seen lots of home offices in which someone pulls a book off a shelf and everything else falls over, or where there isn't enough space near the fax machine to easily insert documents and collect incoming faxes. These small glitches in work flow can turn into major sources of stress when you are experiencing work pressure.

Clear all old clutter out of your home office area. If you cannot remove these things from the room, at least move them out of your field of vision.

Realize that a home office does not have to be a separate room. A home office can be part of a room, as long as you have a permanent work space that is dedicated to your work. However, sharing a space with a room that has a lot of family traffic during work hours may be distracting.

Have a dedicated work area. Do not dismantle your home office and use it for something else when the work day is over. You need to have an area in which you can keep things organized and free from other people's interference. If you are a corporate telecommuter, this will probably be required by your employer to prevent security problems and concerns about family members using company property. If you work for yourself, this will be necessary if you want to take the home office tax deduction. Having a separate work space is also important from a productivity standpoint. If you perform only work tasks in your work area, you are more likely to feel like working when you are there. It creates a trigger similar to what exists in a corporate office.

Create a "safe" trash can. Some people are nervous about throwing things out because they think they'll need it later. This tendency can lead to a lot of home office clutter. If this is your problem, try what I do. I've created a "safe" trash can. Nothing goes into the safe trash can except for paper. No apple cores, no soda cans, nothing that I wouldn't want to have to see again if I need to look in the trash can.

I empty this trash can only every few weeks, so there's a grace period after I throw something out during which I can retrieve it. This system has made it much easier for me to pitch stuff.

Keep your home office from becoming stuffy. Now that you work at home, you are in charge of ventilation, too. If your office becomes stuffy, you will have difficulty concentrating and being productive. It's easy for this to happen. Sometimes when I go out to do errands and come back home, I cannot believe how hot and stuffy my apartment is. But when I was sitting at my desk before I went out, I didn't notice. Keep a fan in your office and always have a window open somewhere in your house to keep air circulating.

EQUIPMENT PLACEMENT IN THE HOME OFFICE

Where you put your computer and other equipment in your home office will dramatically affect your comfort and the well-being of your equipment. In the ergonomics section of this chapter I will go into detail about how to choose a chair and sit at your computer, but the following instructions will give you some basics on placement of items in your office.*

△ Make sure your equipment is placed on sturdy tables or secure shelves.

△ Use a surge protector for all equipment. An uninterruptable power supply is necessary if you live in an area with a lot of surges or power failures.

△ Extreme cold or heat can temporarily or permanently affect your computer, so do not place it too near a window, a heater, or in direct sunlight.

△ Do not put a thermal fax machine in the sun. Sunlight and heat will darken the paper.

△ Make sure when you set up your fax and printer that you have space near these machines for incoming faxes to land, outgoing faxes to be stored, and a place for you to staple or organize papers. This will cut down on stress in your home office.

△ Minimize glare on your computer screen. If your screen faces a window, the light will create glare that will tire your eyes. If a window is behind your computer screen, there can be too much contrast between the sun and the dark screen, which can also hurt your eyes.

*Some of these equipment tips are from Georgene Pijut of Georgene's Home Office Design Company in White Plains, New York.

△ Place equipment so that you can reach it conveniently, either from your chair (without twisting or moving in a way that may hurt your body) or somewhere in your office that you can easily get to. You are better off getting up to use a piece of equipment than reaching awkwardly for it from your chair.

△ Set up lighting that doesn't strain your eyes. There are two types of lighting, *task* lighting and *ambient* lighting. Task lighting is what shines on your work. It should be placed directly above what you are working on to eliminate shadows. Do not have task lighting in front of your computer screen, since this will create glare. Ambient lighting lights the room and should ideally be reflected off the ceiling so that it does not create glare off your computer screen.

DEVELOPING AN ORGANIZATIONAL SYSTEM

In order to keep the home office you have created from becoming chaotic, you need at least two things: a good filing system and a place for everything. These systems will make it possible for you to take care of all of the varied responsibilities that are part of working in a virtual office.

Filing

When it comes to filing, there is no right way to do it. A good filing system has a structure that makes sense to the person who will use it. When you're determining how to label and organize your files, it's important to listen to your own sense of organization and not get caught up with conventional ideas of how files should be labeled.

Ilise Benun, a Hoboken, New Jersey–based office organizer, says the only right way to file is a way that will make it easy for you to find things again. She says that when she goes into someone's office to help redo files, she asks her client to imagine he is looking for the item about to be filed. By doing this, the person can determine how he would think about the item. This approach helps people create a system that reflects their sense of organization.

When I'm filing something, I don't agonize over the right thing to call it. I file it under the first word that comes to my mind when I create the file. Chances are, if that word came to mind when I was filing it, it will when I'm looking for it. The only rule is that you should keep your work files and personal files in separate file cabinets. This will not only keep you more organized, but it will also make you less likely to be distracted by personal matters during work hours.

You will also need a system for keeping up with filing. My aunt Nan realized that I could never devise one, so one Christmas she gave me a certificate for filing services. When I am behind on my filing, I can call her in for some intensive help. She sorts me out until I need help again. If you can create a system for keeping up with it yourself, great; otherwise enlist some help.

Information Flow To operate successfully on your own, you also need a system for moving information through your office and an office design that reinforces that system. I'm not talking about the "touch it only once" kind of rules that sound sensible, but which I have never been able to apply. I mean you need to develop a system for placing things in your home office in their various incarnations. You need a place for incoming and outgoing mail, and projects in their various stages of completion. This system will obviously vary greatly from one office to another; the important thing is that your system works for you.

Decide from the start where you will put incoming mail, current projects, future projects and any other items that tend to collect on your desk. Then create an office setup to manage these items. Your system may be something as simple as stacked baskets or files stacked upright on your desk in a holder. Think carefully about your work flow and then go to an office supply store (yes, for this the office supply store is your best bet) and determine what solution best fits your work. As is the case with designing the configuration of your home office, don't expect to find the answer easily. You may have to combine two products from the store, or buy one item and change it to suit your purposes.

You will also need a system for handling phone messages. I recommend putting people's names and numbers directly onto your to-do list so that you will remember to return their calls. If you do not use a to-do list, establish a place in your office for writing down incoming messages. You may want to create a file on your computer or use something as simple as a spiral notebook. Something that you keep around for a while after the day you use it is a good idea, in case you need to get your hands on someone's number a few weeks or months after they originally called.

To make your life run more smoothly, request in your outgoing message on your voice mail or answering machine that people leave their number for you. This will save you from having to look it up. If you need to keep track of calls you make and want a long-term record of calls you place, you should definitely create a file or notebook where you regularly record this information.

I encourage you to keep as much information as you can on your computer and keep paper to a minimum. This is important in a home office where you may not have administrative help to keep things orderly. Phone numbers are a good candidate for computer storage. I keep all of my phone numbers on the computer. I keep them in three different files, each one representing a different piece of my business. When I need a number, I use the search function in my word processor to find it quickly under the person's last name. I also have a sheet of numbers I call frequently posted on the wall near my desk. Many people use personal organizers to keep phone numbers organized. The choice is yours. The important thing is to create a system for accessing things you need to get to frequently.

I hate to use the phrase, but it fits: "If you don't have a place for every-thing, everything will be out of place." This is reality. You need to have adequate storage space for files, books, supplies, and anything else you have in your home office. This will save time and will cut down on stress. Furthermore, it will prevent you from slipping into slovenliness. Virtual offices can be messy because there is no need to keep things neat for the sake of a boss or coworkers. Prevent this from happening by having enough space for the things you need to store.

Storage

HOME OFFICE ERGONOMICS

A few years ago I began feeling pain in my wrist and shoulder from all the hours I work at the computer. If I worked in an office I'd have asked my manager for help figuring out what to do. But since I work at home, I had

---

Storage Tips

✔ **Buy only top-quality file cabinets.** Cheap file cabinets tilt forward if you open both drawers and will warp over time. The investment in a good file cabinet will always pay off. Look for discounted office furniture (under "Office Furniture, Discount" in the yel-low pages); it is relatively easy to find name-brand stuff for less this way.

✔ **Don't buy a two-drawer file cabinet unless you plan to work at home short-term.** Those small file cabinets are fine for personal files, but won't cut it for business.

✔ **If you have enough room for one in your office, buy a lateral file cabinet** to create more surface space for yourself.

✔ **Have sufficient shelving.** To get around the potential high cost of shelving at office supply stores, buy shelves at discount stores like IKEA.

✔ **Store things you do not use regularly.** In her book *Organizing Your Home Office for Success*, Lisa Kanarek has advice for how to keep your office free of clutter. She sug-gests moving all of your knickknacks and all of the things you use only once a week to secondary surfaces like a file cabinet or a shelf. Anything you use once a month should be stored in a file or put away on a shelf. Items you use less frequently than that should be in a closet.

to investigate it myself. After consulting about a dozen ergonomics experts and manufacturers of office furniture and equipment, I found that there were steps I could take to cut down on bodily wear and tear from long hours at the computer.

Getting better took a lot of energy and a willingness to change my work habits. I was willing to do just about anything, though, because I was in so much pain I couldn't hold my toothbrush or turn a doorknob! One of the first things I needed to do was build up my upper body strength very carefully. The physical therapists I went to explained that one of the reasons I was experiencing wrist pain was that my upper back was weak. Because my upper back was not strong enough to take the strain of all the typing I do, my wrists and forearms were being strained. But building upper-back strength when my wrists were so sore I could hardly hold my toothbrush was not easy. I used very light weights and did exercises prescribed by my specialist. I also began carefully stretching my hands and arms, and took ibuprofen to ease the inflammation in my wrists. To keep from bending my right wrist, the one that was most damaged, I wore a wrist guard when I typed and at night when I slept.

I also changed the way I use my computer mouse and the way I type. I purchased a desk attachment that holds the keyboard very low, almost in my lap. It also has a wide platform in front of the keyboard that allows my wrists to slide from side to side, instead of stretching for keys at the side of the keyboard. The same system also includes an extender board that keeps my computer mouse at the side of my body, so I don't have to learn forward to reach it. I also bought a new office chair that adjusts in every possible direction. I created a system that works for me. When I work on other people's computer setups, or on a portable computer, my symptoms return.

If you are experiencing any kind of pain from working on a computer, consult a physician. These symptoms only get worse and rarely, if ever, go away on their own. It took a lot of trial and error to find a solution for my problem, but the work was well worth it. Use the general advice and the resources that follow to assemble a comfortable and safe work configuration for yourself.

Sitting at Your Desk

Without the proper chair, you are almost certain to experience some strain on your body. At a minimum, a chair should support your lower back. To determine if your chair supports you sufficiently, put your hand on the small of your back and see if it's permanently bolstered by the backrest. If it is not, adjust your chair until it supports the natural curve of your back. But make sure your chair is not forcing you to arch your back or sit in an unnatural position. Some people use lumbar cushions for extra support in this region. Be careful, though, because many lumbar cushions are too large and will actually strain your back. A chair should also give you upper back support. To get the support you need, the chair should come up to at least the top of your shoulder blades. Regardless of how well supported your back is, you'll probably feel better if your desk chair doesn't have arms. Resting your elbows on chair arms can push your back and shoulders into stressful positions.

Another common problem is sitting up straight or leaning forward when you're at your desk. Both of these positions put strain on the back and wrists, among other things. Instead, you want to lean back slightly in your chair, at about 110 degrees or whatever feels comfortable to you. The overall position you should assume in your desk chair is arms at your sides—not stretching forward or sticking out behind you—with your elbows bent in approximately a 90-degree angle. When your hands touch the keyboard, make sure your fingertips are at the same height as your elbows. It's crucial that your wrists not bend upward or downward when your hands are on the keyboard. You want to maintain what's called a *wrist-neutral position*, which means that your wrists lie flat while you type. This position may be difficult to achieve without some kind of *extender board* that brings your keyboard closer to your body. An extender board is basically a tray that slides out from your desk and lets you determine how close the keyboard will be to your body. You can buy one of these or make your own out of a sheet of wood.

Another important part of sitting correctly is keeping your thighs parallel to the floor with your feet firmly planted on the floor. If your feet dangle, you'll put pressure on your thighs and restrict circulation in your legs. If you can't adjust your chair so that your feet reach the ground, buy a footstool or pile up some phone books to make your own.

If you buy a new chair, make sure that it is as adjustable as possible. You'll probably have to spend a minimum of two to three hundred dollars to get a good chair, but consider it an investment in your business because it will make you more productive.

Correct Computer Keyboard Positioning

The right computer keyboard will also go a long way toward preventing strain. There are about a dozen different keyboards on the market and as many opinions about which is best. But one thing ergonomic experts agree on is that a keyboard should allow you to keep your wrists straight when you type. How you move your hands on the keyboard can also affect your potential for injury.

Again, the correct position for your arms and hands is to have your upper arms at your side, not in front of you or behind you, and have your wrists flat when you type. It's important to take pains—excuse the pun—not to stretch your fingers when you type, as you were probably taught in your touch-typing classes. Instead, move your entire hand and arm when

Finding Ergonomic Products

Chances are, you'll need to try a variety of products until you find what's comfortable for you. Some office supply and furniture stores are starting to stock ergonomic products, but the bulk of this merchandise is still sold through special dealers or through the mail. Following is a list of resources of ergonomic products.

- ✔ AliMed Ergonomics
  (800) 225-2610
  Call for a catalogue.

- ✔ Ergosource
  (800) 969-4374
  Footrests, keyboards, headsets, monitor supports, antiglare screens.

- ✔ Global Computer Supplies
  (800) 227-1246
  A variety of ergonomic products.

- ✔ Hello Direct
  (800) 520-3311
  Headsets.

- ✔ Medtech Surgical
  (800) 769-9515
  Antiglare screens, wrist rests, keyboard and mouse extender boards, magnifying lenses.

- ✔ Neutral Posture
  (409) 822-5080
  Chairs.

- ✔ Plantronics
  (800) 544-4660
  Headsets.

- ✔ Proformix
  P.O. Box 22, Route 22 West
  Whitehouse Station, NJ 08889
  voice (908) 534-6400; fax (908) 534-9161
  Keyboards, mouse extender boards, document holders, and other ergonomic products. Contact the main office to find a dealer in your area.

- ✔ The Summerland Group
  (305) 745-4303
  Designs entire offices that are ergonomically oriented.

- ✔ Yellow pages
  Most well-established office furniture manufacturers such as Knoll, Herman Miller, and Steelcase sell ergonomic chairs. You can sometimes find discounted brand-name equipment. Look in the yellow pages for ads for these companies.

you need to reach keys at the side of the keyboard. Give your hands and arms a break by typing lightly on the keyboard instead of pounding the keys. Pounding puts stress on the fingers and can also damage your elbows and shoulders.

If you use a portable computer, you may need a support device that keeps your wrists from bending back. Wrist supports attach to the front of the computer and form a plane with the edge of the keyboard. But a word of caution: If you use one of these, make sure you rest the fleshy part of your palm, not your wrists, on the extension.

It's not enough to have a comfortable keyboard. The computer mouse caused most of my problems. Injuries from the mouse are common because the motion of reaching forward and to the side to use the mouse can strain the shoulder and wrist. One way to solve this problem is to bring the mouse closer to your body by getting an extender board for it. This enables you to keep your upper arms at your side, with your arms bent at a 90-degree angle.

Other options are to buy a flatter mouse model or a mouse that tilts to the side. Wrist rests that attach to your mouse are also available, but again, make sure your palms, not your wrists, rest on the supports.

The top of your computer monitor should be at eye level. If it's higher than that, your head will tilt back and you may get headaches. If your monitor's too low, you may develop problems with your neck. *Avoiding Eye Strain*

To reduce eye strain from using the monitor, make sure your lights are not shining directly on the computer screen. This goes for light from a window, too. Avoid having a window behind you or near your monitor, or an overhead light that reflects down on a screen. Experts say the ideal lighting combination is a desk lamp that shines directly on your desk and an overhead or room lamp on the other side of your office. Look for more on where to place a computer monitor in your office in "Equipment Placement in the Home Office" earlier in this chapter.

An antiglare screen can also be an eye-saver. It significantly tones down the glare that comes off your computer screen and will reduce wear and tear on your eyes. If you use a glass antiglare screen, try not to touch it; you will create smudges that will hurt your eyes.

Another potential ergonomic nightmare comes from awkward use of the phone. Cradling the phone between your ear and shoulder will sap your energy and strain your body. The best ergonomic investment I've ever made is buying a telephone headset. It frees up my hands for working while I'm on the phone and eliminates cradling the phone. Headsets are available in stationary or cordless models. *Avoiding Neck Pain from the Phone*

Stopping Pain Before It Starts

You'll help yourself avoid computer strain if you stretch your shoulders, arms, wrists, and fingers several times a day. Just twenty minutes of work can strain your body, so take frequent breaks to ward off injury.

If you want to make sure you aren't straining your body, you can buy a product called Pocket Ergometer, a portable biofeedback monitor that registers stress on the body audibly. It's $300 now, but Biomechanics Corporation, Melville, New York-based manufacturer, is working on a much less expensive version. You can also get a software package called Life-Guard [TVM Technologies, (516) 676-2545] that reminds you to take periodic breaks based on keyboard usage.

Getting Medical Help

If you are already feeling pain in your hands or arms, stop working immediately and get medical attention. Some common stretches will aggravate the problem, so you shouldn't start stretching before you have the problem looked at. Lots of different health professionals, from neurologists to physical therapists and chiropractors, work with these injuries. You can start with your doctor and get a referral for a specialist, but beware of doctors who dismiss these problems as complaints about hard work.

De-Stressing Your Home Office

If you're on the phone a lot, you're probably listening to too much touch-tone and dial-tone noise. This is a form of repetitive stress; getting rid of it will make you less harried. For relief, you should flip the switch on your phone from push-button to rotary; most phones have this option.

This last tip isn't ergonomic, but it does have to do with comfort. My home office is less stressful and more comfortable since I did one simple thing: I turned the ringer on my fax machine down all the way, so now faxes come in silently.

SETTING UP A MOBILE OFFICE

If you work in your car, you will need to be even more fastidious in setting up and maintaining an office than people who work in home offices. You will have fewer support services and less storage and working space than those of us who work at home. The key to setting up and keeping an orderly mobile office is to develop a system and then use that system routinely. The following steps will help you do both.

1. Set up the car to suit your needs. If you want to run an efficient mobile office, you must design it the way you would any other office. All of your supplies must be on hand and easily accessible, and the office must be designed to suit your needs. With this in mind, make a list of what tasks you will be completing in your mobile office. Then make a list of all of the supplies, storage devices, and equipment you'll need to make it possible.

To do this, be creative; don't look for the answer in an office supply catalogue. Think about how you would handle the organizational problem if you could do anything you wanted. I know a woman who created a wooden platform above her emergency brake that she uses as a mini-desk. Another woman I know permanently secured her tape recorder to her dashboard so that when she needs to use it, her hands are free.

2. Turn the trunk of your car into a file cabinet. You can replicate a file cabinet in your trunk by purchasing a vertical file box. This will keep your files and paper supplies upright and organized and will prevent wear and tear on the things you carry with you. There are many options for storing your files vertically which you can find in office supply catalogues or stores. Plastic file-storage boxes and small portable file boxes are two other options.

3. Because you will be using your trunk as a storage place, keep all of your personal belongings out of the way. Use a milk crate, box, bag, or any other trunk-organizing device to keep your baseball mitt, windshield-wiper fluid, and beach blanket from getting mixed up with your sales presentation materials.

4. Have a place for everything. If you notice that clutter is piling up or you are at a loss for how to cope with some aspect of your work in the car, stop and deal with it. There is lots of gadgetry on the market to help you do this. For example, the Brookstone catalogue [(800) 926-7000] offers a windshield-mounted pen and notepad and a suction-cup "Eye Glass Vault." The Beverly Hills Motoring Accessories catalogue [(800) FOR-BHMA] offers a mobile desk that includes storage for a laptop computer, fax, cellular phone, and beverages. Keller Design [(800) 683-1227] sells a car tray, and Mobile Planet [(800) MPLANET] sells a mobile desk that is big enough for a portable computer.

5. More mundane but important products for every mobile office are stamps, stationery, a calculator, paper clips, a small stapler, a small scissors, a trash bag, a cup holder, a mirror, some snacks, and napkins. Use a box, briefcase, or bag to keep these items together.

6. Use a cassette recorder to take down thoughts or notes from conversations you have on your cellular phone, rather than trying to write while you drive.

7. Keep paper to a minimum. One way to do this is to keep as much information as possible on a computer or other electronic device. Use technology for storing to-do lists, phone numbers, directions, and other information. One mobile person I talked to said he simplified his life when he stopped writing directions down on paper. Instead, he obtains general directions that he can remember and calls his destination when he gets close for the details of how to get the rest of the way.

It may not be possible to record all phone numbers on the computer as soon as you get them, but make an effort to enter them as soon as possible. Some mobile office workers keep the portable computer open on the passenger seat and enter phone numbers at traffic lights, in traffic, in rest areas, and in parking lots.

The Three Biggest Mistakes You Can Make in Your Mobile Office

✔ **Not enough supplies in the car.** Take time to restock your car with promotional materials, sales materials, stationery, and any other supplies you need on a regular basis. Set up a regular time each week to restock.

✔ **Too much junk in the car.** In the same way you need to clear out a home office before you set up shop, you should clear out your car. If you have golf clubs from the weekend, or other personal items that are taking up space, remove them.

✔ **Not the right car.** Lisa Kanarek says many of her clients buy new cars or vans and say, "Why didn't I do this sooner?" Obviously, buying a new car is not always an option. But when you are shopping for a new car, features such as four doors, a hatchback, and a big trunk are important considerations for a mobile office.

These tips are from Lisa Kanarek, consultant, speaker, and author of *Organize Your Home Office For Success* (New York: Plume, 1993).

---

8. Buy a car with extras. Some cars, such as the 1995 Chevrolet Blazer and Tahoe and GMC's Suburban and light truck models, have extra electrical outlets in addition to the cigarette lighter. Others have large lockable center consoles or other storage bins that come in handy when you need to stash equipment out of sight. The Dodge Ram and Caravan have two. All Saabs have removable cup and coin holders in the center console that, when removed, make room for a portable computer. Chevrolet's Tahoe sport utility vehicle has a vinyl security screen that slides across the rear compartment to conceal whatever you have there. The Tahoe also has a center console with a small storage bin.

9. Double your power. Purchase a Y-connector for your car's power outlet so you can plug in two machines at once.

10. Rent the right car. Request a model with auxiliary power outlets.

11. Look for surface space. Some cars now have fold-down or pull-out trays.

12. Consider lighting. Look for large center dome lights as well as map lights, in case you need to do some work after dark. To keep bright sunlight off your computer screen, the most effective kind of tinting you can have on your car is solar-tinted glass. See your dealer for more information.

See also "Setting Up a Home Office" at the beginning of this chapter for more tips that apply to mobile offices.

MOBILE OFFICE TECHNOLOGY TIPS

A good setup in your mobile office is important, but there is more to working successfully in your car than having the right gadgetry and office supplies. You also need to be aware of how to maintain and get the most out of the technology you need to do your job on the road. The following tips will help you accomplish both.

1. **Put your computer in sleep mode instead of turning it off** when you are running on battery power and need to take a break. This saves you the battery power that your system would use to start up the system again.

2. **When you are using a portable fax card in your computer over a hotel phone line, be careful.** Some hotels have digital phone systems which send out higher amperage than typical lines during ringing, which can burn out fax cards. To avoid this, either stay in hotels that cater to business travelers (because they have phone systems that will not harm your card), or get an acoustic connector [available from Unlimited Systems in San Diego, (619) 622-1400], a device that slips over the phone to eliminate this problem.

3. **Watch out for extreme temperatures.** If you leave your portable computer or cellular phone in the car and the temperature drops too low, the equipment may develop problems. The same goes for direct sunlight or high temperatures. If your equipment is exposed to extreme temperatures, allow its temperature to stabilize before using it. A good rule of thumb is, when you are comfortable in the car's temperature (because of air conditioning or heat), the device will be usable again.

4. **Think about crime.** Theft is a huge problem for mobile workers. Take equipment with you if you want to keep it.

5. **Take care of your thermal paper.** If you have a portable fax in the car, be careful not to leave thermal fax paper (the stuff with the strange coated surface) in a warm car or in sunlight. Heat and sunlight will ruin the paper by turning it dark.

6. **Take advantage of power where it's available.** You can get some extra power from your computer by plugging in your computer and modem at the airport. Most airports have electrical outlets scattered throughout the waiting areas. You may have to search a little or ask

maintenance workers to point you in the right direction (they know where vacuum cleaners are plugged in for cleaning). Most public phone banks have a few jacks for plugging in your modem. If you are willing to spend some money, American Airlines Admirals Clubs in thirty-eight airports provide electrical outlets, free local calls with data hookups, free faxing and photocopying, and free international calls at overseas locations. Membership is $250 the first year and $150 annually after that.

7. **Never place items on top of the dashboard.** If you have an accident, these objects will hurtle toward you.

8. **If you plan to put your computer on the glove compartment lid,** be sure the glove compartment lid is strong enough to support it. Otherwise you run the risk of having your computer fall.

9. **If you have a car with bucket seats, set up your office in the back.** Fold down the rear seats to create a flat surface. Be sure to secure the seats so that they do not flap up once you have placed your computer and other equipment on them.

10. **To keep your computer batteries charged,** ask for a table near an electrical outlet if you go to a restaurant for lunch.

TECHNOLOGY

How to Evaluate, Buy, and Maintain Electronic Office Equipment

This chapter will help you make decisions about technology by providing you with the questions you need to ask yourself and explanations of the features you should consider before making a technology decision. I will not be mentioning product names because technology changes too rapidly for any recommendations I could make now to be meaningful by the time you read them. I am also leaving out a discussion of online services and the Internet and certain other technologies for the same reason. For product reviews and up-to-the-minute information on technology, you can read computer magazines such as *PC Magazine*, *Mobile Office*, *Home Office Computing*, and *Computer Shopper*. *Consumer Reports* is also a good resource.

COMPUTERS

Only you know the best system for your business based on your needs, your budget, your desire to travel with your computer, and a number of other factors. The best general advice I can give you is that you should make a list of what you will be using your computer for and then read some computer magazines or talk to friends who know about computers to research what kind of system best suits your needs. If you do not know anyone who can help you, look for a computer salesperson who is willing to listen carefully to your needs before offering a solution.

When it comes to money, don't scrimp, but don't go for broke either. You want a system that will meet your needs now and a few years out, but you may not need the top-of-the-line or latest system. You'll have to make three major decisions when it comes to choosing a computer: power, memory, and disk space.

Power is how fast the machine processes information and how fast it runs software applications. When you hear people talk about a 486 or a Pentium machine, they are talking about the type of microprocessor the machine has, and therefore how fast it can work for you.

Memory, also known as *RAM*, is the machine's temporary storage area for programs and data. RAM will also affect the speed with which your computer can work your software. In order to get a feel for how much memory you need, ask some computer users you know for advice instead of relying solely on what a computer salesperson tells you.

Hard disk space is permanent storage room for software and data. The rule with hard disk space is to get about twice as much as you think you could ever need.

Following are computer features to consider before making a purchase:

Monitor. You should choose a computer screen (monitor) carefully. Monitors vary widely in price, but I suggest a quality monitor that will minimize wear and tear on your eyes. As of the writing of this book, the standard optimum *dot pitch* (distance between dots of similar color) is 0.28 millimeters or less. Retailers often put a cheap monitor with 0.39 dot pitch with a system to lower the price. If this is the case, ask about the cost of upgrading to a better monitor. A color monitor is a must. The standard monitor size is 14 inches; however, you may want to consider a 15-inch or a high-resolution 17-inch monitor if you spend a lot of time in front of your computer, particularly if you do a lot of graphics work or need to view multiple Windows applications on the screen at one time.

Multimedia. Almost all computers now come with a multimedia package that includes a sound board, a CD-ROM drive, and speakers. The sound board lets you play audio and the CD-ROM allows you to display moving video images and will enable you to use the many reference guides available now such as phone directories and encyclopedias. Be sure that the CD-ROM drive that comes with your computer is at least double speed.

Modems. If the computer you're buying comes with a modem—a device that lets your computer transfer data over the phone line to other systems, including online services—make sure it's a fast one. To find out what "fast" is when you are buying your system, ask people who use modems before you buy.

Faxing. An internal fax modem can be effective if you know you will send *only* faxes that were produced directly from your computer. The drawback of an internal fax is that unless you have a scanning device, you cannot fax out a piece of paper that you have in your hand. In addition, when someone sends a fax to your internal fax modem, you will most likely have to print it out before you can work on it. See also "Fax Machines" later in this chapter.

Portability. Buying a portable computer makes sense for more people than ever before because manufacturers now offer *docking stations* and *port replicators*. By plugging your computer into these devices, you are able to use a regular-size desktop monitor and keyboard while they are connected to your portable computer. In this scenario your portable computer is your only computer, meaning that you do not have to worry about copying files onto floppy disks before you leave the office. When you return to the office you have the comfort of using a larger keyboard and monitor.

Expansion slots. Expansion slots enable you to enhance and change the system you own and make your system last longer by adding things to the system on cards that fit in these slots. Things you might want to add to your system include a fax-modem card, a hard drive, or a sound card. I suggest four open slots on your computer.

You have lots of choices of where to buy your computer. The major ones include the following.

Where to Buy a Computer

Mail Order Houses. If you know what you want, you may be able to get the best price from a mail order company. These companies will sell you a computer over the phone, ship it to you, and in some cases, provide phone support and service support through a local organization. But do not assume that mail order is the best deal; as with any other retail venue, compare prices before buying from a mail order firm. Ask about how repairs and service will be handled. Some vendors require you to send a system back when it needs repairing; others have local service contracts. Be wary of small mail order companies; you want to be sure the company you are buying from will be around for a while. To find mail order companies, look in a publication such as *Computer Shopper*.

Computer Stores. Your local computer store can be a good option, if the store is interested in working with individuals and not just large companies that are buying thousands of units. You will know if they are interested in your business easily enough. See what kind of response your visit to the store elicits. Computer stores have the potential benefit of offering personalized service and support. In some cases a computer store will have higher prices than a mail order company or a superstore, but not always. Even if a system from a local computer store costs slightly more, it is usually worth the price if they provide good service. If you can have someone come to your home office and set up your system and deliver service in your home office, you may determine that a little extra money is worth it. The potential drawback of a local computer store is that selection may be limited.

Computer Shopping Advice

✔ **Always negotiate.** You can usually save on something—labor to set up your system, a carrying case, etc.—if you negotiate. Research prices before you go to the store and bring any ads you can get your hands on that quote prices from other stores or vendors.

✔ **Shop at off-peak hours.** If you shop on a Saturday afternoon, you are bound to get the least amount of help. You may also find a frenzied sales person who is not in the mood to make a deal. If you can, shop during the day (not at lunchtime, though). Otherwise, try weeknights.

✔ **Ask questions.** If a salesperson is not answering your questions fully, ask to speak to someone else or go elsewhere. Don't feel stupid for asking questions.

✔ **Clarify who is providing service.** Make sure you understand who will help you with a technical problem or a broken part. It may be the retailer or the maker of the computer. If a salesperson wants you to buy an extended service program, make sure that it is necessary and that you are not already covered by the manufacturer during this period.

✔ **Beware of great deals.** Computer salespeople may have been told to push a particular product because the store is overstocked on an item, or because it will be discontinued soon. This can just mean you are getting a good deal, or it can mean you'll be stuck with something you don't need. Make sure you understand why you are purchasing each portion of your system.

Superstores. Superstores can offer the benefit of good selection and a good price. Some salespeople in superstores are very knowledgeable, although you may wait a bit for service because these stores tend to be busy. Superstores' greatest appeal is the wide variety of products they carry; you have a chance to compare products before buying. If you choose to shop in a superstore, go during off-peak hours to increase the likelihood that you will receive personalized help.

Electronics Stores. These stores sell calculators, stereos, and computer equipment. Many of these stores are in the business of beating any other retailer's price, so you may be able to save some money if you find the system you want at one of these retail outlets. The potential downside of these stores is that their salespeople do not always know as much about computers as those at some of the other retail options.

Office Supply Stores. Office supply stores will vary a great deal in whether or not they can knowledgeably help you with your technology needs. They have the potential advantage of being designed in many cases to cater to small- and home-based business owners. If you are not receiving the kind of assistance you need with technology, ask if there is someone else in the store who knows more about these systems. My experience has been that there is usually at least one person in the stores who is knowledgeable.

Buying a portable computer is more complicated than buying a desktop system. There are many more considerations for a system that you will carry with you, and features vary widely from one portable computer to the next. Not all systems are alike; you should try out as many systems as possible before purchasing one. Consider the following features before choosing a portable system.

Choosing a Portable Computer

1. Weight. Realize that you will probably be carrying a power supply, a surge protector, and other equipment your computer requires along with your computer. Add to that the weight of your carrying case, papers, and luggage, and it all starts to get heavy. In order to cut down on weight, think carefully about what you will really need on the road. For example, you may be able to do without a floppy drive in your computer.

2. Keyboard. Unlike desktop keyboards, which are pretty much standard, portable keyboards vary drastically from one system to another. Variables include the feel, size, location of keys, palm rest (whether or not there is one), and shape and position of the pointing device. The best keyboard for you will be determined according to personal preference based on your business (whether you use number keys or letter keys more) and a variety of other factors. By trying different systems you may begin to get a feel for what will work best for you, based on how it feels and what kind of work you will be doing on the system. Also see "Home Office Ergonomics" in chapter 6.

3. Cursor control. At the writing of this book most computer vendors are turning away from portables using mice and are moving toward trackballs or, in the case of Apple, a touch pad that is built into the screen. The reason for this is that a mouse on a portable computer is one more thing to remember to pack when you leave your office, and when you're on a plane there is no surface to put the thing down on. Also see "Home Office Ergonomics" in chapter 6.

4. Screen. It is important to go to a store and evaluate the screen of any portable computer you are considering. Put the system in sunlight, darkness, and other shades of light to see how the screen performs. Move the cursor around the screen to determine if it

---

Where to Buy Portable Technology

You can find specialized mail order houses that sell only technology for mobile work. You can find ads for these catalogues in magazines like *Mobile Office* and *Mobile Computing*. Because it is crucial to test the screen and keyboard of a portable computer before you buy it, another good place to find these products is any retailer that has a large selection, including superstores, where you can try a lot of different machines before you buy one.

jumps when you do. Screen choice, like keyboard preference, is personal and will be determined by what you will use the system for. If you want a color notebook, be aware that it will be expensive and weigh more than a regular portable.

5. Battery life. Rich Malloy, editor-in-chief of *Mobile Office* magazine, says you may want to divide the amount of time a vendor touts as battery life for a computer in half. This is because the battery life quoted by a vendor will be for a system charged in ideal conditions. Rarely can you and I attain that ideal. You may want to purchase an extra battery pack when you buy your portable if you will need to work for hours on your computer. Lithium-ion batteries are reputed to last longer than nickel/metal hydride. Letting your battery run down completely before recharging can also increase how long the charge will hold.

6. Power sources. Power sources can add weight and bulk to your portable, so inquire about the size and weight of the AC adapter of your computer before you make a purchase.

Leasing Computer Equipment

If you don't have cash but need a computer for your business, leasing is a method of financing and affording what you need to get your business off the ground or to expand it. Even if you have capital to invest, you may want to consider leasing because you can avoid tying up lines of credit and money you may need for other components of your business. But there are also downsides to leasing. When the lease runs out, you don't own anything and you will have paid more than the purchase price for the equipment.

When you lease a computer you must first consider what you need, just as you would if you were buying a system. If you lease from a mail order computer company or a large computer retailer, they will customize one of their systems for you with prepackaged software and the hardware configuration of your choice. Once you establish a purchase price, your vendor will translate that into a lease payment based on the terms you've requested. You select equipment you want to buy and then set up the lease terms with the vendor.

You may also lease from a company that is in the business of leasing all kinds of business equipment, including computers. If you go with a leasing company, you get a system from the vendor of your choice and work out a leasing agreement for that system with the leasing company. In this scenario, you must still get service and support for the system from the computer vendor, rather than the leasor.

At this book's printing, the monthly payment on a 36-month lease term ran just under $40 per $1,000. So if you lease a $3,000 system, expect to pay around $114 per month, in addition to a security deposit which is equal to two months' leasing fees. Some computer vendors offer a buyout at the end of the lease, which is usually a percentage of the purchase price of the computer. Currently, monthly payments for the business-use portion of leases are tax-deductible, which means if you use your computer solely for business you can deduct the entire cost of your lease payments.

Following are some features to consider when leasing computer equipment:

Service plans: Many computer leases come with a one-year on-site service plan. If you plan to lease for more than one year, be sure to extend the service plan to the terms of the lease. If you don't, you are responsible for all repairs after the first year. Also be sure that the lease contract spells out when the service will be performed. Ideally, it should be on the next business day.

Lease terms: Most lease plans run 12 to 36 months, but 36 months is the most common. If you go with a shorter lease term like 12 months, your monthly payment will be significantly higher (well more than twice the monthly payment on a 36-month lease). On a 12-month lease, the total of your lease payments will be nearly as much as the total for a 36-month lease. So unless you have a compelling reason for leasing for only one year, I do not recommend it.

Buying Used Computer Equipment

A used computer that has been cast off by a cutting-edge technology user, or by a business that is going under or moving, may be more than sufficient to perform the tasks you require. These tasks could include things such as administrative word-processing work, a voice-mail system, a back-up system, or faxback capabilities (a setup in which people can request faxes on frequently asked questions). If you buy a used computer through the right channels, you can find a system that is both reliable and cheap.

If you are in the market for a computer to function as your primary machine on which you will do all of your business work for the foreseeable future, it is often better to buy a new system that comes stocked with the software and has the functionality you need now as well as the capability to run all the software packages you may want to add in the not-too-distant future.

Following are some of the things you should consider when buying used PC equipment:

Where to Shop: Computer exchange companies match buyers and sellers of used computer equipment and publish price information on online services and in computer magazines. You contact an exchange and tell them what you are looking for. They provide you with general price information on the systems in which you are interested. You then enter a bid for a system; if the seller accepts your bid, you pay the exchange directly for the system. A significant advantage of using a computer exchange is that once a final price has been negotiated, the seller must send the equipment to the exchange for testing and inspection. The United Computer Exchange can be reached at (800) 755-3033. American Computer Exchange's number is (800) 786-0717.

Upgrades: If you locate a well-priced, high-quality used computer that is missing a component you need like additional memory or a fax modem, you may want to consider buying it anyway. Memory is relatively easy to add, and you can buy an internal or external fax modem at a modest price.

Computer Maintenance, Problem Prevention, and Damage Control

When you work in an office and something goes wrong with your computer, you call the technical department and someone comes to fix it. But in a virtual office, a computer problem can be disastrous because there is no one there to fix things. Telecommuters who work for a corporate boss are at an advantage over entrepreneurs because they will still most likely be able to contact the technical department for help. In some cases, if you telecommute from home and can log into a network, your technical department may be able to diagnose and fix your problem remotely.

▶ If you are telecommuting and still have a corporate technical department to call on, be sure that you have their number handy. Post it on the wall near your computer, rather than in a computer file, in case you have a computer error and cannot access files. It also makes sense to have a few numbers of people to get in touch with. One person may be out for a few hours when you are in a pinch. Also make sure you know the procedures and hours of the help desk.

▶ Keep the manuals for your software and hardware handy, to make it easier to solve problems expediently. Not only will it take less time to find the answer to a relatively simple problem in a manual, but it will also get you points with the technical department. This will be important when you need a call back in a hurry for help with a complex technical question.

▶ Keep diskettes of any software you are running handy. Oftentimes diskettes, not just a copy of the software on your hard drive, are necessary in order to fix a software glitch.

▶ Know as much about your system as possible. Even if you have a technical department to hold your hand, you will probably have to know more about your system when you work at home because you will have to work through the problem over the phone with the technical people. To make your problem as easy as possible for the technical department to handle, take a deep breath before calling them for help. Technical people need your help to figure out what is wrong, so you need to give them information, not complain about the fact that you are having a problem.

▶ Write down any error messages you get before you call and tell them about any changes you've made to your system recently, no matter how minor. Small changes you make to your software or hardware can cause problems weeks later.

▶ Be patient. Computers are like the human body in some ways and technical people are like doctors; they may have to try a few things before they find the one that works. Do not be impatient if the first few things do not work. If you are difficult to work with, your pleas for technical help may not be answered as quickly next time.

Technical Help When There's No Tech Department

Home business owners take note: The advice I gave telecommuters to use with their technical departments also applies to your approach to technicians at software or hardware companies. In addition, the following tips will help you keep your technical problems to a minimum.

✔ If you are a home business owner and you run into a technical problem, the first place you should turn is the software or hardware vendor who sold you the equipment. Have their phone numbers in an easy-to-access spot so you do not have to look through manuals for a phone number during a crisis.

✔ Hire a consultant who will fill the role of a corporate technical department by coming to your home office. The best way to find a good consultant is through a referral from a friend or colleague, or by contacting a local computer users group which will have listings of local experts in various technologies. Keep in mind that a referral from a users group is not an endorsement, so hire carefully. Look for some-

one who asks a lot of questions about your system and your problem. Authorized service providers are another option. These are usually computer stores or service organizations that specialize in certain kinds of hardware and software. Look for them in the yellow pages under "computers" and be sure they are authorized by a computer vendor.

✔ Post your problem on the technical bulletin boards of an online service if your problem doesn't need immediate attention.

✔ Research the location and hours of the nearest computer facility at which you could work for a day or an afternoon in case you have a technical problem when you are working under deadline. Many of these places are open twenty-four hours a day. As with your other emergency numbers, post this information somewhere other than in a file on your computer, so you can easily put your fingers on it when you are having a problem.

(Continued)

✔ Try to anticipate when a problem might occur. Part of coping with home office computer problems is figuring out how to anticipate them. One step is to use some of the gadgetry on the market that will alert you to problems before they reach the critical stage. Programs called *utilities* periodically test and analyze your system for things like errors on the hard drive. You can also get virus detection software that checks your system for viruses whenever you switch it on.

✔ Take precautions. Keep your keyboard covered when you're not using it, to avoid debris buildup; don't eat or drink at your desk; clean your floppy disk drive regularly (using compressed air); and regularly back up your hard drive and frequently used floppies so you don't lose all your data if you have a problem. To keep all of your office equipment looking good and working well, you can purchase the Dust-Off Office Care Kit, which contains eight items for cleaning your phone, computer, keyboard, monitor, laser printer, and fax machine. It is sold by Falcon Safety Products [(908) 707-4900]. Scrubex sheets can keep your laser printer, copier, or fax machine from breaking down. They are solvent-coated sheets that pick up the residue that can cause printer problems. To order Scrubex sheets, call (800) 331-8000.

✔ To prevent mishaps from blackouts, brownouts, or electricity quirks (one of the most common causes of damage to computers in the home office), you can also buy an uninterruptable power supply. This device will maintain power in your office for twenty or thirty minutes during a power outage, so you have time to save what you're working on.

PRINTERS

If you have made the decision to buy a computer, you are likely to need a printer. Most of the work you do on the computer can be printed. Letters, proposals, brochures, spreadsheets, graphs, and graphics can be produced on a printer. To decide which kind of printer best suits your needs, you need to ask yourself these basic questions: What will I be printing? What level of quality do I require? Do I need color capabilities? Printers come in three types: dot matrix printers, ink-jet printers, and laser printers.

Dot matrix printers are the most basic, yet they are fast and loud—they work in much the same way as old typewriters: pins strike a ribbon to form characters on a page. It used to be that dot matrix printers printed on those long rolls of computer paper, but today most can accept sheet-fed paper. Contrary to popular belief, today's dot matrix printers are capable of printing letter-quality—not just those old computer dot characters you remember.

Ink-jet printers are very popular in the home office because they are a step up from dot matrix printers in terms of quality, but they don't carry the high price tag of laser printers. And—very important—they are quiet. The ink-jet printer operates by spraying drops of ink from a print head nozzle onto the page. The general rule is, the higher the number of nozzles, the higher the quality of print. But don't expect the level of quality you'd see from a laser printer. For many people, ink-jet printers are really the perfect compromise. If most of your work involves printing letters, text, and basic graphics, then an ink-jet printer may be sufficient for you. Ask your computer salesperson to demonstrate so that you can compare the print quality of ink-jet and laser printers firsthand and determine if you are satisfied with the level of quality an ink-jet printer provides. Bring some of your letterhead stationery or whatever other paper you will be printing on so that you can see a demonstration on your own paper. Keep in mind that ink-jets require print cartridge replacement periodically, and cartridge price varies depending on the make and model. So if you print large quantities, check prices with your printer dealer so there are no surprises.

Laser printers are what you need if you are printing client letters or proposals that must look top-notch. Laser printers are faster and have higher resolution than ink-jets. The standard laser printer is capable of 300 dots per inch (dpi); however, you can go up to 600 dpi. The quality of resolution you'll see in 600 dpi is comparable to magazine print. The drawback to laser printers is that with high quality comes the most expensive price tag. However, the old adage, "You get what you pay for," is worth considering. For many businesses, a laser printer is indispensable. Like inkjet printers, laser printers require replacement of the ink cartridge from time to time, so check cartridge prices with your dealer before buying.

COPIERS

When you are thinking about purchasing a copier, consider such things as speed, volume, size, cost, and any special features you may need. There are three different types of copiers: portable copiers, desktop copiers, and office copiers.

Portable copiers weigh around fifteen pounds and produce from one to three pages per minute. The low per-minute page production rate is offset by the lowest sticker price of the three types of copiers. So if you only make ten or even twenty copies per day, the portable copier may be for you.

Desktop copiers are in the midrange of copiers in terms of price and performance. They usually weigh about twenty or thirty pounds and stand approximately one foot in height. The advantage of a desktop model over a portable is that a desktop produces twelve to fifteen pages per minute. The disadvantage is that the price tag is usually twice that of a portable.

Office copiers produce thirty to sixty (or more) pages per minute and weigh upwards of 200 pounds. They cost two to three times as much as the desktop models.

As with all of the technology I've discussed, there may now be features on the market that did not exist when I was writing this book. For this reason, ask your salesperson to update you on the latest features, and decide if the bells and whistles are necessary to the running of your business. If you cannot decide what you need, ask for a demo model. Some copier dealers will place a demo machine in your office so that you can test-drive it for a week. Here are the features to consider:

Speed: Speed is important for businesses that rely heavily on a copier or make many copies at one time. When you are evaluating your needs, think about when you use a copier and if time is a factor when you are making copies.

Duty cycle: This factor is as important as speed. It is defined as the number of copies the machine can make over a period of one month without overstressing it or jeopardizing copy quality. Generally, portable copiers have a duty cycle of less than 500 copies per month, or approximately fifteen copies per day. Most desktop models have a duty cycle of 5,000 copies per month, and office copiers can go as high as 20,000 to 50,000 copies per month. Keep in mind that some portable models have a total life expectancy of as few as 5,000 copies—so be sure to ask about this before buying.

Zoom function (enlargement and reduction): The zoom function enables you to enlarge or decrease the size of an original, and may be particularly useful if, for example, you often copy newspaper or magazine articles that you want to fit onto an $8\frac{1}{2}$-by-11-inch sheet of paper, or if you have small print that needs to be enlarged from an original.

Label printing: This feature enables you to copy addresses directly onto labels. Keep in mind, however, that if you produce addresses from your computer, you should first check to see if your printer can print labels. Why print and copy to a label sheet if you can print labels directly from your computer's word-processing software?

Stapling and collating: These features are especially important if you put together many packets of information that need to be collated and stapled. For example, if you produce copies of a weekly report or series of articles for your customers, these features can save you a lot of time.

FAX MACHINES

As with any other technology purchase, you need to examine your needs before buying a fax machine. Think about how frequently you will be sending or receiving faxes, what you will do with the faxed material, and who you will be faxing to. There are two basic types of fax machines: thermal fax machines and plain-paper fax machines.

Thermal fax machines are the less expensive alternative, and their *footprints* (the amount of space they take up on a table or desk) are usually smaller. The other advantage to thermal fax machines is that you don't have to buy ink cartridges, which can translate into significant savings if you fax a lot of pages per day. The disadvantage is the paper—and this can be a *big* drawback for two reasons. Print on thermal paper fades over time, and light and heat also turn thermal paper dark.

Plain paper fax machines may cost a few hundred dollars more than a thermal for an entry-level machine, but if you fax regularly you'll thank yourself for making the investment. Plain-paper fax print mechanisms are ink-jet, laser, or LED. Plain-paper fax machines use regular paper like the kind used in a copy machine. The advantage of this is that you can make edits or notes on your fax without having to copy it (notes made on thermal paper fade quickly), you can save the original fax without worrying that the print will fade over time, and you don't have to deal with the slippery inconvenience of thermal paper. The one disadvantage is that you occasionally have to buy an ink replacement cartridge. So check the price of these cartridges before you buy.

When you are choosing your fax machine, you should consider cost, type, size, cost of maintenance, and ease of use. A good salesperson will ask you a lot of questions. Following are some of the features you should ask about.

Auto redial: If a line were busy or did not answer on the first try, auto redial will prompt your fax machine to periodically continue dialing until it makes a connection. This feature frees you up to go about your work, and is standard on most entry-level machines.

Speed autodial: This is standard on most fax machines and is a big time-saver if you frequently fax to the same numbers. The feature allows you to preprogram a certain number of fax recipients so that you don't have to look up and dial their number every time you fax to them.

Document feeder: This is standard option on most machines; I would not recommend buying a machine without this feature. A document feeder enables you to place your original document in a tray without having to stand over the machine feeding in each page yourself.

Paper cutter: If you choose a thermal fax machine, this feature is a must. It cuts each page from the thermal paper roll as it moves to the next page.

Activity logs: A printed activity log provides you with a complete report of fax activity to and from your machine when you request it. This enables you to confirm that faxes went through, or shows you a message explaining the source of an error—for example, "Line busy."

Send and receive unattended: For most people, this is a critical feature. It allows you to send and receive faxes while you are out of the office, so that you never have to be tied to your fax machine.

Polling: The polling feature allows someone to call in and retrieve a document that is sitting in your fax machine feeder. This is convenient if you are trying to send a fax to someone who's on the road and does not know when she will be near a fax machine.

Memory and quick scanning: This feature enables you to fax a document and retrieve it from the machine before it actually goes through. The fax machine essentially scans the document and stores it in memory, sending it at its own speed. This feature is probably not a "must-have," but can be useful if you often read from or review documents with people while you are on the phone. It enables you to go back to looking at your document while

---

Faxing on Your Voice Line

If you do not have a dedicated fax line, the following devices will make it easier for you to send and receive faxes. Before I list them I should say that sharing one line for voice and fax is acceptable only if you fax very infrequently. It is not professional to tell clients that you need to hang up the phone in order to receive a fax.

✔ **Distinguishing between fax and voice calls** is a feature that prompts the fax machine to listen to your answering machine when it answers to detect an incoming fax signal. If the fax machine detects such a signal, it picks up the line and receives the fax. If not, the answering machine records the voice message as it normally would, without any interference from the fax machine.

✔ **Remote activation** enables you to "wake up" the fax from an extension phone. For example, if you answer the phone and hear fax signals on the line, you can press a button on your phone to command your fax machine to answer the call.

you're speaking with someone on the phone and simultaneously faxing it to them.

Storing incoming and outgoing documents: This feature allows you to store incoming documents so that you can print them later, or store outgoing documents so that you can request the fax machine to send them later.

Broadcasting: This feature enables you to send a fax document to multiple recipients that you designate.

I have highlighted the standard features and a few of the more unusual features that are currently available. Fax features are increasing in number almost daily, so when you are shopping for your fax machine, tell the salesperson what you need to accomplish with your fax machine. There may be new functions available. Also see the section on fax modems earlier in this chapter.

MULTIFUNCTION SYSTEMS

A multifunction unit is a printer, fax machine, and copier all in one. Sometimes the machine performs scanning and other functions as well. The advantages are that you can save on space by not having several separate machines in your office. However, a machine that performs a variety of tasks may not do all functions as well as stand-alone machines. For this reason, test all of the functions of a multifunction system before you buy it to determine if the quality level of each is high enough to suit your needs.

TELEPHONES

To determine your needs for telephone equipment, consider the amount of time you spend on the phone and how you use it. If you spend many hours each day on the phone, I'd strongly recommend a hands-free headset. It will not only free up your hands to write or use your computer keyboard while on the phone, but will also save you from unpleasant neck pain from scrunching your head and shoulder to cradle the earpiece.

Here are some of the basic features to consider when buying home office telephone equipment. Be sure to ask your dealer about the latest features.

Touch-tone or rotary: Don't even consider rotary any more. A rotary phone won't enable you to make contact with the touch-tone computers and voice-mail systems that you will frequently encounter at the other end of the line.

Speakerphone: This feature enables you to speak to a caller without holding the headset, and can be particularly useful if you have others present in your office for phone meetings. A speakerphone allows everyone to listen in and contribute.

Built-in answering: Many telephones now come with a built-in answering machine, saving you money and space.

Hold button: If you need to place callers on hold from time to time, this feature is very useful. It doesn't add much to the price of a phone.

Speed dial: Speed dial is a big time-saver. It enables you to preprogram a certain set of numbers that are frequently called. Many phones now include this feature, and it's a real time-saver if you call the same numbers regularly.

Redial: The redial feature allows you to redial a number that was busy on the first try. You can hit the redial button as many times as you need to until you get through. It won't add significantly to the price of a phone and is well worth it.

TELEPHONE SERVICES

You should look at your needs for phone service in much the same way that you evaluate your needs for equipment: Think about how much time you spend on the phone, how you use the phone, and how you will be using your fax and modem. Many phone companies have staffs devoted to helping home office customers determine what combination of phone lines and services they need to set up or expand a home office. They can also help you figure out how to lower your phone bills.

After you've got your telephone system set up, check with your phone company periodically to ask what's new. They frequently come up with new features and savings plans that you might not otherwise know about. Following is a list of some important considerations:

Telephone Service: What Do You Need?

Here's a list of features you should consider when setting up your telephone service. See the discussions in this section for more information.

- ✔ Number of lines
- ✔ Calling plans
- ✔ 800 service
- ✔ Translation service
- ✔ Call waiting
- ✔ Call forwarding
- ✔ Three-way calling
- ✔ Speed calling

Number of lines: One of your primary considerations will be how many phone lines to have running into your home office. I recommend investing in a second line for fax and data transmission. As I pointed out in the section on fax machines, in most cases it looks unprofessional to work without a dedicated fax line. To save money you can install a residential line because most phone companies don't mind if you use this type of line for business.

For most people, I also recommend a separate business voice line to keep your business life out of your personal life and the other way around. For one thing, if you use your business line for personal calls, you will not be entitled to a tax deduction for the monthly charge for having the phone and making local calls. You will also be unable to shut your home office down at night unless you are willing to forgo *all* calls if you do not have a separate line for business, and you run the risk of having your child pick up the phone when a client calls. As more and more people work outside of the office, business associates will be more likely to want to leave messages for you over the weekend; if your business line is being used for personal calls, this will be difficult.

One alternative to installing a second line is a service that distinguishes between personal and business calls by the type of ring sounded by incoming calls. If you are a telecommuter working at home infrequently, you may not need a separate line if you live alone or work at home only occasionally. If you are a business owner starting off in a home office, you may not yet have a clear idea of your needs for phone service; in this case, it may make sense to try to get by with one voice line and one data line until you can afford new lines and you understand your phone needs better. Keep in mind that these decisions affect your stationery, business cards, and any other printed material with your phone number on it. So don't make a big investment in printing materials until you've finalized these decisions.

Calling plans: The best way to proceed with these constantly varying plans is to keep up to date on what is being offered and make sure you are on the most recently offered savings plan that best suits your calling patterns. Experts say you should check with your carrier every few months to find out if your plan is still the best one for your needs. Investigate the perks being offered as well. Frequent-flier miles and other benefits provided for phone usage can lead to savings if you use your phone a lot.

800 service: Your customers can reach you for free when you have a toll-free number. All of the regional phone companies, as well as the major long-distance carriers, offer toll-free service, so shop around and check out prices if you decide you need it. But remember, you pay for toll-free service by the minute, not by the caller.

Translation service: This service will help you if you make a lot of calls overseas from your home office. AT&T has a twenty-four-hour translation service. The translators are fluent in 140 languages and stay on the line with you and your foreign contact to decipher your conversation. The cost is $3.50 per minute plus the price of the call.

Call waiting: This function enables you to receive a second incoming call while you are already on another call. Call waiting is a good option *if* your local phone company offers the override function, which allows you to hit *70 and prevent interruptions during important calls, *and* offers a voice-mail system to take messages while you're on the telephone. Otherwise, call waiting is an annoying interruption and I don't recommend it.

Call forwarding: This feature lets you forward your calls to another number. If you often work at another location or in your car, this benefits you and your customers by keeping you in touch and available. Call forwarding frees you up to work anywhere while remaining in contact with the people who need to reach you.

Three-way calling: This is necessary if you frequently need to conduct conference calls with two other parties. It enables you to place two separate calls and connect them so that you can speak together. Even though you can do the same thing with a conference call, it's more complex to use and costs more. The only drawback to three-way calling is that it's limited to just that—only three parties. More than that requires you to set up a conference call.

Speed calling: With this function, you can program frequently dialed numbers so that you can call them with the touch of a few buttons. Even though many phone companies offer speed calling, you'll find that many telephones can do the same thing, often with a limitation of five or ten speed dial numbers. But if that's all you need, rely on the phone's speed dial feature.

500 numbers from AT&T: A 500 number enables you to receive calls wherever you happen to be through a service that searches for you at a variety or preprogrammed numbers until it finds you. You can program it to ring at a number of phones and it will continue to search until the call reaches you. Because a 500 number is not tied to a location, it is a number you will have for life. Different payment options exist for 500 numbers. For example, you can choose to pay for the forwarding of all calls to your current location, provide only some people with access to a code that will enable them to have charges paid by you, or you can have all callers pay for the cost of making the call to wherever you are.

One thing we all know for sure—you need some kind of messaging capability. Thankfully, most people have finally gotten over the phobia of leaving a message with a machine. Now what kind of machine will you use?

Answering Machine versus Voice Mail*

Telephone answering devices (TADs) are very flexible—you are in control of the programming. You can see at a glance that you have messages waiting, and you don't have to place a phone call to pick them up. TADs are usually far less expensive than voice mail. They let you monitor incoming calls, which is helpful if you want to get some work done while waiting for that all-important call. If you need to keep audio records, it's easy to archive messages—although you might get sick of a filing cabinet overflowing with tapes. If you have a digital machine, you no longer have to worry about snarled tapes or scratchy outgoing messages.

Voice mail's biggest advantage is that it takes messages even when you're on the phone, so your callers don't have to experience busy signals. Message handling on voice mail is more functional—especially the broadcasting and messaging capabilities. A message on an answering device is just that— you can listen to it, save it, and erase it, but you can't send it to another user, add comments, or port it to your PC for later reference.

Business, Residential, or Home Office?

Traditionally, phone service has been available only as a business or residential line. A business line had the advantage of providing a listing in the business directory (although a little-publicized fact is that a residential line customer, in many cases, has always had the option of buying a spot in the yellow pages). Some business lines also enable you to code your calls, which is handy for billing clients. However, a business line has also had the downside of being significantly more expensive than residential service. But now many regional carriers are offering a home office line that allows customers to list their home office number in the business directory for a slightly higher service rate. Check with your local phone carrier to find out what options you have and weigh the price of continuing your residential service and paying for a yellow pages listing versus changing over to some kind of business or home office service.

TADs are still not the most reliable devices. In a *Consumer Reports* survey conducted in November 1991, 40 percent of the respondents

*Excerpted from Telecom Made Easy: Money-Saving, Profit-Building Solutions for Home Businesses, Telecommuters and Small Organizations by June Langhoff (Newport, RI: Aegis Publishing Group Ltd., 1995).

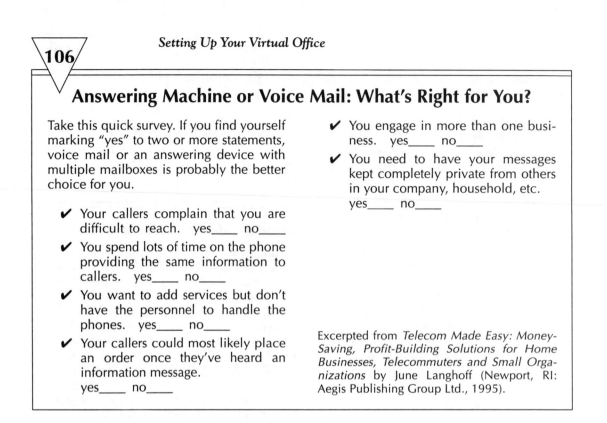

Answering Machine or Voice Mail: What's Right for You?

Take this quick survey. If you find yourself marking "yes" to two or more statements, voice mail or an answering device with multiple mailboxes is probably the better choice for you.

✔ Your callers complain that you are difficult to reach. yes____ no____

✔ You spend lots of time on the phone providing the same information to callers. yes____ no____

✔ You want to add services but don't have the personnel to handle the phones. yes____ no____

✔ Your callers could most likely place an order once they've heard an information message. yes____ no____

✔ You engage in more than one business. yes____ no____

✔ You need to have your messages kept completely private from others in your company, household, etc. yes____ no____

Excerpted from *Telecom Made Easy: Money-Saving, Profit-Building Solutions for Home Businesses, Telecommuters and Small Organizations* by June Langhoff (Newport, RI: Aegis Publishing Group Ltd., 1995).

reported some kind of answering machine malfunction. And, if security is a concern, voice mail is hands-down the best choice. However, if you need to speak to your callers real-time the first time they call, voice mail is no improvement over an answering machine. You'd be better off with a cellular phone or a "follow-me-anywhere" (500) phone number.

CELLULAR PHONES

There are three types of cellular phones: mobile (car-installed) phones, transportable phones, and portable phones.

Mobile phones were the first to gain widespread popularity. A mobile phone is installed in your car and is connected to the car battery. It sends and receives signals from that familiar spiral antenna that sits outside the vehicle. One big advantage to the mobile is that it puts out a strong three-watt signal, making its connections more dependable in weak (such as rural) or congested cell areas.

Transportable phones are similar to mobile phones in appearance, but they are connected to a large rechargeable battery pack and antenna, usually housed in a soft case or bag. Sometimes these are referred to as "bag phones." The advantage to a transportable is that, like the mobile, it produces a strong three-watt signal. The disadvantage is its size and weight. The transportable does not fit in a pocketbook or coat pocket. You need to carry it over your shoulder or in a backpack. If you use a transportable daily, you'll need to recharge the battery pack by plugging it into an electrical socket at night.

Portable phones are quickly becoming the most popular, mainly because of their size. Portable cellulars fit nicely into your coat pocket or pocketbook. Remember the communicators on *Star Trek?* Well, the portable isn't quite that small, but it's very close. The other advantage to a portable is its light weight. Of course, there is a downside: the portable produces only 0.6 watts of power, which can be a problem if you are calling from a weak or congested area. The battery on a portable is small and slim and, depending on the make and model you choose, generally provides you with one or two hours of talk time (time spent actually communicating with someone) and several hours of *standby* (time spent turned on but not communicating with anyone).

I cannot cover all of the cellular phone features here because there are too many, but I have highlighted some of the features you should consider:

Features

> **Battery performance:** The general rule is, the longer a charged battery can operate, the better. If you are investing in a transportable or portable cellular phone, be certain that the battery performance is sufficient for your needs.
>
> **Alphanumeric storage:** This feature enables you to program frequently called numbers and—in some cases—alphanumeric entries so that you can identify these numbers more easily.
>
> **Automatic redial:** This function enables you to redial a number that was busy on a previous try. It's very helpful if you are calling while in the car.
>
> **Speed dial:** This feature allows you to enter a few digits to call a number stored in the phone's memory.
>
> **Ringer select:** Most cellulars have this option. It allows you to preset the volume of the ringer, and—in some cases—select the type of ring you'd like to hear. You can also select a phone featuring a silent vibration, so you can avoid drawing unpleasant attention while in a meeting or a quiet restaurant.
>
> **Retractable antenna:** Not all portable cellular phones have this feature, but it is important. Built-in antennas can be cumbersome and

make it downright difficult to store a portable cellular in your pocket, so make sure you're comfortable with the phone before buying.

Selecting Cellular Phone Service

Aside from selecting the right phone for your needs, you should carefully evaluate the service you will be getting before making a commitment. Keep in mind that you will pay a variety of service fees, including activation fees, a basic monthly rate for service, per-minute airtime usage charges, and *roamer fees*, which are fees charged by other cellular carriers when you leave your regular service area. Each local cellular service will offer you any number of other services such as voice mail, but you should decide if you need those services and are willing to pay for them. Also, remember that airtime is billed from the time you place the call (when you hit the "send" key on your phone), not when someone picks up on the other end. However, if nobody picks up and you haven't let it ring for more than sixty seconds from the time you hit "send," you will not be billed for the airtime. In addition, you pay airtime fees for incoming calls to your cellular phone. Finally, if you do sign a service contract, keep in mind that cellular service providers will stick you with a hefty fee for backing out early, so check the fine print.

Other Important Cellular Phone Features

✔ Low-charge alerter

✔ Rapid battery recharger

✔ Lighted keypad (most have it)

✔ Custom menu programming

✔ Long-distance lockout to restrict the phone to local calls only

✔ Microphone jack and earpiece for privacy

✔ Call timer and alarm

✔ Voice-activated dialing

✔ Built-in answering machine

✔ Paging indicator

✔ Auto credit-card dialing

✔ Call forwarding and call waiting

✔ Data links to interface with computer or fax

✔ Holder and other accessories for mounting a portable in your car

---

PAGERS*

According to the Personal Communication Industry Association, over 25 million Americans carry pagers and the number is growing rapidly. You see all sorts of people using pagers. Here's a small sampling:

*The information on pagers and personal communicators came from the book *Telecom Made Easy: Money-Saving, Profit-Building Solutions for Home Businesses, Telecommuters and Small Organizations* by June Langhoff, which can be purchased in bookstores or ordered by calling toll-free (800) 828-6961.

△ A lawyer uses a silent alpha pager in court to communicate with members of her team.

△ A real estate agent carries an alpha pager to receive listing information on the fly.

△ A field service agent carries a numeric pager to stay in touch with his office.

△ A sales manager downloads and broadcasts the latest price list to her field sales force.

If you decide you need a pager, you'll need both a paging device and a paging service. When you sign up with a paging service, you specify the geographic area where you wish to receive pages. This can be as small as a portion of a city or as large as several nations. You also sign up for the type of paging you wish—basic beeper, numeric (which sends you the telephone number of the calling party), or alphanumeric (which can send a short message). In addition to a service contract, you'll need a pager or PDA device equipped as a paging receiver. [See "Personal Communicators" later in this chapter.]

A caller leaves a message for you via a paging operator, voice mail, or other system. The paging information is entered into the system's computer, which broadcasts the data (which could be a beep, a telephone number, or a short message) over every part of its covered territory, using radio towers and/or satellites to deliver the signal. If your pager is on, it "catches" the broadcast and your pager alerts you. Once you have been beeped, you call in to your paging or voice-mail service to pick up your message, or if your pager has display capabilities, you read the message displayed on your screen. Only you (or someone with your security code) can pick up your messages. All other pagers within your area are locked out from the data being sent to your pager address.

Pagers come in several varieties: beepers, numerics, and alphanumerics.   *Types of Pagers*

Plain old beepers are like radio-controlled doorbells. The pager buzzes or beeps, often quite loudly, to let you (and everyone within a hundred feet of you) know that you've got a page. If you dislike the sound, you can get a beeper that vibrates silently. You call your pager service to pick up the message.

Numeric pagers display the phone number you should call. If your paging service is connected to voice mail, the number displayed will be your voice-mail access number. If your callers page you directly, the number displayed will be the number they keyed in using a touch-tone phone.

415-555-4727

Alphanumeric pagers, also known as alpha pagers, display a brief message (which could also include a phone number) or coded information such as a sender code:

03:   10AM MEETING

POSTPONED UNTIL 2

PM TODAY

Messages are often limited to from one to four lines. This type of pager reduces the number of return calls you have to make.

Determining If You Should Rent or Buy a Pager

You can buy a plain old beeper for less than $10. Numeric pagers range from $50 to $90; alphanumerics range from $120 for a two-line model to about $300 for a four-line version. You can save money if you buy your pager at the same time as you sign up for a service agreement.

You can also rent a pager from your paging company, an option that the majority of pager users employ today. You can usually reduce your monthly charges by three or four dollars if you provide your own pager (you may be able to negotiate an even larger discount). Rental agreements usually provide repair and replacement insurance, either bundled in the monthly charge or for a low additional fee. If you own the pager, you have to either carry your own insurance or be prepared to bear the cost of repair or replacement. If you plan to keep your pager for over two years, and are reasonably careful, you'll probably save money by owning your pager. The trade-off is that you may be stuck with obsolete equipment.

Pager Survey

Take a moment to complete this survey. If you answer "yes" to three or more statements, paging will benefit your business.

✔ Are you losing business to your competitors because you aren't able to return calls quickly?

✔ Do you want to be able to respond to callers more quickly, but need an economical method?

✔ Are you out of the office a lot, but not near a phone?

✔ Do you need to keep abreast of late-breaking developments?

✔ Do you need to be in touch, but don't require two-way communication?

✔ Do you run a service business such as computer repair, automobile towing, plumbing, delivery, etc.?

✔ Do you worry about not being reachable in an emergency?

✔ Do you waste time (and phone change) constantly checking in?

PERSONAL COMMUNICATORS

These are multifunction devices, which may perform calendar, memo-pad, calculator, and scheduler functions, as well as paging and e-mail. These devices go by many names such as PDA (Personal Digital Assistant), PIC (Personal Information Communicator), and PCS (Personal Communications System). Personal communicators often will allow you to send and receive longer messages which you scroll to view, and may work with a communications software package located at your home office.

Many PDAs—including Casio, Sharp, Sony, and Apple Newton models—support paging, either as a built-in function or as an option supplied by a PCMCIA (Personal Computer Memory Card International Association) card device. PCMCIA cards are designed to insert directly into hand-held or notebook computers equipped with a PCMCIA slot. Many of these devices can receive longer messages and, if they have compatible software, you can keep the page as a permanent file in your portable computer. They're great for sending important information such as price updates, stock availability, and market news. Among the companies selling PCMCIA pager cards are MobileMedia, Information Radio Technology, and Motorola.

NUTS AND BOLTS

When you are establishing a virtual office, you have to think about insurance, zoning, taxes, safety, and other nuts-and-bolts issues. The information in this chapter provides general guidance in these areas. It is no substitute for checking with your own insurance agent, accountant, safety officer, or other official or professional who specializes in these areas. The first part of this chapter deals with the needs of telecommuters; the second part addresses the needs of home-based entrepreneurs and some of their special concerns.

INSURANCE RULES FOR TELECOMMUTERS

The best piece of general advice I can give on insurance for telecommuters is to determine what coverage will be extended to you when you work outside of the office. In the vast majority of cases, telecommuters are insured in the same way at their home office as they are at the company office. Following is some general advice about the various kinds of insurance you should investigate.

Workers' Compensation Employees are covered by workers' compensation insurance at home in the same way they are when they're in the office. As with any workers' compensation claim, telecommuters' claims for coverage of medical expenses would be evaluated on a case-by-case basis. Obviously, if an employee is at home and is doing something other than office work outside of the home office—for example, reshingling the roof—the employee may not be covered when the case is examined.

Auto Insurance If you are using your car for business for your employer, tell your insurance agent and obtain an endorsement or a separate policy. Whether you need an endorsement or a separate policy will depend on the state you live in, your insurance company, and your work arrangement. Employers usually do not provide or subsidize extra auto insurance for their employees who work outside of the office. In most cases, mobile workers notify their insurance carriers that they use their cars for business, and pay for extended coverage themselves.

If you work at home and are therefore not commuting as frequently to the office, you should also let your insurance agent know. According to the Independent Insurance Agents of America, you can save a significant amount of money on your car insurance premium if you commute less than you used to.

Equipment Insurance

If you own the computer equipment you use to telecommute, make sure that your homeowner's or renter's insurance covers your equipment. Many homeowner's and renter's policies exclude coverage for equipment used for business, even if the business is not your own. You should also check the amount of coverage your policy provides. Standard coverage in many home owner's and renter's policies is in the $2,000 range, which does not cover very much office equipment. If your employer provided the equipment you use at home, your employer's insurance will most likely cover the property. Also see "Setting Up a Home Office" and "Equipment Placement in the Home Office" in chapter 6.

Liability Insurance

Liability coverage provided in homeowner's and renter's insurance may not cover a mishap that takes place in the course of business. Furthermore, most employers will not cover any mishap that befalls visitors to your home office. Because of the potential liability, many employers discourage their employees from having any visitors in the home office. If you plan to have clients, messengers, or anyone else in your home office for business reasons, you should extend your homeowner's or renter's insurance and obtain liability coverage for business use. You can purchase an endorsement (an add-on to your policy) that provides this liability coverage.

SAFETY RULES FOR TELECOMMUTERS

Some companies have guidelines for setting up home offices to comply with safety standards, and some employers leave safety to the common sense and good judgment of their employees. These are basic safety recommendations:

▷ Make sure wires are not placed where they might cause someone to trip.

▷ Keep extension cords in good condition and out of traffic areas.

▷ Have a surge protector for electrical equipment.

▷ Properly label circuit breakers.

▷ Maintain sufficient ventilation for electrical equipment.

Occasionally companies provide employees with a safety checklist. A checklist for the home office should include the following items:

▲ Smoke alarm
▲ Fire extinguisher
▲ Evacuation plans
▲ First aid supplies

Some employers, such as United Airlines, require pictures of telecommuters' home offices to ensure that they comply with safety standards. Other employers actually send someone out to inspect home offices and investigate possible violations. The most common scenario is for employers to reserve the right in telecommuting agreements to inspect home offices, but never to exercise that right. If they do, they are almost always required to give telecommuters notice before they visit.

UNIONS AND TELECOMMUTERS

If you are a union employee, your union may not support telecommuting of any kind. Some unions fear that employers will take advantage of employees who telecommute. The union stance is often that employees should be compensated more for telecommuting since they are more productive as telecommuters. Unions are also concerned about the fact that not all employees are eligible for telecommuting. This is often an issue during a pilot (or demonstration) phase, because pilots are almost always small and therefore open to few employees. Because negotiating with unions is one more barrier to getting a pilot program off the ground, employers often begin their telecommuting programs with non-union employees.

Some people say that unions' real concern about telecommuting is that a dispersed work force will be difficult to manage and the unions' strength could thereby be diminished. If your employer launches a company-wide telecommuting program, chances are it will already have negotiated with the relevant unions and will have obtained a signed memorandum indicating union support of the plan. Employers that have successfully worked with unions include them early in the program planning stage, and prove that they have specific criteria for choosing employees that guard against discrimination. New York State's Department of Transportation, Region II Office, for example, chooses telecommuters by committee, rather than by manager recommendation. The criteria include the distance the person travels to work, the mode of travel, the difficulty of the trip, and disabilities, among other factors. Employee names chosen by the committee are then passed on to supervisors for approval.

If you want to check with your union, call your company's labor relations manager or the employee relations office of your union.

ZONING REGULATIONS AFFECTING TELECOMMUTERS

Many community laws that prohibit businesses in residential areas were enacted when the typical neighborhood business could be anything from a florist to an auto-body shop. Today, many home-based businesses operate in defiance of the law because their work does not disrupt the neighborhood at all. As a telecommuter, you are very unlikely to be bothered by zoning officials.

I have not heard of a case in which a telecommuter has gotten into trouble with a zoning board for working at home. Even in the case of home-based businesses which add to neighborhood traffic, problems usually arise only when neighbors complain. So if you are working at home as a telecommuter, the best approach to take is to stay on good terms with your neighbors. You may want to tell your neighbors you'll be working at home part of the time, and stress the crime-fighting benefits of having someone in the neighborhood during the day. If you have a fax machine, you may want to offer to let neighbors send an occasional fax. All of this will help insure that your neighbors do not cause any problems for you.

Even though you may not clash with zoning officials, it is a good idea to investigate your local zoning rules before you begin telecommuting. Zoning is regulated locally, so start with your town or city hall. Homeowners associations, co-op boards, and other entities often have rules of their own about working at home, so check with them too. If you live in an apartment building, check with any board or management agent that makes rules about the building.

TAX LAWS FOR TELECOMMUTERS

Because of changes in the tax laws a few years ago, tax deductions for telecommuters are limited. To deduct business-related expenses, telecommuters must meet a difficult set of criteria. Like entrepreneurs, telecommuters must use the home office as their principal place of business. This means you have to earn the bulk of your income from the home office to qualify. If you sell at a client's office or go into the office for the majority of the week, most likely you will not be eligible. For more details on what it takes for a home office to qualify, see "Home Business Deductions" in this chapter, or get Publication 587, "Business Use of the Home," from the IRS. Also see "Tax Laws for Entrepreneurs" in this chapter if you work at home for yourself.

Home-Office Tax Deductions

If you meet the criteria for use of a home office, you still cannot take any deductions unless your telecommuting is *for the convenience of your employer*, not merely because it is *appropriate and helpful*. If you are audited, you will have to present a note to the IRS stating that you are telecommuting at the request of your employer. You also cannot take deductions if you are receiving rent from your employer for the space you work in as an employee.

If you do qualify for home-office deductions, you must report them as itemized deductions on your return. The category of itemized deductions that includes employee business expenses must exceed 2 percent of your adjusted gross income before you can claim these deductions. For example, if your adjusted gross income is $50,000 annually, you cannot deduct the first $1,000 of expenses. Some other restrictions may apply; check with your tax planner.

Mobile-Office Tax Deductions

You must own your car in order to take the current 29-cents-per-mile deduction for business use of your car. You should keep track of your miles with a log, or at the very least, get a record of miles on your car when you have it serviced. Parking and tolls are also deductible, so keep receipts for these expenses, too.

If your principal place of business is your home office (meaning you earn the majority of your income there), then you can deduct the first trip of the day from your home office to a client. If your office does not qualify as your principal place of business, then (believe it or not) this trip will be considered your commute and is not deductible. All of your other trips to clients during the day are deductible. For more information on business use of your car, look in IRS Publication #917.

TELECOMMUTING CONTRACTS

When you are arranging the specifics of your telecommuting contract, it is important to keep one thing in mind: everything is negotiable. Your company may have a set of printed policies and procedures for telecommuting, but that does not mean that you cannot negotiate things. For example, unless you work for a computer or telecommunications company, it may not be standard operating procedure for your employer to give you a computer and other technology to work at home. In this case, it will be up to your manager to determine if you should get what you are asking for. If you can build a good enough case for this, or something else you want—flexibility in your hours or an extra day at home, for example—you may get it.

Telecommuting: Typical Forms to Expect

Written policies will protect both you as a telecommuting employee and your employer. Your company will provide these forms, but it may help you to know what should be contained in them for your protection.

Form 1: Telecommuting Policy

These are the general rules and regulations for your telecommuting program. This document protects your rights and clearly states what you and your employer are committing to. Among the things it should include are that you:

1. Are telecommuting voluntarily and that you or your employer may terminate the arrangement at any time with some notice.
2. Are working under the same salary and benefit arrangements as other employees.
3. Are covered by the company's insurance while you are working in your home office.
4. Have the same job responsibilities and amount-of-work-per-day requirements as your office counterparts.
5. Will abide by agreed-upon work hours.
6. Understand your company's policy toward equipment procurement and purchase.

Form 2: Telecommuting Agreement

The telecommuting agreement contains the details of your telecommuting program. This includes where and when you will telecommute, as well as how things like sick days and child care will be handled. This is usually a standard document with spaces to be filled in with each participant's specifics. At a minimum, the agreement should detail:

1. The date the telecommuting arrangement will begin.
2. The location where you will work.
3. Which days you will telecommute.
4. What your hours will be.
5. How often you will check in with your supervisor and/or check for messages.
6. Who will provide the equipment you use.
7. Who pays for other related expenses.
8. How your performance will be evaluated.

Form 3: Daily Work Plan

Depending on your relationship with your manager, you may want to create a work plan for the days you telecommute. This is a form on which you record the tasks you anticipate completing when you telecommute. Creating agreed-upon results for your telecommuting days will make it possible for you and your supervisor to track the success of your telecommuting program. Listing your intended tasks will also help ensure that you have all of the materials (files, papers, computer disks, and so on) that you will need to work outside of the office. A daily work plan could include:

1. What is your assignment—what end result is expected?
2. When it is due?
3. How will results be measured, i.e., what criteria will be used to determine the merits of your work?

For more on how to negotiate a contract, look in chapter 3 for tips from negotiating guru Roger Fisher, author of the best-selling book *Getting to Yes*.

BUSINESS-STRUCTURING OPTIONS FOR ENTREPRENEURS

The way your business is organized is important because it affects every aspect of your operation, from what you pay in taxes to the extent of your liability and your ability to raise capital. There is a lot of folklore about business structure, so be sure you make a decision only after thorough research and careful consideration of what is best for your business. Your options for business organization include sole proprietorship, incorporation, partnership, and limited liability corporations and partnerships.

Sole Proprietorship

A sole proprietorship is the quickest and easiest form to adopt. If you don't incorporate and don't have a partner, you are automatically a sole proprietor. As a sole proprietor, your net profit is taxed at personal income tax rates and you are personally liable for any debts or losses you incur.

For some businesses, sole proprietorship makes the most sense. If you run a one-person business that has limited liability, you may not need to bother with the expense and time of incorporation or any other more complex form of organization. Sole proprietorship can also be a good choice for businesses in the start-up phase because it does not have a lot of legal requirements. "It's easy to start, it's easy to end, it's easy to change, and it's good for a trial run while you see how your business evolves," says Ed Slott, a Rockville Centre, New York–based CPA and small-business tax expert. "It might not pay to get involved with a corporation or some other entity at the beginning in case you need to make changes in your business."

Incorporation

Incorporation requires more paperwork and expense than sole proprietorship. You may need to hire an attorney to help you incorporate, and you are likely to pay more to have a corporate tax return prepared. In some states, you will also have to pay a minimum amount of tax as a corporation, no matter how much money your corporation makes or loses.

What you get for your effort and investment is protection from liability. A corporation is a legal entity, separate from you and anyone else involved in your business, that enters into contracts, owns property, borrows money, and engages in other business activity. Because the corporation, not you, is involved in these business deals, you and your personal

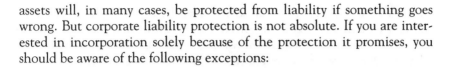
assets will, in many cases, be protected from liability if something goes wrong. But corporate liability protection is not absolute. If you are interested in incorporation solely because of the protection it promises, you should be aware of the following exceptions:

1. It cannot protect you from your own bad acts. For example, if you run a package delivery service, and you fill in for a driver who has called in sick and in the process run into a busload of people, you are personally liable for the damage.

2. It cannot protect you from things you personally guarantee. To make sure you don't inadvertently become personally liable, be sure you put your name, title, and company name on anything you sign.

3. It cannot protect you from owning governmental trust fund taxes (withholding taxes and sales taxes). When a corporation withholds state and federal taxes from employee paychecks, it holds them in trust for the government. The same goes for sales taxes. When taxes are held in trust, all officers and anyone who has check-signing authority are jointly liable to the government for these taxes. That means that as a principal, you cannot hide behind the corporation and will be personally liable for these taxes if they are not paid.

4. It cannot protect you from some state laws. New York state, for example, has a law which says that the ten largest shareholders of a corporation are personally responsible for unpaid employee wages. If a restaurant operates for three years and goes out of business, the owners and principals are personally responsible for any unpaid salaries.

5. It cannot protect people in certain professions. Professionals including doctors, lawyers, and accountants are personally liable in any lawsuit.

Other reasons to incorporate include the ability to gain access to benefit plans only available to corporations, and the image that incorporation creates. When you are trying to raise capital, obtain credit card merchant status, win certain kinds of new customers, or do business in foreign countries, incorporation can be important for appearance's sake.

If you decide to incorporate, you have two options: a C corporation or an S corporation. The primary difference between an S corp and a C corp is the way profits and losses are handled.

S Corporations

With an S corp, you pay tax at the personal rate and your profits are your salary. S corps also limit the number of shareholders in your corporation to thirty-five and stipulate that all shareholders be U.S. citizens and individuals rather than other corporations or estates. However, this rarely applies to small businesses because the average small business has under five shareholders. S corps are generally recommended for small entities.

C Corporations

In a C corporation, profits and losses are taxed to the corporation itself. This means that you'll pay corporate tax on the earnings of the business. However, if you form a C corporation you run the risk of being taxed twice on your profits—once as a corporation, and a second time when the IRS regards that money as a salary or as dividends, or upon liquidation of the corporation. This is one of the major disadvantages of a C corp. Let's say, for example, that your company has profits of $100,000 for one year. If you parcel that money out to yourself or other people who own the corporation with you, the IRS may try to call the money dividends and will tax you as a corporation and as an individual. If you wait until the next year to take all or part of that money as salary, you will already have paid corporate tax on it during the year it was profit, and will then pay tax as an individual when you give it to yourself as salary.

The benefit of a C corp (at this book's printing) is that it enables you to deduct 100 percent of the cost of health insurance premiums for yourself and your employees. An S corp, at this book's printing, can deduct only 30 percent. Owners of C corps can also borrow from the corporation's retirement fund, and have access to certain benefits packages that S corps do not. C corps make sense for companies keeping chunks of cash in the corporate bank account for capital expenditures or payment of debt, because C corps can take advantage of lower initial corporate tax rates.

Partnership　If you have business partners, you also have the option of forming a partnership. If you choose to take this route, it's a good idea to formalize this relationship and create a partnership agreement that will protect all the parties involved. The benefits of a partnership are that you have someone with whom to share the business burden. It will also probably cost less to form a partnership than to form a corporation. If you do form a partnership, each year you have to file a partnership information return that tells the IRS and state officials the gains and losses to be divided among the partners. The partners then report this information and pay taxes on personal returns. The downside of partnerships is that you are legally responsible for your partners' liabilities related to the business.

Limited Liability　A limited liability company has the liability protection of a corporation
Companies　but the tax status of a partnership. In other words, you pay taxes as an

individual, but you are protected from liability as you would be with a corporation. Most states now allow limited liability companies. To verify whether your state allows them, check with your state department of taxation. To form an LLC, you have to file forms with authorities whose titles vary from state to state. The paperwork has to be completed meticulously, so hire an attorney to help you. Limited liability partnerships are also available.

Most of us have heard of the allure of incorporating in Delaware. But for a small business operated at home, it usually doesn't make sense to incorporate there. The state's incorporation fame is based on the fact that it offers potential tax breaks and, in some cases, more corporate statutory protection from liability. However, in order to incorporate in Delaware, you must appoint someone in Delaware to be an agent for your corporation. There are companies in Delaware which provide this service for a fee. You will also have to pay an annual franchise fee, which is corporate tax to the state of Delaware. Furthermore, if you incorporate in Delaware and do business in your home state, you will have to file an application in your home state to do business as a foreign corporation and will then have to pay a franchise fee as well as income taxes in your home state. If someone sues you and your business is incorporated in Delaware, you will be forced to hire legal counsel to defend yourself in Delaware. Furthermore, most states have adopted corporate statutes that are often as flexible as Delaware laws.

Incorporating in Delaware

Many people ask me if they can save on legal fees by incorporating themselves instead of hiring an attorney to do it. The answer is, you may be able to. However, incorporating requires a lot of paperwork, and it is not always apparent how the forms for corporation should be filled out. For example, the State of Connecticut has approximately nineteen different forms that must be completed to incorporate. If you have access to an attorney to answer specific questions, you can do it yourself, but it will be time-consuming. You may also need a statutory agent to sign your incorporation papers and this is usually an attorney. Finally, you have to consider whether spending time on incorporating is a good use of your time. Often, you're better off putting time and energy into your business and paying an expert to complete your legal work.

Incorporating without Hiring an Attorney

Choosing an Attorney

It's a good idea to have an attorney on call when you run your own business. You may not need legal advice on a regular basis, but when you need an attorney, you need one fast! For that reason, you should find one ahead of time. That way, you'll have had the opportunity to carefully select someone who understands you and your business as well as someone you feel comfortable dealing with. An attorney's advice and assistance may be critical for your business in any of these instances:

▲ Deciding whether to incorporate—and then filing the complex paperwork

▲ When a complicated contract must be written, deciphered, and signed

▲ When you are threatened with a lawsuit

▲ When you need help collecting a debt

▲ When you need information on regulations pertaining to your business and assistance in compliance with them

Referrals are the best way to find just about any service you might need; finding an attorney is no exception. Talk to other small business owners, your banker, your accountant, or other trusted advisors. You can check with your local bar association also, although not all of them verify if an attorney who claims to have a specialty does in fact have extensive experience in that area. A bar association referral, will, of course, guarantee that an attorney has passed the bar exam.

You should ask the following questions of an attorney:

Is there a charge for the consultation?

What, if any, specialty does she have?

Has he handled needs like yours before? (Otherwise you'll pay for learning time.)

What and how does she charge?

Does the practice include other small businesses? What kind?

How long has he been practicing?

An attorney's fees will vary depending on the location of the practice, the experience of the attorney, the specialty, and whether you're dealing with a large firm or a small legal office. The range can go from under $100 an hour to more than $300.

You can save money by doing preparation work yourself. Be organized for all meetings with your lawyer; make all non-legal phone calls and do research yourself to save on legal time, because the clock is ticking. Prepare a contract and show it to your attorney, rather than asking her to prepare it. With all of the books and software programs about law on the market, you can learn to handle a lot of legal matters yourself and pay for an attorney's time only when a legal representative is necessary. Do this only if you calculate that doing it yourself would be less expensive once you add up the cost of your time.

You have a few options for how you will pay for legal help. Most small-business owners pay attorneys when they need them. In other words, if an attorney does two hours of work for you, you pay for that time. It's a good idea to have a relationship with an attorney whom you know you can call when you need to. If you establish a relationship like this, the attorney will probably bill you once a month for services rendered. If you didn't need any legal services, you won't pay anything.

Another option is to have an attorney on retainer, but that is rare for small-business owners. On *retainer* means you pay a fee to an attorney to be available to do an agreed-upon collection of duties for your company on an ongoing basis. If you head into heavy litigation or a special project, additional fees are negotiated.

It is sometimes possible to obtain a prepaid legal plan, in which you get a variety of services for a flat annual fee. Ask your local bar association if this is available in your area, or contact the American Prepaid Legal Services Institute at (312) 988-5751.

INSURANCE FOR HOME-BASED ENTREPRENEURS

Insurance is in the same category as bookkeeping for home-business owners—called "Neglected Matters." Sometimes it's because they have not been able to find the coverage they need; other times, cash-strapped home-business owners cut corners by choosing not to have insurance. But a lack of insurance can permanently shut down your home-based business, not to mention wreak havoc on your personal assets. So my general advice is, consider insurance a business expense, not something you buy if you have money left over. This section will help you figure out what you need and how to make decisions about it.

How to Find an Insurance Broker

Because of the challenges to finding home-business insurance, it's important to find a broker who is committed to helping you. Some brokers will not take on small businesses because they are too small to be lucrative. Others don't want to be bothered. That's fine; just keep looking until you find the right broker. Here are some ideas for finding and evaluating a broker.

Start with your current insurance company. See what they offer. If your agent cannot help you, ask for a referral.

Contact a trade association. They are usually familiar with insurance problems in your industry and may even offer an insurance plan from a large insurance company that has been designed for your industry. To find your industry association, look in *The Encyclopedia of Associations*, by Gale Research, Inc., which can be found in any reference library.

Ask for a referral. Ask people in your field or other home-based business owners. You can also get leads from home-business associations or associations for the self-employed.

Check with smaller storefront insurance agencies. They often look to small businesses for their bread and butter.

Evaluating Your Insurance Needs

1. Investigate your current renter's or homeowner's insurance and evaluate what business coverage it provides. The average residential policy covers approximately $2,500 worth of business property.

2. Extend your current coverage if appropriate. If your business assets exceed the amount of coverage you currently have, you can sometimes extend your property coverage to the value of your assets (if you are incorporated, this may not be possible). Make sure your policy covers business-related property; if you travel a lot, make sure your coverage for loss outside of the home is adequate.

3. Obtain liability coverage. Most homeowner's and renter's insurance will not cover mishaps in your home if they are related to business. You can, however, purchase a rider (an add-on to your policy) that provides this liability coverage. This is important insurance because it protects you if a customer or client falls in your house or a messenger is injured on the premises. You can get this insurance even if you live in an area that is not zoned for home businesses.

4. Buy a business owner's policy if necessary. If you have employees, require coverage for mishaps out of the home, or are incorporated—and in some cases if you use a name other than

---

Why It's Difficult for Home-Based Business Owners to Get Insurance

1. There are insurance agents who handle only commercial policies, and representatives who handle only consumer's home insurance. There is sometimes confusion about who sells home-business insurance. In some cases, the company you buy your property insurance from may not even write business policies, and your commercial broker may not write insurance for the home, so neither one feels equipped to provide a home-business policy.

2. Insurance writers do not like to cover home-based businesses with large inventories because they are worried about security. They feel that inventory is more secure in a storefront or warehouse location with security guards, gates, and sophisticated alarm systems.

3. Insurance companies worry that if a home business hits rocky times, it's easy for the owner to throw in the towel and engage in insurance fraud to make back some of its money. In their eyes, it's easier for a home-business owner to claim that inventory has been stolen because a robbery at a home is easier to fake.

your own—you will have to buy a business owner's policy in order to obtain liability coverage. This is also true if your business assets are so great that they cannot be covered by extending your homeowner's policy. This is similar to the kind of policy a business outside of the home would purchase; it provides important coverage for items such as product liability, general liability, business interruption, and property damage.

5. **Extend your car insurance.** If you use your regular car in the course of your business and you infrequently have customers in your car, most insurance companies will let you pay a little more for business use under your personal auto policy. Auto policies do not cover the contents of a car, so if you travel with valuables, make sure your product policy covers loss outside your home. If other people will be driving your car for the business, put their names on your policy. If your employees use their own cars in the course of working for you, you may need to get a non-owned-auto insurance policy that provides coverage in case something happens when they are working for you. If you have a van that is used primarily for business, you will most likely have to buy a separate business auto policy.

6. **Determine if you need professional liability insurance.** Professional liability insurance is the service equivalent of product liability and includes coverage for malpractice and errors and omissions. Some states and professions require it by law. Even if you are not mandated, it is wise to have it if the service you provide could inadvertently harm another person. The professions for which it is recommended or required

Evaluating an Insurance Broker

✔ **Look for a broker who asks a lot of questions** about your business and your needs. You should not be asking more questions than the broker who is selling you a policy.

✔ **Ask for references** and check all references to find out how responsive the agent has been to each person's needs.

✔ **Check with the State Insurance Department.** It has a list of brokers with complaints against them and can also verify that an agent is properly licensed.

✔ **The Insurance Information Institute recommends putting a potential broker to this test.** Ask him what he would recommend if you had a problem (fire or disaster of some kind) late on a Sunday night—for example, who you should call. If the broker does not say to notify him, that is a bad sign. The III says you should have a broker who is willing to be there for you. That doesn't mean the broker must visit the site of your disaster when it happens, but in the opinion of the III, he should be interested in helping you contact the proper people when a problem occurs.

✔ **Shop around and compare.** Keep in mind that brokers make a commission from the policy they sell you. You can buy from either an agent who sells for one company or an agent who brokers lots of companies' products. Your best bet is go to several brokers and compare what they offer you.

✔ **Look for someone who is willing to do some research** to find the insurance you need for your business. Many are, in the hope that although you may be a small business now, you'll grow. Insurance needs vary depending on the business and the business owner. It's difficult to know what you need or even where to start when you are trying to find insurance for your home-based business.

include, but are not limited to, computer technicians, systems analysts, accountants, hairdressers, lawyers, and consultants.

7. Determine if you need product liability insurance. Most business owner's policies include this coverage. If for some reason you do not have this coverage through a business policy, and your product runs the risk of inflicting harm on other people, you may need to buy product liability coverage separately, which can be expensive. A "product" is anything that is tangibly used, touched, or consumed. It's recommended for businesses including, but not limited to, toy makers, candy manufacturers, caterers, cake decorators, food sellers, and garment manufacturers.

8. Obtain workers' compensation insurance. Most states will require you to have workers' compensation insurance for any employees. This is the insurance that covers employees in case of a work-related accident. Some states also require you to purchase disability insurance which covers employees in case of *any* accident, no matter where it happens. New York mandates disability insurance and worker's compensation insurance for all employees (not to be confused with contract workers). The only exception is part-time domestic help, which is covered under homeowner's insurance. In New York, a corporation with three or more officers also must provide workers' compensation for those officers.

9. Consider disability insurance. Disability (or loss-of-income) insurance covers you in case you cannot work because of illness or injury. You can insure up to 60 percent of your gross income. If you want to cover yourself for disability, you can also set yourself up as a corporation, and cover yourself with workers' compensation.

10. Buy extra equipment coverage. If your computer equipment isn't adequately covered by your other insurance, you can buy a rider or separate policy to cover it. Not all insurance companies offer this kind of coverage, but one of the vendors specializing in it is Safeware—(800) 800-1492. Computer data is expensive to cover, but in some cases insurance companies will write a policy that will partially pay for time spent on data restoration.

11. At least consider life insurance. If you have only yourself to worry about, even insurance agents admit that you may be better off putting your money back into your business than investing it in life insurance. If you have a family or other people depending on you, life insurance is recommended.

Home Business Insurance Policies

It used to be that those of us working at home had two options for insuring our offices. We could extend our homeowner's insurance to cover our home offices, or we could get a small-business policy for our home businesses. For a lot of people neither choice is ideal. Extending your home-owner's policy covers you only for accidents; small-business policies offer lots of coverage, but force you to pay again for the structural coverage already included in a homeowner's policy. But now there's a third option: home-business insurance.

Home-business policies tend to be cheaper than business-owner's policies because they are usually not available to businesses with lots of expensive equipment or a good chance of being sued. One carrier won't cover computer consultants who write custom software packages, none of them cover doctors, and they aren't interested in businesses like construction. You also can't get one of these policies if you have employees. For example, the In-Home Business Policy from RLI Insurance in Peoria, Illinois, is available to "small retail and service risks operated from a residence that present minimal product liability, professional liability, and off-premises exposure."

Home-based business policies also do not usually provide very high levels of coverage for things like inventory. You can always increase the amount of coverage a policy provides, but then you remove one of the major benefits of a home-based business policy: economy. Home-based business policies tend to be more economical than small-business insurance, but get expensive very quickly when you extend coverage.

If you do not currently qualify for a home-business policy, find out what you can do to change your status. Some business owners with inventories too valuable to be covered by a home-business policy rent inexpensive storage space off the premises, thereby reducing their risk. Flammable materials in the home, or other potential risks, can also be modified so that your business qualifies.

Home-business policies on the market include In-Home by RLI, which is available through independent insurance agents. To find a broker who sells RLI's insurance, contact the Independent Insurance Agents of America and

Health Insurance Warnings

✔ Many business or industry associations offer members the option of being part of a group insurance plan. This can be a good way to go, but these policies are also often overpriced, so don't automatically assume that your professional association is giving you the best deal.

✔ The same goes for HMOs. They aren't always the least expensive option because they historically have been more liberal about who they insure; the cost of covering these people may be passed on to you, although that is changing in many states.

✔ You may choose to buy insurance through a PPO, an organization which allows you to choose a doctor from a list of providers or go outside of the network as long as you are willing to pay a deductible. If you buy coverage through a PPO, be sure to check for hidden expenses such as "hospital admission expense."

✔ COBRA coverage through the job you used to have is also not a guaranteed bargain. Your employer's corporate policy is probably packed with things like drug treatment and other coverage you may not need. If so, you may do better finding your own insurance.

ask for Mike Beach—(800) 221-7917, ext. 5387. Homework, from Continental Insurance in New York City, was being acquired at press time by CNA Insurance Companies in Chicago, and can be obtained through CNA agents.

Health Insurance Lots of home-based business owners have given up on finding health insurance. They say they don't know where to find coverage and they can't afford it anyway. But it is important to have health insurance when you work for yourself at home; otherwise an illness can wreck you financially. Here are some facts on your options and tips that can help you avoid hidden costs and find the best deal (keep in mind that state insurance laws vary and these are general rules).

If you are evaluating a private insurance policy, check into a few things.

△ **The financial stability of the company.** If you aren't going with one of the giants, you want to make sure the company will be around for a while. To determine if a company is stable, you can run a check through one of the services that rates life and health insurance companies. These services include Moody's Investor Services, Standard & Poors, A. M. Best, and Deff & Phelps.

△ **The company's license.** Check with your state office of insurance to make sure the company you are considering has a license. While you're at it, check with the office to determine if any complaints have been lodged against the company for taking a long time to pay or refusing to pay claims altogether.

△ **Limited coverage.** Scrutinize the coverage itself and make sure that it doesn't have a low coverage limit for major operations like heart and liver transplants, or for parts or systems of the body.

△ **What you're losing for being part of a group policy.** Group insurance is heavily regulated and may be packed with features you don't need. Also, insurance companies cut prices only for groups of about 500 or more. So if you need to cover only yourself or your family, stick with an individual or family plan.

ZONING REGULATIONS FOR HOME-BASED ENTREPRENEURS

Most cities, municipalities, towns, hamlets, and so on have rules about working at home, and frequently prohibit it. Some local authorities are changing or talking about changing rules forbidding home-based business, but in many cases local ruling bodies routinely look the other way as more and more home businesses spring up and add revenue to the city coffers. I have actually heard from home-business owners who told me that when they called their local zoning boards to ask about the rules for working at home, they were told, "You didn't hear it here, but if we don't know about it, we don't mind."

I'm not recommending that you break the law. Businesses *are* shut down and fined for operating illegally at home. Whenever I talk about zoning authorities looking the other way, someone in the audience stands up and tells a story about a home-based operation being shut down. However, at this point, businesses being shut down for violating zoning regulations are the exception, not the rule.

When you decide to work at home, you should investigate your local zoning rules by calling the smallest ruling entity in your area. The department that handles zoning varies from one area to another. If you aren't sure who to contact, your city or county clerk's office can usually direct you to the right ruling body. Zoning will vary widely from one neighborhood to the next. Not only will there be a difference in whether or not home businesses are allowed, but zoning departments also vary widely on what they require you to do before they will permit you to operate.

Homeowner's associations, co-op boards, and other ruling entities can restrict you from operating a business at home, even if zoning officials give you the OK, so check with all ruling entities. If you live in an apartment building, you should check with any board or management agent who makes rules about the building.

You may not run into trouble from zoning authorities unless you employ more than one person or hang out a sign advertising your business. Placing ads for your business in the yellow pages or the local paper may also get you into trouble, but most home-business owners take the risk.

Most zoning problems arise when neighbors complain about a real or perceived increase in traffic in the neighborhood because of a business, or when a neighbor is mad at someone and turns her in to the zoning board as revenge. In other words, keep your neighbors happy and you probably will not have trouble with the zoning board.

Getting Along with Your Neighbors

To cope with your neighbors, I suggest being open about your home office. Unless you are already at odds with your neighbors for other reasons, most people will be intrigued by your business venture. You can help win their support by inviting them to look at your home office and letting them know you can now send a fax for them in a pinch. You can also point out the crime-fighting benefits of having someone home all day. Some people think it's asking for trouble to let your neighbors know what you are doing, but I think the chance of agitating your neighbors is higher if you hide what you are doing from them.

Another way to minimize problems with your neighbors is to make sure you provide adequate parking for clients or employees who come to your house on a regular basis. If possible, make arrangements so that no more than one person comes to your house at any one time. Try to squeeze these people into your driveway, if this applies, or ask them to park in a parking lot and walk to your home office, if possible. You should also try to restrict employees' and clients' hours to traditional work hours when possible. (Most zoning rules strictly prohibit employees in the home office unless they are immediate family members who live in the house. The reasoning behind this is that employees in the home increase traffic in residential areas.) Keep deliveries to a minimum by ordering supplies in bulk or getting a post office box where you can go to pick up packages that have been dropped off during the day.

If you run into zoning roadblocks, you have the option of applying for a zoning variance. Variances are granted by zoning boards in one of a few instances: if you can prove that the business you want to start is similar to one that is currently allowed in your area; if you can show that a zoning ordinance preventing you from working at home will deprive you of your livelihood; or if you can show that a home office would do no harm to the neighborhood. Getting a variance can be very expensive and time-consuming, but if you choose to apply for one, you should file your case with the zoning or planning board.

Businesses Prohibited at Home

There are some home businesses that fall into what I call the highly prohibited category. Running them often breaks more than just zoning rules, and may get you into trouble.

▶ Food handling, processing, or packaging companies are taboo. Believe it or not, all of those catering companies and baked-goods companies you know may be operating illegally. You can run a business at home preparing food only if the health department inspects your kitchen. The problem is, it's almost impossible for a residential kitchen to stack up because the health department's standards for capacity, quality, temperature control, and size cannot usually be met by standard kitchen equipment. Most caterers get around this by using an industrial kitchen somewhere else or operating on the sly.

▶ If you have a soft spot in your heart for small furry creatures, that's fine; just don't give a business working with them a spot in your home. If you do, you'll be breaking many of the urban laws that prohibit you from running any business at home in which you raise or breed animals.

▶ You can't fix cars either. Auto-body and repair shops cannot be run from the home because there is a fear that banging, soldering, and repairing will be noisy and disruptive to neighbors. The increased traffic that is bound to be part of an auto-body or repair business is also a reason that these businesses are not welcome.

▶ Manufacturing or processing of any kind is also out, including any business that creates fumes, dust, vibrations, or pollution.

▶ Speaking of pollution, beauty shops are also off-limits because they have a tendency to pour chemicals down the drain and engage in other anti-neighborhood activity.

▶ Any business that operates with an assembly line, even as short as two or three people, is often not allowed because the aim is to prevent sweat shops from starting up again in this country. This law restricts anything as simple as a few people putting clothes together.

Evaluating a Neighborhood for Home-Business Friendliness

If you're planning on moving to a new neighborhood and you want to work at home, you need to ask a lot of questions. Some neighborhoods are more home-business-friendly than others, and you should know how a community rates before you move in.

First you should look at what it costs to set up a business in your prospective new hometown. Total fees for things such as home-occupation permits and business licenses can range from about $25 to $650, depending on the area. Some governments see home businesses as simply an opportunity for revenue generation, while others regard home businesses as a positive addition to a community and encourage them by making it affordable to operate one. For example, a business license fee in some areas will be based on your annual gross income, while other communities charge a flat fee. The flat fee is not only cheaper, in most cases, but it requires less paperwork and time on your part. Another discrepancy among communities is that some insist on a home-business inspection, and will charge you for it, while others don't bother.

As I said in the zoning section, rules can change dramatically when you move even a few miles away. Not only will there be a difference between whether or not home businesses are allowed, but zoning departments also vary widely on what they require you to do before they will permit you to operate. Some zoning boards will ask for pictures, signatures from neighbors, and everything but a letter from Newt Gingrich, while others will require you to do very little to gain approval. Homeowner's associations, co-op boards, and other ruling entities also have rules about working at home, so check with associations and investigate the rules before you decide to move in.

Local taxes are another differentiating factor between hospitable and inhospitable areas. Some cities don't even have taxes, while others derive significant income from residents who work at home. New York City, for example, charges a 4 percent tax on the net income of any incorporated business that makes more than $10,000 annually.

You'll also want to ask a lot of questions about phones. The number of lines you are allowed to have coming into your home can be restricted by the town, a homeowner's association, or sometimes simply the number of lines the phone company has available in your community. Also, because of the increasing importance of computer online services you may want to investigate how easily you can access these services from a potential new home office. If it's a long-distance call to get online, you should be aware of that before you move in.

Of course, you should be concerned about convenience of services when you move into a new house, but this is especially important when you're working at home because you'll need to get out a lot to the post office, printer, overnight delivery service, and any other service you use on a regular basis. Also, technical help should be readily available for those inevitable hardware problems. Crime is another common consideration. No one wants to move into a high-crime area, but those of us working at home may need to be even more concerned because we usually have invested significant sums in home-office equipment that burglars would love to get their hands on.

The bottom line is, when you're moving, ask a lot of questions. Where you live can have a lot to do with how easy it is to run a home-based business.

TAX LAWS FOR HOME-BASED ENTREPRENEURS

As a self-employed person you must pay city, state, and federal income tax just like anyone else, but you are responsible for paying it directly to the government. Federal income taxes must be paid in estimated quarterly payments. These payments are due in four installments, on April 15, June 15, September 15, and January 15. These federal taxes will cover your self-employment tax, which includes social security and Medicare. Self-employment tax makes working for yourself expensive because when you had a boss, your employer paid for half of these taxes and you paid the other half. You will now be responsible for all of it. If your state has an income tax, you must pay it quarterly also. Cities may have their own tax rules.

Generally speaking, you must pay estimated quarterly installments if you expect to owe at least $500 in tax for a given year. The laws governing how much tax you must submit during the year require that you pay either 90 percent of the tax you will owe by the end of the year (to avoid penalties), or 100 percent of last year's tax (110 percent if your income exceeds $150,000). This means that you can submit a minimum amount of tax during the year if you want to hold on to some of your money. However, this plan works only if you are able to leave the money intended for taxes alone. Too many people spend the money that they put aside, then run into trouble at tax time.

If you use a tax preparer, he will provide you with estimated payment recommendations based on what you earned last year. If you are figuring your own estimates, base them on last year's tax. For example, if you paid $8,000 in federal tax last year, each quarterly payment should be $2,000. If you start to make a lot more money, see your accountant to obtain updated estimates. If you are just starting up, you may want to consult a tax preparer during the year to determine what you owe.

Staying on top of your estimated quarterly tax payments will save you both money and grief. If you fail to make your payments on schedule and within the guidelines I've mentioned, you will be liable for penalties, plus interest on the money you owe. Your tax preparer should provide you with forms and envelopes for making your estimated payments, or you can order these forms directly from the IRS by calling (800) 829-3676.

At the end of the year, you will calculate all of your expenses on a Schedule C tax form that will itemize all of your expenses for the year.

Employee Taxes

If you have employees on your payroll, your tax situation is significantly more complex. You'll have to keep track of FICA, unemployment, disability, and workers' compensation—just to name a few. All of these require separate calculations and timelines for payment. These rules are very strict, and unless you're in the payroll business, you should hire an accountant to keep you legal and punctual with all these payments. You should also check with your state's office of taxation to find out about state income tax, unemployment, and workers' compensation.

The only exception to the rules for tax responsibilities for employees you have is your children or grandchildren. You do not have to pay social security or unemployment taxes on salaries paid to minors. Children do not have to pay income tax on their first $3,000 worth of earnings.

If you pay an independent contractor more than $600 a year, you have to file a 1099 form with the IRS and send one to the person you paid. You can get these forms from your accountant or from tax officials. The 1099 reports to the government that this person was paid as a non-employee. This gives you the right to deduct those payments as an expense and tells the IRS to look for that money as income on your non-employee's Schedule C form.

Sales Tax   A state sales tax ID number is basically a business version of your social security number under which you collect and pay tax for any service or product you sell that qualifies for taxation in your state. The state department of taxation provides sales tax ID numbers, and it takes about a month to get one. The rule of thumb for sales tax is that most services are exempt and most products are taxable except for food and drugs. However, for the last few years, states have been gradually adding to the list of services that are taxable. Check with your state department of taxation to determine if the product or service you sell is taxable in your state.

If you close your home business or never get it off the ground after you have already procured a tax ID number, make sure you notify the department of taxation. If you don't, you will continue to get computer-generated estimated bills and fines! Also, if you buy a home-based business from someone else, make sure you have a bulk sales tax clearance done, which is an OK from the tax people that there are no liens on the business.

Home-Business Deductions   If you work for yourself at home, you are eligible for a break on your taxes *if* your house, apartment, or other living quarters is your "principal place of business"—that is, where you spend the majority of your time and make most of your money. This requirement resulted from a 1993 U.S. Supreme Court decision which ruled that deductions are off-limits to people who spend only a portion of their time in a home office.

Another catch is that if you want home-office deductions, you must use your home office exclusively for business. This means you cannot work at the kitchen table or in a den that your family uses at night. There are a few exceptions to this rule, including day-care centers, which tend to take over the house.

If you are eligible for a tax break as an entrepreneur, deductions may include a percentage of your rent or the cost of owning your home, based on the percentage of square footage your office takes up, as well as things like homeowner's insurance, utilities, cleaning service, and repairs. If you are a telecommuter, see "Tax Laws for Telecommuters" in this chapter.

Business expense deductions include supplies, advertising, car expenses, depreciation of equipment, legal fees, and travel. Phone bills are a big potential deduction, but they are tricky. If your business line is also your personal phone, you cannot deduct the cost of having the phone or making local calls, even if the bulk of the calls are business-related. On that line, only long-distance calls are deductible.

IRS Publication 587 covers all information on working at home. To get it, call (800) 829-3676. For answers to general questions, call (800) 829-1040.

If you owed more than you expected to this past tax season, or if you have a suspicion that you would save money on your taxes if your accounting practices weren't so slipshod, try the following suggestions.

1. Don't Spend Cash. If you didn't have as many deductions as you thought you would, you may not be keeping track of all your expenses. Lots of us spend small amounts of cash on things like taxis, tokens, pens, coffee with clients, food for entertaining clients in our home office, and other expenses, but don't document them sufficiently enough to deduct them at year end. The amount of money you spend on these things may seem too insignificant at the time to bother recording, or you may get a receipt but forget to record the expense.

If this is your problem, save money this year by doing a couple of things. First, do not spend a lot of cash. Write checks or use a credit card for as many purchases as possible. My accountant told me that every time I make a purchase, I should think about whether I want to be able to deduct it. If I do, I should pay by check or credit card to increase my chances of remembering to include the expense in my year-end calculations. To minimize the amount of cash you spend, set up accounts with businesses you frequent, get a check-writing card for your grocery store, and start buying things like stamps over the phone so that you can pay by credit card—(800) STAMP-24.

2. Reimburse Yourself Frequently. To make sure you keep track of the cash you cannot avoid spending, reimburse yourself for cash expenses. Every week or two, tally your cash receipts and write yourself a check for the amount you have spent. Attach the canceled check to these receipts, with a note on top breaking out how much cash you spend in each expense category. This will help you tally your expenses at the end of the year, and will make the person preparing your return feel confident in taking all of the deductions you are due.

3. Separate Your Business and Personal Expenses. If you don't have one yet, you should also get a separate bank account and credit card for your business. If you do not, there is a chance that the IRS could claim that all money deposited in every account is income, which means you'll pay tax on things like reimbursements from your insurance company. The government may also be more likely to challenge business expenses if your personal and business charges are intermingled.

4. Make Bigger Quarterly Payments. If you are in financial shock because you had to pay a lot of tax for last year on April 15 along with your first quarterly payment for this year, it is time to start making bigger quarterly tax payments.

Year-End Tax Preparation

In the middle of December, right when you are running around trying to finish your holiday shopping and get all of your holiday cards written to your clients, you need to make time to do one more thing. Take a look at your income and expenses for the year. Why look at your income and expenses in December? Because if you wait until January or February, and then discover you owe a lot of taxes for this year, it will be too late to do anything about it.

1. Tabulate your income for the year by looking through pay stubs, bank statements, or whatever records you use for your business. Be sure you don't count loans to your company as income.

2. Tally up your expenses by looking at your receipts, credit-card bills, and checkbook. Don't forget cash expenses, and don't double-count—look what happened to Webster Hubbell in Whitewater. Throughout the year, you should have been writing expense checks to yourself every week or month from your business account to keep track of your cash expenses. If you didn't, try to remember what you've spent cash on (and have receipts for), and resolve to reimburse yourself by check next year. Throughout the year, staple these checks to the receipts they cover to keep your records straight. Simple software programs designed for personal income tracking can help you keep your business organized if it's small enough. Microsoft Money and Quicken by Intuit are two popular programs; there are plenty of other more sophisticated packages if you need them.

3. Send all of this information to your accountant. You could get a tax book and figure out what percentage of your expenses are deductible, but I don't recommend it. First of all, tax laws are complex and are constantly changing. Second, even if you could calculate everything properly, you should be using your time for your business and delegating your tax responsibilities to someone who does taxes for a living.

By examining the financial condition of your business now, instead of next year, you can take action that may save you on taxes. If you haven't paid all the taxes you owe from this year, you may avoid some penalties by paying them before the year is out.

4. If you find yourself with a large tax liability, you can do the following before the end of the year to help defray what you owe:

Open a *Keogh account*, a retirement plan for the self-employed that must be funded before the end of the year.

Take advantage of the equipment-expense deduction. If you face a large tax liability, you can purchase equipment this year that you were planning to buy next year, thereby generating another deduction.

Defer a payment to your business until the next year.

Pay business expenses for next year early. Bills for electricity, legal fees, or another business expense can be paid ahead of time to reduce your income. Ask suppliers if you can prepay their invoices.

Take advantage of tax deductions available to businesses that employ their children. If your kids legitimately work for your home business, this is a way of moving money to someone who is taxed at a lower level. But don't try to fool the IRS by saying you employ a child if you don't. The IRS requires a lot of verification when you claim to employ a child, and it doesn't look too kindly on things like three-month-old employees.

CHOOSING AN ACCOUNTANT

Probably the best advice I can give you on the subject of taxes and your finances in general is this: Hire an experienced accountant who specializes in small businesses. You may not need to do this right away while your business is small and hasn't yet taken off. But eventually you will need help. Under ideal circumstances, your accountant is a trusted member of your close circle of advisors. This person should be a wise business counselor as well as a tax planner.

You will want to retain someone you feel comfortable with. And do make sure she is a good listener! If your accountant is going to help you structure the financial future of your business, she had better understand your plans and believe in your vision.

Don't be afraid to shop around for the best person. Ask other business owners who they use and talk to your banker or attorney for recommendations. Sometimes your local college's accounting department can be a good source of referrals. Call the society of certified public accountants in your state. Many, though not all, have referral services.

What to expect in the way of fees will vary a great deal depending on where you live, how complicated your business is, and the experience level of the person you are considering. A very rough estimate of what you will pay would range from $75 to $125 an hour. At these prices, you'll want to be sure to do all the routine organizing work yourself, and consult your accountant only for his expertise and counsel. Once your business is established it is ideal to have more than one accountant or financial advisor to speak to when you are making important business or tax decisions. Financial and tax decisions are so crucial it is preferable to see if two experts concur and, if they don't, weigh their advice and make your own decision.

BUSINESS CONTRACTS

All business agreements should be put in writing—even if you're working with a close friend or relative. Many people think the act of writing up a contract is a statement of mistrust between parties, but that is not true. A contract is a professional way of spelling out in writing who gets what, when, and how, and just exactly what each party is responsible for. I respect people who request that we work with a contract. Furthermore, confusion and misunderstandings between people—even the best of friends—are perfectly natural. Having a contract to refer to for clarification will help keep you on good terms with your business associates and your friends.

Writing a
Contract

At the minimum a contract should include details of what you are agreeing to, including money, quantities, time frame, date of delivery, and payment terms. It should also spell out what will happen if parties do not deliver, or if the deal does not go as planned in some other way. Knowing what unexpected things may happen and how to word them to cover yourself in a contract is best handled by an attorney. They have seen so many deals gone bad that they will be able to point out possibilities that you might not think of. It is tempting to leave these things out, especially when you are eager to get going on a project and feel nothing but goodwill toward the person you will be working with. But you will thank yourself in the long run if you take the time to construct a good contract. To save money, you can draft a version of a contract and pass it on to your attorney to check it over for you and include the "what ifs."

Once you have created a contract, you should sign it and forward it to the other parties for their signatures. People routinely do business based on contracts with faxed signatures, but mailing a contract is still preferable. There are some courts that will not accept faxed signatures if the contract is in dispute and you have to go to court. You can attempt to get around this by asking the other party to mail you the original, but according to Ethan Finneran, a New York City attorney, it could then be interpreted that you do not believe the faxed signature is valid. If you do request that an original be sent to you, you should wait for it to arrive before starting work on what is in the contract.

The Basic
Contract

The basic contract is an agreement between two or more parties for a service or a product, or anything else to which you are agreeing. The tradi-

Basic Contract

Agreement made [or entered into] this _____ day of _____, 19_____, between [or *by and between*] _____[name] of _____[city], referred to as [or *called* or *designated as*] _____ [descriptive word, such as *owner* or *employer*] and _____ [name of other party], of _____[city], referred to as ____ [descriptive word, such as *contractor, employee,* etc.] or who is agreeing and brief description of what is being agreed to _____. Brief description of other intentions _____.

A. _____[*owner* or *employer* or other descriptive word adopted in commencement of contract] agrees:
  1. _____.
  2. _____.
  3. _____.

B. _____ [*contractor* or *employee* or other descriptive word adopted in commencement of contract] agrees:

  1. _____.
  2. _____.
  3. _____.

C. It is further agreed between the parties as follows:
  1. _____.
  2. _____.
  3. _____.

This agreement shall be binding on the heirs, executors, administrators, successors, and assigns of each of the parties. The parties have set their hands [and seals] the day and year written above [or specify day, month, and year].

[Signatures of both parties to contract]
In presence of _____ [if attesting witness or witness necessary or desired.]

tional contract can be used whether someone is providing something to you or you are providing something to others. The basic contract and all other sample contracts are presented as a guide and are only a starting point for a contract. I recommend that you consult your attorney before you enter into any agreement.

Confidentiality/ Noncompete Agreement

The confidentiality/noncompete agreement is an agreement that protects you when you work with another party and they learn confidential and/or proprietary information about you and/or your business. For example, if you build inventions, another party you are working with on a project may learn some of the secrets to a new product you are building. A confidentiality/noncompete agreement helps to prevent that party from disclosing any information obtained in the course of doing business with you. It is also designed to bind someone from competing against you for the same or very similar products or services in the future.

However, keep in mind that unscrupulous people will steal your ideas even if they have signed an agreement. Many people have com-

Confidentiality/Noncompete Agreement

The undersigned, representing _____ [company name], hereby agrees that he/she will not disclose proprietary information acquired pursuant to this meeting or any other discussions he/she has had with _____, representing [your business] and other [your business] representatives, to any other party. This agreement shall not apply to any information which was in undersigned's possession prior to the time of our mutual disclosure; which was in the public domain prior to our mutual disclosure; which becomes part of the public domain not due to any unauthorized act or omission on undersigned's part; or, is supplied to the undersigned by a third party as a matter of right. The undersigned agrees that he/she will not now, or at any future time, divulge or appropriate to his/her own use or the use of others, reproduce, transmit or provide information regarding [your business] business or plans for business or any part thereof to any person or persons not connected with [undersigned's organization].

The undersigned agrees that he/she and undersigned's organization will maintain information in strict confidence, not use [your business] information for his/her own benefit or disclose it to third parties, and return property and information to [your business]. In addition, the undersigned agrees not to use information gained in this or any other meeting or discussion to compete with [your business], or to use the information gained from this or any other meeting or discussion with [your business] to create a product that is similar to the one that is being discussed.

Signed,

_____

Representing:_____

Dated:_____

plained to me of this. The thief will risk the chance of being sued if the idea is good enough. With this in mind, reveal only that information that pertains to your working relationship.

Be sure to have the other party sign the confidentiality/noncompete agreement as soon as your working relationship begins—even when you are in the early stages of discussion about a project. It is a very common form, and people should not be offended by a request to sign one.

The confidentiality/noncompete agreement and all other sample contracts are presented as a guide. I recommend that you consult your attorney before you enter into any agreement.

OBTAINING CREDIT CARD MERCHANT STATUS

Chances are that accepting credit cards for customer purchases will help you compete and increase sales in your home-based business. But it can be difficult to get the OK from banks to accept these cards.

For the most part, banks don't like to grant merchant status to home-based businesses, which would allow them to accept credit cards for purchases. They think we'll fold in the face of credit-card fraud, and they'll be stuck paying for merchandise someone bought from us with a stolen card. But even though banks don't like us, you should try them first because they have the cheapest rates. Start your search at your bank. If it rejects you, contact your industry association for names of banks that work with companies like yours, or ask other home-based business owners where they got merchant status.

When you approach a bank, keep in mind that it is looking for proof that your home-based business is professional and sustainable. Most banks provide explicit written guidelines for how to apply for merchant status, but there are a few things you can do to get an edge. For starters, give the bank a list of some big-name customers who'll vouch for your stability. And register your business with Dun & Bradstreet. It will bolster your image.

To reassure a bank that it won't be left in the lurch, offer to put some cash in a CD or bank account equal to the amount you expect to get in monthly charges. Set up this account so the bank has access to the money, and after six months of paying your bills on time, have the arrangement dissolved. It's also a good idea to get a copy of your credit report first, before a bank looks at it. If it has negative marks on it, try to clear them up or at least explain them. This will help you get approval and obtain a better rate.

An alternative to the bank is an *independent selling organization* or ISO. An ISO goes between a business and a bank to set up merchant status and assumes the risk for businesses that are considered a gamble. If you go out of business or can't pay for some reason, it's the ISO's loss.

As you might guess, ISOs charge more than banks. They'll take a higher percentage of all the money you make, and will charge other fees. But the reality is that ISOs are the most likely route if you work at home. The cost of using an ISO varies widely from company to company, so shop around. And look out for ISO scams. To verify an ISO's legitimacy, ask for the name of the bank it works with and call the bank to check it out.

Trade associations and business groups are another resource. They sometimes offer Visa and MasterCard access to members and, at the very least, they can recommend reputable ISOs, banks, or other organizations that have worked with people like you.

Also, American Express merchant status is easier to obtain in some cases, so you may want to try AMEX first—and then use that relationship for leverage. It will cost you more to accept any credit card, but if the market will bear it, you can always raise your prices to cover the cost.

For more information and a guide to ISOs and banks, read *How to Achieve Credit Card Merchant Status* by Paul Mladjenovic. It's $29.95 and you can get it by calling (201) 714-4953 or (800) 98-SUCCESS.

DETERMINING YOUR PRICE

There is no definitive answer to the pricing question because prices are set based on a variety of factors. I have a friend in the restaurant business who keeps raising his prices every year. He says the higher he raises them, the longer the lines for a table at his restaurant. On the other hand, I've priced myself out of business and I know lots of other people who have too.

A commonly used pricing formula is: Direct costs plus overhead plus profit equals your price. Other people advise doubling your wholesale price. But formulas can be problematic because they don't give detail. Lots of people follow this formula and lose money. The following points explain how.

▲ The price you can charge for anything is tied to what customers are willing—or expect—to pay. This may seem obvious, but a lot of entrepreneurs forget that no matter how much their product or service is worth in their eyes, if people won't pay that much for it, it won't sell. You can easily check this out by looking at your competition and by calling companies or individuals you know to ask them what they would be willing to pay.

▲ Your customers don't always make their purchasing decisions on the basis of logic. Sometimes, they'll equate quality with price—in some cases, if your price is too low, they will see your product as low quality. They may be suspicious that they're getting something not quite up to standard, and avoid buying at your "bargain" price.

Once you know what your costs are and what your customers are willing to pay, you have to make some decisions about where you want to place yourself in the pricing spectrum. Do you want to position yourself as a discount, no-frills vendor who makes money on volume, or as a high-end provider who makes more profit per job? If you decide to go for the high end of the pricing spectrum, you will need to add value to what you are selling. This means providing extra services, products, or resources along with your product. But don't panic, thinking, "How can I afford that?" Often adding value means bringing attention to something you are already offering such as guaranteed online service, quick turnaround, high-quality products, or extra features. Bringing attention to these in your marketing is often enough to justify a higher price to consumers.

Service Business Pricing   If you are in the service business, you should research what your competition charges and then place yourself in the spectrum accordingly. If you have a specialty, put yourself at the top end of the spectrum. Otherwise you may be wise to put yourself in the middle of the range.

It can be dangerous to price yourself too low. Consumers' tendency is to wonder what is wrong with a service that is low-priced. They may wonder if you have the expertise necessary to do the job. If you have a service business, you also need to decide whether you should charge by the hour or by the job. The answer to that depends on your business, but here are some examples of circumstances in which one method is better than another:

If the job is one where your client may want changes to the project after the fact or mid-job, you're better off charging by the hour. Say you have a word-processing business and you spend a few days typing a lengthy thesis for a graduate student. You've quoted him a flat price, based on your estimate of how long it will take you to type the

Figuring Your Expenses

Some people come up short because they forget to calculate all expenses. Here are some general categories to factor in when you are determining costs.

- ✔ The cost of your furniture and equipment
- ✔ Stationery, business cards, and office supplies
- ✔ Magazine subscriptions
- ✔ Cost of membership in professional organizations
- ✔ Postage and express mail delivery
- ✔ Telephone and fax charges
- ✔ Printing
- ✔ Software
- ✔ Travel and transportation fees
- ✔ Consultant fees
- ✔ Your time

200-page document. After you've finished the work, he comes back to you with several revisions that he wants you to make in the finished paper. If you'd been charging by the job, you would be in for hours more work at no more money. If you are charging by the hour, you'll be compensated for the extra time added to the original job. Of course, you might also negotiate a straight hourly rate for the changes.

It's often a good ideas to charge by the job when the quoted hourly rate for your service might make a customer balk. For example, if you're writing copy for an ad brochure and you know it will take you two hours to do it, quoting $75 an hour may sound too high. But quoting a flat $150 for your service will sound more reasonable.

Knowing how long it will take you to do a certain job is the key in figuring out how much to charge. If you don't yet have the experience to know how long a job will take, find others in your line of work and ask them for an estimate.

Service businesses also frequently require a portion of their payment up front, since there is usually no way of taking back a service once you've given it. You have to determine if that is appropriate based on your business and your customer base, but a common practice is to request one-third of a payment when a contract is signed, one-third halfway through the job, and one-third on completion. I strongly urge you to use this method whenever possible.

Wholesale Pricing   Like any pricing question, determining what to charge to retailers who will resell your product requires some homework. In general, retailers will not buy from you if they can get the product for less from someone else. Retailers also have to be able to double the price that you are charging them (the general retail price formula is wholesale price times 2) and still get customers to buy. "If it's priced too high and retailers cannot get normal markup, they won't purchase," says Phillip Messing, certified public accountant and lecturer at The Entrepreneurial Center, Inc., in Purchase, New York. "The key with wholesaling is you have to get your product cheap enough so that you can sell it to retailers at a good price."

To make sure you fulfill these two requirements, do the following to set your wholesale prices.

△ Investigate your competition at the wholesale level by calling them for prices, attending trade shows, and talking to trade associations. To find trade shows, look in industry publications.

△ Talk to retailers. Ask retail shop owners where they purchase and what they pay, or go to stores and divide the retail price by two to determine the wholesale price.

△ Call the association for the retailers you want to sell to and find out what the markup rate is. That will help you determine what the retailers you'll be selling to will be willing to pay.

BUSINESS LICENSES

Certain businesses need to be licensed and some geographic areas require all businesses to have a license. Whether or not you need a license to operate your home-based business depends on the type and location of the business. For example, doctors and lawyers, hairdressers, masseuses, plumbers, and social workers need licenses to operate whether they work at home or for a multinational corporation in a big office park.

There are a few different ways to find out about what permits and licenses you'll need. First, most states have an office of business permits and licenses. Second, contact the association for your chosen industry. To find your industry association, look in *The Encyclopedia of Associations*, by Gale Research, Inc., Detroit, Michigan. Go to the local library reference desk to find this book, look up the organization, and call it for information or a recommendation of where you can find information on industry requirements.

To find out if you need a license, contact your state office of licenses or the department of commerce's small business division. Most have an office for permits and license requirements. They will either give you the answer or direct you to the local agency that can help you. Sometimes you'll need a local license as well as a state license to operate but the state office can tell you that as well. In general, the only reason to get a business license is if you are required to by law.

BUSINESS CERTIFICATES

If you don't need a business license, you may still need to, or want to, get a business certificate or register as a DBA (Doing Business As). These are two different names for the same procedure. In many states, if you are a sole proprietor operating a business under a fictitious name (any name other than one that contains your full name), you must get a business certificate. If I called my home business Alice Bredin's Home Decorating Company I wouldn't need to get a business certificate, but if I called my business City Home Designs, I would need to register it. "It's a way for government to find you to sue you if someone is hurt in your business," said Steve Gersz, an attorney specializing in business law at the Rochester, New York, firm of Underberg & Kessler. If a state has an occupational license rule you will have to get a DBA even if you use your full name as your company name. California is one of those states.

You may choose to register as a DBA even if you don't have to by law. A DBA will help you open a business bank account and may reassure some clients that you have lasting power. If you don't have a DBA and you open a bank account under your name, if a client makes a check out to your company name, your bank may not cash the check.

In most cases, you register for a business certificate (DBA) at the county clerk's office. In a few cases you register with the state or city, but a call to county clerk will resolve the question. Fees vary and range from as low as $10 to above $50. The county clerk's office cannot restrict you from choosing a name that is already in use, but they will tell you if someone else has your name, and will usually discourage you from using the same one.

There are also special permits and regulations that apply to some businesses. If you advertise kosher products, for example, you need a permit from the state. If you use hazardous substances for, let's say, a printing business, you need a federal permit. Home improvement contractors are regulated under a statute that requires them to be bonded. Some travel agents need to be bonded, too.

Other Regulations

Where to Find the Information You Need

✔ Local requirements: city or county clerk's office

✔ State requirements: state office of permits and licenses or state Department of Commerce

✔ Federal requirements: Contact your industry association

Some state departments have packets of information on particular businesses; for example, New York State's Department of Social Services has packets of information on state regulations for daycare centers. Call the Department of Commerce Small Business Division, or the state office of licenses and permits. In some states you will have to publish your intent to do business in an official notice. This is regulated by the states, but the county clerk's office will be able to tell you if this is necessary when you obtain your DBA.

SECURING A NAME

The first step to take in securing a name is to look in the Yellow Pages to see if the name you want is already taken. When you go to the city or county clerk's office to register your name (in some states it will be done at the state level), they will do a search to determine if anyone is using the name locally. Most clerks cannot stop you by law from using another DBA's name, but they will usually advise against it. The other circumstances that will prevent you from using your chosen name is if someone else has a trademark on a name, or some other legal right to it. When you go to register your name, you will want to have a few extras ready in case someone else is using the name and isn't in the phone book.

If you want to search for yourself to see if someone outside of your locale is using a name you're considering, you can do a trademark search (see Trademarks). Keep in mind that if you register your name as a DBA, this does not prevent another company from using it. If you want to protect your name you must secure a trade name or trademark. Even if you are incorporated (which is done statewide) your name is not protected unless you obtain a trademark.

If you do business in a variety of states and have a permanent or even a temporary selling site in more than one state, you may be required to register in those areas. If you have a mail order business based in New York that sells nationally, you don't need to register your name anywhere other than New York. (You might want to trademark it so that no one will compete with you nationally under the same name.) If you have offices in several states or counties, or even if you travel from trade show to trade show, you may be required to register your business name. If you are a corporation, you have to register as a foreign corporation in any state outside the charter state in which you have an office.

INTELLECTUAL PROPERTY PROTECTION

There are three forms of intellectual property protection: patents, trademarks, and copyrights. The three are often confused and hopefully I'll clear some of the confusion up in this section.

Patents

When you have an idea for a great new product, the first stage is usually excitement. Stage two is often concern about how to protect your idea when you begin shopping around for resources to help you bring it to market and have to share the idea with other people.

The simplest way to protect yourself—although it is by no means fail safe—is a noncompete/nondisclosure agreement (see page 140). This is a document in which people pledge they will not compete with you or provide information about your product to other people. Of course, many people sign these agreements and break them, but their existence may at least discourage potential thieves.

A more involved process that can provide significantly more protection is a patent. If you are considering a patent, it is important to realize that the patenting process can be lengthy and expensive, so before you embark on it make sure you have researched your product and determined that it has a market. You should also determine that the product you are interested in is not already patented before you spend time and money on the application process. To do this, you can go to the U.S. Patent and Trademark Office in Washington, DC, or search the patent libraries located across the country.

A patent allows the inventor the exclusive right to make, use, and sell an invention throughout the United States during the term of the patent. Any other party that makes, sells, or uses the patent invention during the term of the patent—without consent of the patent holder—is infringing on the patent.

There are three forms of patents: design, utility, and plant. Design patents are granted for any new, original, and ornamental design for an article of manufacturing. Design patents cover the aesthetic appearance of an invention such as the appearance of a fax machine or a lamp. Design patents have a term of 17 years in the United States. Some people believe that design patents are the weakest form of patent because a competitor can avoid infringing on your patent by changing the design very slightly. Utility patents cover the functional features of an invention and are granted for any new and useful process, machine, manufacture, or composition of matter, or for any new and useful improvement. For example, the switching mechanism in a lamp or the electronics in your fax machine could fit this category. A utility patent lasts 14 years. The third type of patent, a plant patent, protects a new form of greenery or plant.

In order to get a patent you must file an application with the U.S. Patent and Trademark Office where examiners determine the originality of your invention and request through a series of steps. To patent something takes between one and three years and can cost between $3,000 and $10,000, including legal fees. The fee the Patent Office charges will vary depending on the size of your business and the number of claims in the patent application. You must apply for a patent within one year of the time a product is first offered for sale or disclosed publicly.

While you can complete all of the patent paperwork yourself to obtain a patent, it is recommended that you consult with an attorney during the process because the protection you create may not stand up to litigation. If you want to save money on legal fees, draft patent papers yourself and have an attorney review them, rather than having the attorney draft the papers from scratch. You can also use the services of a patent agent. To get a list of patent agents who are registered to practice before the Patent Office, contact the Superintendent of Documents, Government Printing Office: 202-783-3238. For help patenting on your own, you can get a book like Nolo Press's *Patent It Yourself*.

If you choose to go with a company that promises to patent and market your product for you, be careful. There are reputable companies on the market, but there are also scam artists looking to profit from other people's lack of knowledge. If you are considering one of these companies, try to use one that comes recommended by another entrepreneur or knowledgeable source. You should also contact your state attorney general's office to be sure the company is reputable before handing over any money, and ask the company for about a dozen references you can speak to.

The protection you'll get from your patent is effective only when a patent is granted, not during a patent-pending period. Also, a patent only protects you in the United States. A U.S. patent will not stop someone in another country from manufacturing and selling your product outside the United States. If you want to protect yourself in other countries, you need a patent in each one.

For patent information and applications call 703-557-4636 or write to the U.S. Patent and Trademark Office, Washington, DC, 20231 or to have questions answered call 703-308-HELP.

Trademarks   A trademark is any word name, symbol, device, or combination of these things used to identify and distinguish one's goods from those manufactured or sold by others and to indicate the source of the good, even if that source is unknown. Trademarks also apply to sayings such as "The Friendly Skies of United," and the soda phrase "Uh-huh" and to configurations such as book package designs. Trademarks also encompass trade names (the trademark for a corporate entity) and a service mark (used for services rather than products).

You don't have to register with the U.S. Patent and Trademark Office in order to trademark your good or service. Trademark protection commences as soon as you begin using your trademark. However, although you don't need to register your trademark, I recommend it because it provides procedural advantages if you need to sue someone for infringement. You can file an "intent to use" application with the Trademark and Patent Office which will protect you from the date you file as long as you do eventually file your application. This is useful if the time between when you choose a name and actually bring a product to market is lengthy because it reserves the name until you get the mark into commerce.

Obtaining a trademark takes about one year and costs approximately $1,000 in fees and legal costs. Trademarks last as long as the owner of the mark continues to use it; however, the registration for the trademark must be renewed every ten years. In addition, in the first ten-year period in which you have a trademark, you must demonstrate during the fifth and sixth year that the trademark is being used. Thereafter, you must only renew every ten years. Trademarks are usually passed on in wills or carried on through a corporate entity. Like a patent, a trademark protects you only in the United States.

You can check to see if a trademark is currently in use by looking on CompuServe, in the Thomson & Thomson's Trademark Scan online, or by accessing the same database through Westlaw, a law-related on-line service, or on Knight-Ridder's Dialogue Information Services, an online service that provides direct online access to databases including Trademark Scan. Thomson & Thomson can be reached directly at 800-692-8833 to conduct an over-the-phone search for a fee that ranges from $80 to $500. Some librarians can also do a trademark scan for you for a fee, or you can do your own search in the Directory of U.S. Trademarks in the library.

State trademark registration is easier and cheaper but it only provides you state protection. The benefit of a state trademark is that in states with strong laws prohibiting the counterfeiting of state trademarks, trademark owners can bring state action for infringements.

For trademark information and applications call 703-557-3158 or write to the U.S. Patent and Trademark Office, Washington, DC 20231. To have questions answered call 703-308-HELP.

Copyright

This information may help you understand when copyright can be used and how to make sure you don't infringe on someone else's copyright.

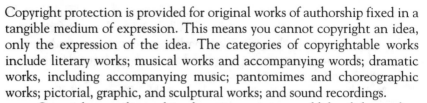
Copyright protection is provided for original works of authorship fixed in a tangible medium of expression. This means you cannot copyright an idea, only the expression of the idea. The categories of copyrightable works include literary works; musical works and accompanying words; dramatic works, including accompanying music; pantomimes and choreographic works; pictorial, graphic, and sculptural works; and sound recordings.

Copyrights are limited in duration to a term of life of the author plus 50 years. For work created by employees for hire, they are good 75 years from first publication or 100 years from creation (whichever expires first).

You do not have to register with the U.S. Copyright office in order to have copyright protection. Rights commence upon creation of the work. Until 1989, a copyright owner was required to include a copyright notice on all products and failure to do so could result in a loss of copyright rights. That law no longer exists and creators now own a copyright unless a contract states otherwise. However, before you can start action against a copyright infringement, you must register a copyright claim. As of January 1994, the filing fee is $20 per application and it takes about six weeks for the copyright office to process the application and issue a registration. The U.S. filing achieves rights in all countries that honor U.S. copyrights. The copyright office in Washington, D.C. can provide you with a list of these countries. If infringement occurs in another country, however, you must sue in that country.

To make sure I protect my copyright, I am in the habit of writing Alice Bredin, copyright, and year of publication after work that I own the rights to. Although this is not necessary by law, copyright lawyers say its a good idea. "It's not necessary, but it puts the world on notice, so it's a good idea," says Greg Battersby, an intellectual property attorney at Grimes & Battersby, Stamford, Connecticut, and co-author of *The Toy and Game Inventors Guide* (New York: Kent Press, 1995). You should place the copyright notice somewhere that gives "reasonable notice" of its existence. That means on the first page of a manuscript or on the label of a record. If you take this precaution, the recommended form is your name, followed by the *Copyright*, and the year in which you created the work.

The fight over copyrights is heating up as creators and those who pay them to generate work do battle in the new territory of electronic rights. Realizing that once something is placed on the Internet its value for future distribution in other venues is greatly reduced, creators are trying to hold onto these rights. Employers, also realizing the value of these rights, are more determined than ever to make sure the copyright is theirs.

As an independent contractor or freelancer, you usually own the rights to what you create unless you sign a contract giving rights to your client. If ownership is not stipulated in a contract, the creator owns the copyright to the work. Before you sign any contract, be sure you know who will own the work you create during your employment. Oftentimes, the entity paying you will try to lay claim to all work, not just what you were hired to create, during the term of the contract, so be on the lookout for the clause in all contracts. If you hire someone to create work for your business and you want to own it—public relations material or ad copy, for example—you will want to have the agency or individual sign an agreement assigning rights to you.

If you publish something on a regular basis, such as a newsletter or magazine, you may be able to register a year's worth of work at one time. The possibility of what is called a *group registration* will depend on whether or not all the work in the periodical has the same author. To find out more about group registration ask the Copyright Office for its publication *Group Registration of Contributions to Periodicals*. The *Registration for Serials* publication explains rules for periodicals.

Software copyrighting is a little more complicated because registering for a copyright of software may make your source code available to anyone who wants to look at it. To protect yourself, you may want to patent portions of your code and have it blacked out in your copyright. For more information on copyrighting software, ask the Copyright Office for the publication, *Copyright Registration for Computer Programs*.

The myth about the efficacy of protecting work by mailing yourself a sealed copy of the work is just that. Mailing work to yourself does not provide protection because you could easily mail yourself empty envelopes and then open them and insert anything you want. Instead, you can protect yourself by having a notary public sign and date your work or by registering it with the Copyright Office.

If you find information in a magazine or online that you want to use for something you are creating, chances are you cannot, even if you pay to access it.

You may have heard the term *fair use*. This rule says that portions of works may be reproduced for educational, news, commentary, or research without infringement under some circumstances. Fair use is decided on a case-by-case basis using the following criteria:

▶ Purpose of use. For example, whether it is commercial or for non-profit, educational purposes.

▶ The nature of the copyrighted work.

▶ The effect of the use upon the potential value of or market for the work.

▶ How much of the entire body of the work is used.

Public domain information (work not covered by copyright) is typically federal government publications and work with expired copyright.

For more information on copyrights contact the Copyright Office Information Line at 202-707-3000 or write Copyright Office, Library of Congress, Washington, DC 20559. To obtain an application, write to Applications, Superintendent of Documents, U.S. Government Printing Office, Washington, DC 20402, or call 202-783-3238.

Part Four
LIFE IN THE VIRTUAL OFFICE

Structuring Your Unstuctured Work ◄
Environment

Encouraging Productivity and Coping ◄
with Distractions

Coping with the Psychological Issues of ◄
Working Alone

Maintaining Visibility ◄

Communicating Effectively through Technology ◄

STRUCTURING YOUR UNSTRUCTURED WORK ENVIRONMENT

9

Most of us are accustomed to structured environments with clearly delineated schedules. Our childhoods were spent in school and our adult responsibilities on the job have, in most cases, been defined by the beginning and ending of a corporate work day. The virtual office presents a schedule that we must design and control ourselves, which can generate stress. This chapter covers techniques for managing stress, as well as time-management techniques and advice for insuring that you control your virtual office, not the other way around.

MANAGING STRESS

There are two ways to look at the stress of a virtual office: how you manage it, and what mechanisms you can put in place to maintain a work/life balance. Managing stress requires that you identify its source. To do this, keep a "stress diary" for a few days to pinpoint areas in which you need to reduce your stress. A stress diary is a log in which you rate events on a scale from one to ten, to determine what raises your stress level. A ten is something that generates a lot of stress, and a one is something that does not create any stress. You can also gain insight into your sources of stress by asking someone who knows you well what they have observed generating stress for you.

Once you have determined the source or sources of your stress, you can begin to assemble a "stress package." A stress package, according to Allen Elkin, Ph.D., director of the Stress Management and Counseling Center in New York City, is a plan for reducing the amount of stress you have in your life. The actions you can take to cut down on stress fall into three categories.

1. Environmental change. These are changes you can make in your environment or work habits that will help you reduce your stress. These include actions such as managing your time more effectively, lessening your workload, or telling people they cannot call you after 9 P.M. about work matters.

The most stressful jobs are, not surprisingly, the ones in which you are under a lot of pressure and have very little control over your schedule. Even if you cannot control the input of stress into your life, you can gain some relief by finding ways to introduce greater control over your schedule. This may mean new time-management or task-organization strategies, such as cutting down on meetings, outsourcing work, getting an assistant, or delegating.

2. Personal change. This means altering the way you look at situations. Again, Dr. Elkin suggests a test, this time to rate your stress reaction. Keep a log for a few days of circumstances that generate stress for you. Rate both the event and your reaction to it. For example, if you miss the train, you may give that a rating of five in terms of how dreadful an occurrence that is. If you rate your reaction—to something that in reality is not such a big deal—at a high eight or nine level, you know your reaction to stress is out of whack. This will help you gauge how much of the stress in your life is coming from *you*.

Chances are, a fair amount of your stress is self-generated. We all have a tendency to "catastrophize" and "awfulize" situations, according to Dr. Elkin. Using the train example again, this means that when you miss the train, you say to yourself, "This is terrible, this always happens to me, what is wrong with my life, now my whole day is ruined," and so on. Another common syndrome is "can't-standitis." This is when something you do not like becomes something you cannot stand; you emotionally exaggerate. Just recognizing these tendencies will help you gain some relief from them. But to further combat them and change yourself, Dr. Elkin recommends putting situations in perspective by asking yourself if you will remember an event in three years, or even three days. You should also begin talking to yourself differently and trying to recognize whether or not your have control over a situation. If you do not, try not to get upset about it.

3. Lifestyle change. According to Dr. Elkin, a lot of our stress comes simply from not eating or sleeping properly. The ideal for sleep is to wake naturally. If an alarm gets you up, you are tired. Sleeping late is not an option for a lot of us, but you should try to increase the amount of sleep you get by going to bed earlier, if you cannot sleep later. When you are tired, you will be more easily annoyed and therefore more stressed.

What you eat is also important for managing stress. If you do not eat breakfast or generally do not eat well, you are asking your body to perform without giving it what it needs. You are therefore increasing the stress you are placing on your body.

AVOIDING OVERWORK

Overwork is an occupational hazard of virtual-office workers because we make our own schedules and have access to our offices at all times of the day and night. Without the formal division of office and home life, work can encroach on the amount of time we leave for ourselves and our personal lives. But a virtual office doesn't have to lead to overwork. Even if you have an office at home, a phone and a computer in your car, and a beeper, you can still restrict the amount of work you do. But the responsibility lies with you. A lot of people use technology as an excuse to give up control over their work life and simply say, "It's the information age; I can't be out of touch!" There is an undeniable reality that technology has ratcheted up the pace at which we are expected to respond to business demands, but you still can, and should, set limits on your work life. Take the following steps to help yourself control the amount of time you work.

1. **Learn to determine what is *not* urgent.** There is a tendency in the technology-laden business world to believe that everything has to be done immediately because the technology exists to transmit things without delay. Because of this, people tend to treat everything as urgent rather than determining what is urgent and what can wait. To learn to do this, begin asking questions about projects before you agree to "get something right out." This applies to requests from clients *and* bosses. As long as you are conscientious, people will respect you for setting limits on what you can accomplish in a given time frame.

2. **Do not try to prove that your work arrangement is working.** Lots of telecommuters and entrepreneurs feel pressure to perform miracles or risk being returned to an office or failing at a business venture. Don't succumb to this pressure. Your output should increase automatically when you work outside of an office because you will have fewer interruptions and you will not be commuting.

3. **Have a set beginning and ending time for your day, as if you still work in the office full-time.** There is always more work to complete, but that does not mean you should exhaust yourself working just because you have all of your work tools at your fingertips. There will be times you need to work long hours, but in general, you should set strict beginning and ending times for your work days to avoid burnout. If sticking to a strict end time is impossible, create some leeway for yourself by committing to working no longer than thirty minutes beyond your stated end time. You can also build a stop time into your day by scheduling meetings outside of the office at the end of the day, or by making other appointments that

force you to stop working. If you work at home, "close" your office when you leave it. This means turning down the ringer or unplugging your phone, shutting off the computer, and turning off the light at your desk.

Having office hours will train many of your professional associates to get their requests to you during these hours (of course, there will always be exceptions). When you receive calls on weekends or after work hours, ask if you can return the call during business hours.

If you are a mobile worker, make it difficult to work at night by leaving your equipment or supplies in the car (if the temperature is not too extreme and the crime rate in your neighborhood is low). One woman told me she leaves her computer in the car at night because the cold weather deters her from going outside to get it.

4. Designate a time each day when you are not reachable. If you are always wondering if the phone will ring in your house or car, you will never be able to relax completely. For that reason, get into the habit of choosing when you will allow the phone to intrude and when you will not. This means turning the ringer off sometimes. It will be difficult to do this the first few times you try, but eventually you will wonder why you haven't done it before. Start by turning it off for just an hour and work your way up to more time.

5. Give your home and cellular phone number to a very few business contacts. It is confusing for people to have too many numbers for you, and stressful for you to be reachable everywhere you go. Provide the majority of people with only your voice-mail number and check it frequently.

6. Get to know yourself. By knowing your work tendencies, you can develop techniques for managing yourself. For example, if you know that you are an overachiever and usually do more than what is asked of you, you may gradually be able to scale back the effort that you put into projects. If you acknowledge that you are not good at prioritizing, you can find someone to help you. Take the self-management and overachiever/underachiever quizzes in chapter 2 to identify your tendencies.

7. Establish a clear idea of what is expected of you. A large portion of the energy that people expend in work is spent on the wrong tasks. When you are given an assignment, whether from your boss or a client, ask as many questions as are necessary to obtain a clear picture of what is expected of you. Sometimes the easiest way to get a straight answer is to find out what is *not* expected of the project. This will help you cut down on overwork by limiting the time you waste on unnecessary work.

8. Learn to say no. If you consistently say "yes" to things that you later wish you had declined, set up a mechanism for helping yourself to say "no." When you are faced with a request, ask people if you can call them back in a few minutes. Take that time to think carefully about how you should respond. If you decide not to, you can work up your resolve to say "no" before returning the call.

9. **Create goals and use these goals as a matrix for deciding what to take on.** If you know what you are trying to attain, it will be easier to prioritize and prevent overwork. For example, if visibility in your department is your short-term objective, you may want to respond immediately to all requests for work that will help you attain this goal, and be merely conscientious with other projects. If one of your goals is to cut down on the amount of time you work and improve your health, then you may have to accept that a choice assignment may go to someone else.

10. **Stop and think before you make a phone call, write a letter, send a fax, or have a conversation,** and evaluate whether you should be spending time on that activity. Ask yourself what would happen if you didn't do it. If you can live with the consequences, do not complete the task. This streamlining is essential to gaining control of your schedule.

11. **Take yourself away from your work environment.** People who work in virtual offices particularly need regular breaks from work. A break can be a day on the weekend spent hiking or driving in the country, or any change in your environment. Have at least one full day a week during which you do not check your messages or do any work. See "Learning to Take Vacations" and "Short Breaks" later in this chapter for more information.

12. **Avoid using all the extra time gained by not commuting to complete more work.** Do not work from 7:30 A.M. to 7:30 P.M. if this was your work day, including commuting time, when you worked in an office. Evaluate your work by what you accomplish, not your hours.

TECHNIQUES FOR PRESERVING OR CREATING BALANCE

It is easy for work/life balance to get out of whack. We live in a culture that places a great deal of value on work accomplishments. High praise for someone often includes, "She is a hard worker." What's more, working a lot can actually become addictive. It begins with a drive for money or success, and is fueled by the adrenaline high that can come from working under pressure and the gratification that is often part of professional accomplishments. Working a lot can also be an easy way to avoid confronting what may be troubling you in your personal life.

Warning signs that you may have a problem with balance can include: You consistently work to the point that you are too tired to go out; you have nothing to talk about except your job; and your family and friends are consistently doing things without you because you are working.

You can regain balance by making gradual alterations in the amount of time you spend on non-work-related activities. At first, this may require a formal scheduling of non-work activities, but with time, creating balance can become natural to you again.

1. Set your sights on personal achievements or milestones when you are making your weekly, monthly, or yearly business goals. Be careful not to think of yourself only as a professional.

2. Identify the things in life that give you satisfaction and pleasure. By identifying what brings you joy, you will be better equipped to insure that you do not miss out on these things in the name of work. The activities that bring you satisfaction can be big or small. They may be drinking a cup of coffee and reading the paper, playing with your kids, or taking a hot bath. Bigger ones include maintaining a social support structure of friends you have fun with or pursuing a hobby. To identify what can help you maintain balance in your life, make a list of all the small things you enjoy and all the bigger things that matter to you. Include activities on this list even if you are not currently engaging in them. When you are making this list, remember what used to bring you pleasure and let yourself imagine what you would enjoy doing. Keep this list where you can see it to reinforce these habits.

3. Consciously set priorities. You may say that your priority is family and friends, but find yourself spending very little time with them. Dr. Elkin says if this is happening, your conscious and subconscious priorities may be at odds, or you may be sabotaging your ability to attain your goals. To get at what you truly value in life, try the following exercise: Ask yourself what you would do if you had six months to live or if you won the lottery, or ask yourself what you would like people to say about you after you die. Write these things down on a piece of paper. Then bring yourself back to the reality of your life: You probably didn't hit the jackpot and have years left before your number is up. But examine your list and see if you can introduce a little bit of these things into your life. Try to visualize what your life would look like if you could have anything you wanted. Chances are you have to work, so try to imagine how you can mesh work with a lifestyle that you would enjoy.

4. Get active about your activities or hobbies. If you want to exercise regularly or do something else that keeps getting pushed aside because of work, you have to actively integrate it into your schedule. This may require some creative thinking about how you can modify your schedule. It may mean spending money on a membership or a series of tickets to something because you know that having spent the money will encourage you to follow through. It could also mean finding a health club that is open until midnight or pursuing your hobby with another person because you are less likely to let another person down.

5. Think of something fun you would like to do and write down fears of what would happen if you did it. Once you look at the fears, you may see how unfounded they are.

6. Take time to relax. Imbalance has a lot to do with fear and anxiety and the biggest cures for these two ailments are relaxation and meditation. Katherine Crowley, the New York City–based psychotherapist who works with entrepreneurs, recommends building some time into your schedule for relaxing. Try scheduling a time once a week in which you will just relax, rather than work or engage in social obligations. This relaxation will put you in a state of mind in which you will be more open to taking steps toward regaining balance.

ACKNOWLEDGING YOUR ACCOMPLISHMENTS

If you work all day but do not complete everything on your to-do list, do you give yourself credit for what you have accomplished, or do you think about everything you haven't done? If you think about everything you have not accomplished, you are not alone. Most of us have that tendency, and therefore feel as though we have never done enough. Not acknowledging your accomplishments can cause you to feel bad about your work, push yourself to do too much, and eventually burn out.

When you work in a virtual office, the onus is on you to give yourself credit for what you've accomplished. Learning to do this will require you to change your habits if you are accustomed to judging yourself harshly for what you have not accomplished. Try the techniques below to make small, gradual changes in how you treat yourself.

▷ **Take a few minutes at the end of each day** to go over what you have accomplished, even if it wasn't remarkable. Think back over your day about the not-so-obvious accomplishments, such as the faxes you sent, the phone calls you returned, and the appointments you completed successfully.

▷ **Acknowledge work in progress.** The number of days you spend chipping away at work in progress will far outnumber the days you spend winding up a huge campaign or making a big presentation. Get in the habit of giving yourself credit for making slow but steady gains on ongoing projects, instead of celebrating only major accomplishments. Record minor gains in a log if you want to.

▷ **Tell somebody about what you have done.** It is sometimes tempting not to take time to do this, and just keep on slogging. If you are having trouble acknowledging your accomplishments, force yourself to call someone and talk about what you've gotten done, even if you only modestly work it into the conversation.

▷ **Reward yourself.** A reward does not have to be a trip to Hawaii, just a small token of your appreciation for yourself. It is amazing how many cards and bouquets of flowers we buy for other people and how stingy we are with ourselves.

▷ **Realize how difficult it is to acknowledge accomplishments.** You cannot just read this advice and suddenly change your behavior. In order to change, you will have to practice the things listed here and make a concerted effort to alter your behavior. See also "Being a Good Boss to Yourself" in chapter 11.

LEARNING TO TAKE VACATIONS

For those of us working in the virtual office, there is a great risk of never taking any time off. This is a common problem and it's got a name: *overcompensation*. It's a fear that if we aren't constantly tending to business, it will fall apart. The irony is that people who get away from work may actually be more successful than those who are always available. The key is that taking a break sends a message that you are confident enough to remove yourself completely and know that your job or business is secure enough to survive. *Not* taking breaks sends an equally *bad* message. If you're a telecommuter, skipping vacations may indicate that your telecommuting program is not working out so well. Here are more reasons why it's a good idea to take time away from the home office:

▲ A complete break cures burnout. Your mind needs downtime to think creatively; this kind of thinking solves problems and generates new ideas.

Tips for Getting Away

If you're having difficulty scheduling time off, remember that it will never be a good time to go away. Just schedule a trip and stick to your plan. You'll be amazed at how your schedule will then change to accommodate your plans. If you are apprehensive about going away, start small by scheduling a trip over a long weekend when most people take a break. Force yourself to get work done before you go by pretending that you can't take anything with you. You'll be surprised what you can accomplish if you have to.

Once you get away, don't make business calls during your vacation. I'm sometimes guilty of this, but I try to avoid it because it pollutes my vacation and takes away from my rejuvenation time. Even calling in to check messages can trigger work thoughts for days afterward. For the same reasons, don't give out a phone number where you can be reached.

▲ If you spend too much time at home alone working, your stress level will rise and you may become difficult to work with. No one can afford to be difficult to work with.

▲ Clients don't look for other resources and your contacts don't shrivel up just because you take a vacation. Realizing this will provide you with a renewed sense of confidence in your staying power.

▲ Your customers may begin to wonder about someone who cannot get organized enough to take a break.

SHORT BREAKS: ONE OF THE VIRTUAL OFFICE'S BENEFITS

Taking advantage of working independently, even if you are still employed full-time, is an important part of thriving in the virtual office. It is the small perks, short breaks, and minor opportunities to enjoy the flexibility you have that enable you to manage the increased stress and responsibility that can go with working on your own.

Lots of people forgo this opportunity because they think if they do not work hard all the time, their virtual office arrangement will not be a success. Actually the opposite is true. Building small breaks into your schedule to enjoy the freedom of working on your own will help you avoid burnout and overwork. This safeguard will enable you to thrive long-term in your virtual office.

The first step is to figure out what you want to do during your breaks. Maybe you've had your nose so close to the grindstone that you haven't thought about it in a while. To jog your memory, think about all the things you wished you could do when you had an office job. It might be beating the crowds by shopping mid-week, taking a nap after lunch, getting out of town on a Friday before the traffic gets bad, spending more time outside in the afternoon, or going to an occasional matinee. There will always be crunch times when you have to forgo your time off, but make sure guilt doesn't prevent you from enjoying your flexible schedule on a regular basis.

If you need it, post a reminder sign near your desk that says "Enjoy Your Freedom." For more structured breaks, schedule your fun. A home-based public relations executive I know has two nonbusiness lunches every week, an artist I know takes every Tuesday afternoon off to shop galleries, and my friend who runs a general construction firm at home leaves early every Friday for the country.

VIRTUAL OFFICE TIME MANAGEMENT

The rules are the same for time management no matter where you work. If you had difficulty with time management when you worked in a traditional work environment, you will most likely still struggle with the same problems on your own. But there are some characteristics of a virtual-office environment that may make it easier for you to apply time-management techniques than in the past. Working on your own, for instance, may give you the opportunity to complete tasks when it suits you most. You can now probably work more in sync with your energy levels and according to how you believe tasks should be prioritized. The flip side of this freedom is the potential for chaos in a virtual office if you do not learn to manage your time. Without the momentum of an office environment, inertia can strike, your work day can become unfocused, and your priorities can become unclear.

There is no magic trick to time management. It requires a commitment to examine your current habits and make some changes. You will need to synthesize some time-management basics and then develop a system that works best for you.

Time-Management Secrets from the Pros

I have two friends running businesses from home who have the kind of lifestyle that every home-business owner dreams of. They take months of vacation every year, their businesses are booming, and they supervise their companies—they don't toil in them. If they weren't such good friends, they would make me kind of sick.

They both started their businesses from scratch, and although each business is very different from the other, my friends have a few things in common that I call "The Secrets to the Good Life in the Home Office." They are a combination of time management and life philosophy.

1. They say "no" a lot because they realized long ago that there will always be more demands on their schedules than they can manage. This includes saying "no" to social invitations and to any projects they aren't sure they can complete well and make a lot of money on.

2. They rarely answer the phone. They prefer to collect their messages and call people back when they have had a chance to prepare an answer. They believe it is more efficient.

3. They get a lot of sleep. They are firm believers that you cannot be effective during the day unless you are rested. If you are tired, you are more likely to half-finish a project or be inefficient in all your work.

4. They do not tolerate inconvenience. If they have a problem, they find a solution for it right away. Both of them spend a lot of time alone thinking and strategizing to find these solutions.

5. They delegate. They do only what they do well themselves, and find people to do absolutely everything else for them. They know that spending money on hiring people to complete work for them makes the money in the long run. They spent money on house cleaners, technical experts, errand runners, and bookkeepers long before they had a lot of money to spare. They knew early on that they couldn't do it all *and* run profitable businesses.

6. They expect a lot from their employees and associates. They put a lot of energy and money into being fair and generous to the people who work with them. In return, they demand that these people do an almost-perfect job. Their standards are high and they refuse to work with people who cannot live up to them. This often causes them short-term inconvenience, but always rewards them with a long-term gain.

7. They do not always make themselves available to their employees. They are likely to tell employees that they do not have time to figure out solutions for them. They lay out explicit expectations up front and then encourage people to determine the best strategy for meeting these expectations.

8. They are explicit in their instructions and communications. They

Easy-to-Use Time-Management Techniques

✔ Evaluate each task you are embarking on and determine if you can get away without doing it. I am not recommending being irresponsible, but I *am* suggesting being stingy with your energy.

✔ Delegate tasks.

✔ Plan your day—when you will take breaks and when you will take care of certain tasks.

✔ Think about new ways of doing things. I read my mail only once a week. Just because it arrives every day does not mean I have to look at it every day. This trick may not work for you, but you should try thinking about what habits you can change that would enable you to use your time better.

✔ Prioritize. Figure out at the beginning of the week or the day what you want to accomplish. If you do not accomplish these things, look back and determine why not. It could be that you were unrealistic about the amount of time projects would take, or that you were devoting your time to other activities, or any number of other reasons. Think about how can you do better the next time you set your goals.

✔ Do not beat yourself up for not getting a lot done. Most of us have a tendency to think we can accomplish more than we can.

do not want to discuss or explain things five times, so they take the time the first time to make sure their instructions, requests, and communications are clear. This requires a little more time up front, but is more efficient in the long run.

9. They are honest. Both of them are very nice people, but they are not afraid to tell someone when they have a beef. They don't waste time beating around the bush to spare someone's feelings.

10. They love to defy convention. They are both eccentric in how they approach their personal and professional lives. They both refuse to wake up early, and they both have a list a mile long of their personal theories and strategies for how to do everything better.

Delegating So You Can Get More Done

I meet a lot of people who do everything themselves. "I do it all myself from start to finish," they proclaim with satisfaction. The subtext seems to be that they are strong and enduring because no job is too large or too small. But they're missing the point. Just because you can do everything yourself doesn't mean you should. In fact, you should delegate as much work as you possibly can. But I encounter lots of resistance when I encourage people to farm out some of their responsibilities. The three most common reasons people say they can't delegate are:

1. Money: Paying someone to do some of the work often means you'll make less money in the short run. We all have to operate our businesses within our financial realities, but it's short-sighted to avoid delegation because of the investment it requires. This approach keeps a lot of people treading water in their businesses instead of moving ahead. As soon as you begin using the time you have freed up by delegating to find other business, you'll make more money. You'll still be making some money on the tasks you contracted out and you'll be making money on the new work too.

When you work at home, delegating is effective for both professional or personal responsibilities. For example, if you make more money per hour than it costs you to pay someone to clean your house, there is no reason why you should still be doing it yourself.

2. Time: Another reason people say they can't assign tasks to someone else is that they don't have time to train someone. This is often a smoke screen for something else, like a fear of giving up control. If this is your rationalization, write down all of your tasks and how long it would take to teach someone to take care of them for you. Then choose one or two jobs that are the easiest to teach and start with them. This will gradually get you used to letting go of minor or routine responsibilities.

3. Quality: Lots of people tell me they can't give up any of their responsibilities because no one can do them as well as they can. This is the oldest excuse in the book; but it's not a reason to avoid delegating. A person you hire may not do something as well as you can do it, especially initially. But you have to think about the job this person can do for you once she is trained. Remember that people *learn* to do jobs well; you didn't start out as efficient as you are now.

If you determine that only you can complete certain tasks perfectly, you have two choices: save them for yourself and delegate other tasks, or settle for having something done well instead of perfectly. Lots of times a very good job is sufficient.

Do not let a lack of room or equipment in your home office stop you from delegating, either. Just because you want to have someone do work for you does not necessarily mean that you have to bring them into your home office. If someone has the computer programs you need on his system, why not let him complete the work for you from wherever he is?

Quick Reference for Time-Management Troubleshooting

You can use the following list of problems and solutions to troubleshoot when you're having time-management difficulties. Problems are listed in bold and the solutions are numbered in a list following them. You may not find every solution to each problem applicable to you, so pick and choose to find the best solution for your personality, your schedule, and your business.

Problem: I do not write a daily list of tasks for each day's work.

Solutions:

1. Begin to think of structure as something that will make it easier to attain your goals.

2. Keep a running daily to-do list, as well as a list for the next day, the next week, and so on, so that you can add tasks as they come up.

3. Get software or a paper planning device to give you a place to make the list.

4. If you don't feel comfortable making or keeping a to-do list, find a format (a chart or a color-coded system, for example) for planning your daily activities that fits your style.

5. Consider that a to-do list may free up your mind to work on other things.

Problem: At the beginning of the day I do not usually have a clear idea of what tasks I want to accomplish by day's end.

Solutions:

1. Create weekly goals. These will help you determine how you should spend your time each day.

2. Make a to-do list at the end of the work day, when important tasks are fresh in your mind. This will help you get started in the morning.

3. Each day before you begin work, prioritize your tasks.

4. If you have difficulty prioritizing, try describing your responsibilities and goals to another person. Together you can clarify what should come first.

5. Out of all of your daily tasks, consider what accomplishments would make you feel good at the end of the day. Write these at the top of your list.

Problem: I am reluctant to give myself a concrete schedule for completing daily work tasks.

Solutions:

1. Estimate the amount of time it will take to complete each task on your to-do list.

(Continued)

2. Think about your energy levels, probability of interruption, and so on, and choose the best time to complete each task.

3. Based on this information, map out when you will work on each project.

4. Keep in mind that many successful artists, writers, and other creative types have very regular work schedules.

Problem: I do not like to plan out exactly how my day will proceed.

Solutions:

1. Leave some unscheduled time in your life for spontaneous activity.

2. Be willing to adjust your schedule when opportunities arise.

3. When it comes to dealing with other people, don't be too rigid with scheduling.

4. Realize that planning does not rule out spontaneity.

Problem: I do not have a clear point of demarcation that signals the beginning of my work day.

Solutions:

1. Choose a start time which will mark the beginning of your work day.

2. Even if you aren't sure what you will begin working on, go to your desk at your designated start time.

3. Schedule the start of your day to coincide with another activity such as your family leaving the house, the end of a radio or TV program, and so on.

4. Schedule a morning phone call or in-person meeting after which you will begin work.

5. Realize that if you start on time you'll set a positive tone for the rest of the day.

6. Recognize that postponing the beginning of the work day can generate more stress than jumping right in.

7. If the start of your day is routinely delayed because of nonwork activities, try working for a few hours first and then take a break to do those nonwork things.

Problem: I do not have a clear point of demarcation that signals the end of my work day.

Solutions:

1. Choose a time at which you will finish work.

2. When you finish for the day, straighten up your desk, shut off the computer and phone, and turn off the light.

3. Schedule an activity at the end of the day that forces you to close up shop.

4. Recognize that overwork will eventually lead to a loss of productivity because of burnout, illness, and so on.

5. Be aware of the fact that home-based workers tend to overwork.

6. If you have a pressing project that requires overtime, tally the extra hours and give yourself comp time later in the week.

7. Pay for tickets to a series of shows, tuition for a class, or something that will routinely get you out of the house at the end of the day.

Problem: I routinely put off starting difficult tasks.

Solutions:

1. Force yourself to work for thirty minutes, after which you can take a break.
2. When facing a difficult task on your schedule, take a deep breath, sit down at your desk, and take one action toward completing it.
3. Break the project down from its large, perhaps intimidating form into small, less threatening steps.
4. Dress that part. Dress up for making sales calls and dress down for redoing your file cabinet.

Problem: I have difficulty sticking to the schedule I have created for myself.

Solutions:

1. Check the clock and acknowledge when a project is running overtime. Evaluate whether you are able to adjust your schedule and still complete other important projects, or if you should move on.
2. Look at the clock when you begin a project and assess how much you can realistically accomplish by your end time.
3. When you are considering making a personal phone call or taking a break, consult your schedule to determine if you have time.
4. Do not take phone calls when they threaten to disrupt your schedule.
5. Postpone responses to non-urgent requests for information or assistance until you have accomplished what's on your schedule.
6. Give yourself a reward, like a trip to the sauna or steam bath, when you stick to your schedule.

Problem: I am not able to break each work project down into the tasks it will take to accomplish it.

Solutions:

1. Map out all of the steps you must take to complete the project.
2. For each step, make a list of tasks necessary to reach it.
3. Create a schedule for completing each task, assigning a rough time frame for completion of each task.
4. Get comfortable mapping out projects and creating tasks by practicing with a simple project, such as doing the laundry.

Problem: I sometimes lose track of my priorities by focusing on small tasks and administrative details.

Solutions:

1. If you are in the habit of doing the easy stuff first, try the reverse for just a few days or a week. Tackle tough or crucial work first and leave administrative details for later.
2. Design your schedule so that the last hour of every day is devoted to taking care of small tasks and administrative details.
3. Set aside certain times of the day or week to tend to administrative details. The rest of the time, consider them off-limits.
4. If administrative tasks are taking up a lot of your work time, delegate them.
5. Track the time and money (in time spent) you spend on administrative work.
6. Recognize that focusing on details can be an avoidance tactic.

(Continued)

Problem: I have difficulty limiting the amount of time I spend talking on the phone.

Solutions:

1. Buy a phone that tracks the amount of time you are on a call.

2. Look at your watch every time you get on the phone and make a mental note of when you want to end the call.

3. Request that friends and family call you after work hours or only during certain times of the day.

4. For one morning or afternoon, try not answering the phone and see how much you accomplish.

5. When you're on the phone, ask yourself if this is an income-generating call (sales, networking, bill collection). If not, make it short.

6. Remember that talking on the phone takes a lot of energy. Don't devote too much of your finite daily resources to it.

7. Learn to recognize telephone bloodsuckers and limit the time you give them.

8. Always know why you are calling someone before you call.

9. Keep a log of the amount of time you spend on the phone.

Problem: My meetings and appointments seldom begin and end on time.

Solutions:

1. Allow yourself extra time when getting to a meeting so that the meeting starts on time.

2. At the beginning of the meeting, state the amount of time you have available, the meeting's agenda, and how much time you will allot to each topic.

3. Toward the end of a meeting, state the amount of time left and assess what is left to be discussed.

4. Make a conscious decision to be known as a professional who begins and ends on time.

5. Don't be afraid to stick to your time frame even if the people you are meeting with are more casual about time.

GOAL SETTING

Goals are crucial to success in any business, but they are particularly important for entrepreneurs and telecommuters because the virtual office has myriad distractions. But very few people set goals. Most people believe that goals are important, but less than 5 percent of us write down our goals or have action plans for attaining them. Fear is often the culprit. People don't like to write goals down on paper (a crucial part of goal setting) because they are afraid to commit to their goals. If this is your problem, try to remember that a goal can be changed at any time after you write it down. Also realize that goal setting gets easier the more you do it. When you have set goals and attained them, the power of goal setting will compel you to set more. If you avoid goal setting because you don't know how to do it, the following suggestions should help.

There are many ways to set realistic long- and short-term goals. A sales trainer I recently spoke to suggests taking thirty minutes each month to set one or two personal goals, one or two family goals, and three to eight business goals. I use a method I learned many years ago from Business Strategy Seminars, a Manhattan-based support group for entrepreneurs and start-up business owners. I set weekly goals and three-month goals, and I keep my weekly goals posted on the wall near my computer. You can develop your own routine or choose one of these to get started. A crucial component to any method you adopt should be the selection of goals that are both attainable and challenging.

One way to generate short-term goals is first to consider your long-term goals. Is there a certain dollar amount you want to earn or a number of clients you need to sign up by a certain time? If there is nothing that comes to mind immediately, take a few minutes and think about what professional goal you would like to attain. Once you have determined long-term goals, you can work backward. If your goal is to make $100,000 this year, you should make a list of what it would entail to make that money. If you do not know, enlist the help of peers. Once you have made a list of all that it will take to achieve that goal, you can break those small steps down into short-term goals.

When you write your goals down on paper, make sure they are specific ("get new clients"), measurable ("get three new clients"), attainable (aim high, but do not set yourself up for failure), relevant (are the goals you are making going to help you attain your goals, or are they just going to keep you busy?), and within a specific time frame ("get three new clients by November").

If you are a telecommuter and work at home for your boss, show these goals to your boss to make sure you are on track with the goals of your team and your company. If you work for yourself, show your goals to a peer or friend. Make sure this person is supportive of you, but will also be tough with you and not just tell you what you want to hear.

If your system of setting goals does not initially seem to be working for you because you are not attaining very much of what you write down, do not give up. Keep setting goals for several months and you will find that your goal-setting skills will improve.

ENCOURAGING PRODUCTIVITY AND COPING WITH DISTRACTIONS

Nothing can be done to eliminate distractions in a virtual office. The best way to deal with these distractions is to minimize them as much as you can, determine which ones you are most vulnerable to, and develop techniques for coping with distractions when they arise. This chapter provides techniques for creating the structure you'll need to stay on track with your work as well as solutions for dealing with the distractions you are most likely to encounter.

CREATING STRUCTURE

Structure is an important part of making it easy to resist distractions and be productive. The kind of structure you need will depend on your personality, where you work, what your job responsibilities are, and what distractions you are most vulnerable to. Following are some techniques you can choose from.

▲ **Make lists.** Your brain has room for only a certain amount of information. Do not clutter it up trying to remember things that you could easily write down. Trying to keep too many things in your head will make you absent-minded, because you will be thinking about too much at once.

▲ **Make more lists.** Have long-term project lists for things that do not belong on your daily to-do list, but need to be recorded.

▲ **Be task-oriented, not time-oriented.** It would be more difficult for me to be productive on the editing of this book if I decided to work for two hours than if I decided I would edit two chapters before quitting for the day. Tangible goals encourage me to work productively.

Using time as your measure can lead to a tendency to mark time, rather than complete projects.

▲ **Develop a routine.** Some people like to complete phone calls in the morning; others work first and return calls when they have accomplished other tasks. How you structure your day is up to you, but structure of some kind is usually necessary in order to stay on course with your work.

▲ **Only *work* in your work area.** Do not read magazines, pay bills, or do any other work in your work area. That way, when you enter the work area, you will automatically be in work mode.

▲ **Build breaks into your schedule for food and rest.** Working non-stop is not the path to productivity. Without breaks, you will eventually burn out in the long run and may not produce your best work in the short run.

▲ **Write things down instead of acting on them.** If you find yourself distracted by thoughts of tasks you feel you need to complete while you are working on something else, start writing these tasks down instead of acting on them. Make a list of the phone calls and projects that are vying for your attention and take care of them later.

▲ **Develop a system of rewards for yourself.** Promise yourself you'll take a break if you accomplish a task. Allow yourself a nap if you can get through half of your list of things you need to do for the day. The promise of these rewards will help to keep you on track.

See chapter 9 for more time-management techniques.

THE MOST COMMON DISTRACTIONS

Through letters from my readers and radio listeners, as well as messages I receive through online services, I have assembled a list of the most common distractions. Following are some techniques for coping with them.

Reading: Keep magazines and books out of your home office. Don't make it any harder on yourself than it has to be. If you're reading a great book, don't leave it where you can see it. If your favorite magazine comes in the mail at noon, put it into your mail bin or on the coffee table immediately, before you open it up. Otherwise you're asking to be sidetracked. I often don't pick up my mail until the end of the day because of its potential to distract me.

Lounging: Think of your home office as a separate building from the rest of your house and don't go into your living room, den, or other comfortable parts of your house during work hours. I move between the office, the kitchen, and the bathroom, steering clear of my living room. By staying away from my couch and coffee table, I'm less likely to want to flip through magazines or turn on the TV.

Meetings: Meetings are a huge time-eater. To cut down on meetings, carefully consider each one. Sometimes it's essential to meet face-to-face, especially if you're trying to establish a relationship, but in many cases you can handle business over the phone or by sending a fax.

As a guideline for how many meetings you can do without, keep in mind that I have someone who has been working for me in California for almost a year, and I've never met her. My business partner lives in Connecticut and I see him about once every two months.

Cleaning: I have a soft spot in my heart for this distraction because it is my personal weakness. I used to use cleaning as a tool of procrastination because I could justify it. But cleaning has nothing to do with business and it shouldn't be done during work hours.

There are a few ways of dealing with cleaning. First, you can do what I did and hire someone to clean and do your laundry, to eliminate the distraction altogether. Second, you can tidy up each morning before you start working so you aren't tempted to leave your desk and do it later in the day. Third, you can resolve that the house will stay the way it looks when you start working until the end of the day. That's the way things operated when you worked in an office.

Errands: I know a woman who is always complaining about not getting enough done in her home business. She's also always running out the door to the grocery store or to do some other errand. There's nothing wrong with taking care of some personal business during the week when you work at home, but if you're serious about your work, you should do it only if you are on top of things.

Distraction Troubleshooting

The following list of problems and solutions can be used as a quick reference guide for dealing with distractions. The problems are listed in bold and are followed by possible solutions. Not all of the solutions for the problem you are encountering may be applicable for you, your business, or your work style.

Choose the solution or solutions from the list that you feel will work best for you.

Problem: When people ask me to do things during the day, it is difficult for me to say "no" and I usually agree to their requests.

Solutions:

1. Create a pause between when you are asked to do something and when you respond. This will give you an opportunity to evaluate what you really want to do and to work up the courage to say "no," if necessary.

2. Think about what you are giving up by agreeing to these requests. Determine if you want to do it.

3. Try saying "no" to all requests for one day.

4. Think about what makes you say "yes" to requests. Make a list and evaluate if you want to be motivated by those things.

5. Plan what you want to accomplish during the day so that you are not swayed by others' requests.

6. Remember that people need to respect your work responsibilities. But they will respect them only if you do.

7. Make a list of all the requests that are made on your time during the day and practice saying "no" to all of them.

Problem: When family and friends call during the day, I feel that I should make time to talk to them, no matter how busy I am.

Solutions:

1. Condition your family and friends to call you less frequently during the day by telling them how busy you are when they call and by referring to projects you're working on.

2. Remind yourself that you do not make any money while you are on the phone, nor do you move yourself closer to your goals.

3. Get into the habit of calling people at night.

4. Set aside a time of the day to call your family and friends, and return all calls at that time.

5. Remember that you need to work with your own schedule, not other people's.

6. Evaluate why you feel you must be available for people at all times. What do you think would happen if you weren't?

Problem: Because I do not have a strict nine-to-five schedule, I often find myself saying "yes" to requests from neighbors for assistance during my work day.

Solutions:

1. Determine the time of day requests come in, and make sure you are busy in the office when they do.

2. Send a message to neighbors that you are a professional by talking about your clients, dealings, and responsibilities.

3. Tell an occasional lie about a meeting or conference call at a time of the day when you are needed.

4. Turn requests down with specific business-related reasons why you are not available when they want you.

5. Go to the door with the portable phone on your ear whenever neighbors come by.

(Continued)

Problem: I often sleep in later than I had planned and get a late start.

Solutions:

1. Schedule early morning appointments to get you out of bed.
2. Regulate your sleep and wake times to within fifteen to thirty minutes to make getting up easier.
3. Examine what you are avoiding by staying in bed late.
4. Stock the kitchen with great coffee or breakfast food that you will want to get up and consume.
5. Shift your schedule so that you don't have to get up early.
6. Make sure you eat at least two hours before going to bed, so your food has a chance to digest.

Problem: Because I have a flexible schedule, I assume the bulk of household responsibilities.

Solutions:

1. Recognize that working at home is as demanding as, if not more demanding than, working in an office. You should not necessarily expect yourself to take on more household responsibilities.
2. Create a formal division of labor among household members.
3. Hire someone to clean and take care of other household responsibilities.
4. Establish office hours; decide that household chores cannot be done during office hours.

Problem: TV, magazines, and books often get in the way of my productivity.

Solutions:

1. Keep magazines and books out of your home office.
2. When the mail arrives, put it aside until the end of the day.
3. Minimize the amount of time you spend in parts of the house other than the office. This is where distractions lurk.
4. Put books and magazines you're reading in a drawer out of sight.
5. If possible, keep the TV in a place where you do not regularly go during your work day.

Problem: It is difficult for me to ignore the phone and allow my answering machine to pick it up.

Solutions:

1. Try not answering the phone for just one hour.
2. Recognize that if you answer the phone every time it rings, you are allowing outside forces to determine your schedule.
3. Think about the positives. If you return calls instead of taking them, you will appear more prepared and professional in your phone interaction.
4. Realize that you have to devote uninterrupted time to your business if you want it to thrive, and the only way to do this is to ignore the phone periodically.
5. Evaluate what would happen if you missed a call. Determine if you could live with it.
6. Remind yourself that constant interruptions create a state of psychological stress.

Problem: A messy house or car distracts me from my work.

Solutions:

1. If a mess distracts you, straighten up every morning before you start work.

2. Understand that cleaning can be a form of procrastination. Notice when you want to clean and ask yourself what you might be avoiding.

3. Hire someone to clean.

4. Recognize that you *can* work when the house or car is a mess.

AVOIDING PROCRASTINATION

If you are procrastinating, you may be using any number of distractions as an excuse. There is plenty of opportunity for procrastination when you work on your own. I asked some business owners and telecommuters how they avoid this stress and get themselves moving when they don't want to.

△ Trick yourself. I trick myself into starting tough projects by committing to work for a half-hour and seeing how it goes. I promise myself a break after that if I want it, but most of the time that initial half-hour turns into three productive hours.

△ Focus on how great it will feel to complete the object of your procrastination, instead of how terrible it will be to work on it. It's a matter of shifting your focus from the unpleasant task to the pleasant reward.

△ If a task at hand is unpleasant, think about the goal that the task is part of. Without goals, chances are that too much of your focus will land on your task, and your enthusiasm level for different tasks will vary. If you are always focused on your goal and committed to it, your enthusiasm will vary much less.

△ A friend of mind who produces an investment newsletter from his Manhattan apartment takes another tack. He tells himself how bad things will get if he doesn't do a project he's putting off. He thinks about work piling up and growing exponentially, and that gets him moving.

△ Part of the reason we put things off is that we build them up to be more important and difficult than they really are. A phone call becomes your day of reckoning, a proposal the document that will decide your destiny. If this happens to you, try what a Pittsburgh metal artist I know does when he dreads writing artist's statements for show programs. He works on something related to the statement, like a cover letter, and gradually works his way up to the main task.

△ To work your way up to a difficult phone call, try what a playwright and writer I know does. Use the "starter-call" method. He calls friends and talks to them before a difficult call to get himself talking and revved up.

△ If there are certain projects that you routinely dread doing, determine if you can give them to someone else. Hire someone, swap tasks with someone else, or get a college intern.

△ Promise yourself a reward for completing a job you do not want to do. Give yourself a few hours off, a short TV break, or a call to a friend.

△ If there is no existing deadline for a project, create one. Promise your portion of a project to someone by a certain date; once you commit to it, you will be less able to put it off.

KEEPING YOUR EATING UNDER CONTROL

I was once teaching a seminar on working in the virtual office, when a man raised his hand and asked for advice on how to avoid eating too much at home. His question prompted another man to raise his hand and confess that he wastes a lot of time making elaborate lunches that require a lot of preparation and cleaning time. Two women in the class said their frequent snack breaks are a distraction, and another woman confessed that she had gone up a dress size since she started working at home.

The problem is that when you work at home, the sky's the limit for eating. You have access to all the snack foods you used to eat only at night, and you can chomp freely while you put together an important presentation because no one knows the difference. But if you want to control your eating habits at home, there are a few things you can do.

▶ When you get the urge to snack, ask yourself if you really want food or if you just want a break from work. Since those of us at home don't have coworkers to talk to, we turn to food when we're bored, restless, or tired.

▶ If you determine that you're not truly in need of sustenance, try postponing the snack until after you finish a project you're working on. This will limit the frequency of your snacks and gradually get you out of the habit of snacking so much. If you can't wait an hour for a break, avoid snacking by going outside for some fresh air or walking around your house and stretching. Don't automatically head for the kitchen just because you don't want to be at your desk.

▶ When you do snack, make sure you enjoy it. Take small bites and taste the food, rather than nervously downing a bag of potato chips without thinking about it. One satisfying snack will keep you from wanting another one again soon.

▶ Realize that when you work at home, you cannot stock your house with all of the goodies that you used to load up on when you spent less time at home. Aside from health and weight issues, having a cupboard full of tantalizing snacks will make it difficult to stay at your desk. Instead, stock your kitchen with healthy snacks. A bag of small prewashed carrots or salt-free pretzels is a better snack than cookies, because they won't zap your energy or put on weight. Admittedly, they aren't as satisfying as three or four Oreos!

▶ To avoid the long-lunch syndrome, make large amounts of food for dinner every night so you have leftovers, or cook big pasta dishes on the weekend that you can eat during the week.

▶ Do not skip meals. This is bad for health and energy levels, but it's easy to do when you get really busy. Staying at your desk instead of eating lunch may seem like the path to productivity, but it will prevent you from concentrating later in the afternoon. If you go without dinner, you'll also pay the price. You'll wake up feeling groggy the next morning and you'll be dragging all day.

If you spend a lot of time working in your car, you may have the opposite problem. You probably do not get enough time or opportunity to eat. To make sure you get the food, and therefore the energy, you need, I recommend keeping some snacks in the car for times when you do not have enough time to eat between appointments. Some road warriors even carry coolers with soda and snacks so that they can avoid going without food or eating food they do not like.

DRESSING FOR WORKING AT HOME

Even though one of the benefits of working in a home office is not having to put on a stifling corporate uniform every morning, it pays to take some care when you're getting dressed for your home office, because how you dress will affect your productivity.

I learned a lesson about dressing during a ski lesson. My instructor told me that in order to ski my best, I had to feel good about my equipment and feel comfortable in what I was wearing when I skied. Only then could I focus on my skiing. Dressing up in the home office is the same concept. It's a matter of eliminating all the possible obstacles to doing your best. Feeling good about the way you look will make you feel better about yourself. This good self-image will help you even if no one sees you all day long, because people can sense your attitude about yourself over the phone.

Keep this in mind when you're standing in front of the closet or drawer in the morning. Don't reach for a wrinkled T-shirt, stained sweater, or those pants you wouldn't wear outside the house. Put on something presentable that makes you feel good.

I know some people who put on a business ensemble every morning to run their home business. They say it makes them feel less like goofing off. If you're having trouble with distractions in the home office, you may want to try this, but in general, I don't think confining clothing like ties and panty hose are necessary at home.

Casual clothes that are comfortable should suffice. You may not have anything in your wardrobe that fits this description because all of your clothes are either very professional or very casual. But since you're spending less on professional clothes now that you're working at home, invest some of your savings in nice casual clothes.

Also try to avoid the habit of letting regular showers lapse just because you aren't planning to leave the home office. You don't have to get dressed and shower first thing in the morning, but if you do, it saves you from having to find the time later in the work day to put yourself together. Besides, if you put off getting ready for the day, it's easy to put off everything else too.

If you don't make an effort with your looks you will gradually relax your standard of dress. Eventually you will develop the "at home" look, an unfinished, unkempt look common to home-office workers. While this in itself may not bother you, the downside of this look is that if you assume it for too long, you lose the ability to put yourself together when you need to. Or, if you can put yourself together, it will require a superhuman effort and lots of time.

I dress up when I'm working because I want to feel good if I catch a glimpse of myself in the mirror. It keeps my spirits up. But this isn't entirely based in vanity. I also like to be ready to run out to a meeting at a moment's notice. Dressing up can also be a signal to other people that you are working. Some people I know dress up to let their families know that they are in work mode. This can also help people take your work seriously.

THE IMPORTANCE OF GETTING ENOUGH SLEEP

Part of being productive is getting enough sleep. To find out how to do this, I talked to doctors at the Montefiore Hospital Sleep/Wake Center in New York. They told me that everyone needs a different amount of sleep,

How to Get Sleep When You're Traveling

I just got back from a five-day business trip during which I had trouble sleeping because the room I had was noisier than my apartment in New York City. It bordered a busy highway, and even with a pillow over my head I could hear every car that went by. At one in the morning I finally called down to the front desk for one of three things: a new room, some earplugs, or a fan that would drown out the noise. I got the earplugs and eventually fell asleep, and I resolved to add a section about this topic to my book. Here are some tips on how to insure that you get a good night's sleep when you stay in a hotel.

✔ Unpack your things and organize your belongings. This will make your room more comfortable and will contribute to a relaxed state, which is good for sleep.

✔ Bring earplugs and a blindfold.

✔ If you are cold, call housekeeping and ask for a blanket. Most hotels will provide extra blankets if you ask.

✔ Stay awake until at least 10 P.M. when you are in a new time zone, even if you are tired.

✔ Avoid a big dinner or caffeine three hours before dinner. Something as minor as a piece of chocolate can prevent you from falling asleep.

✔ Do not use alcohol for falling asleep. You may fall asleep quickly, but you will have a less restful night of sleep if you have been drinking.

✔ To fight jet lag, use daylight to reset your body's internal clock. Before traveling east, get some sun early in the morning. On westbound trips, stay outdoors at the end of the day.

✔ Tell the person at the front desk of the hotel, nicely, that you would appreciate a quiet room. It's worth a try.

anywhere from five to nine or ten hours a night. It is up to you to determine how much sleep you need. A rule of thumb is that if you need an alarm to wake you up, you are not getting enough sleep. If you fall asleep within a few minutes at night, you are probably overtired.

Naps can be used to make up for sleep lost at night. Even if you are getting enough sleep, an afternoon nap or rest as short as ten minutes can increase alertness and reduce fatigue. Naps longer than one hour may leave you groggy. Naps taken before 4 P.M. can make up for sleep lost the night before; naps after 4 P.M. steal from the upcoming night. So if you nap late in the day, you may have trouble sleeping at night.

If you are groggy in the morning, your eating habits might have something to do with it. If you skip dinner, you will most likely wake up groggy the next morning. If you do eat dinner, wait two hours after eating before going to bed. Otherwise your food does not have a chance to digest properly and you will feel groggy the next morning, as though you skipped the meal altogether.

COPING WITH THE PSYCHOLOGICAL ISSUES OF WORKING ALONE

Working in a virtual office can exact an emotional toll. When you give up the structure of a conventional work arrangement, you also leave behind a network of coworkers and managers who may have provided you with emotional support. To work successfully on your own, you may need to learn to cope more independently with things such as rejection, self-doubt, worry, and setbacks. This chapter provides mechanisms for doing so.

LEARNING TO COPE WITH ISOLATION

I knew I had a problem with isolation when I wanted to have long conversations with everyone I came in contact with during the day. Every secretary or assistant I talked to learned a little bit about me, and I invited my bank teller to my New Year's Eve party.

Feelings of isolation occur at different times for everyone. Some people feel it initially before they get into a groove at home or on the road, and others feel it only after months or years of working alone. People have told me they have enough contact over the phone during the day so that they never feel isolated, while others say they spend all day with clients and still feel isolated because they lack the camaraderie of an office.

An important first step in coping with isolation is to be willing to admit that you feel isolated. Why bother? Because feelings of isolation can lead to depression, stress, lack of motivation, and eventually burnout. You may even be driven to give up your virtual office if you don't find a solution to the problem.

It is very natural to feel isolated when you work by yourself. It does not mean that you are failing or that your situation is not working out. It simply means that you need to make a few minor changes in your schedule.

Part of what keeps people from finding solutions to the problem of isolation is that they believe it requires radical change. But that is not the case. Short breaks from your routine will enable you to get some of the social interaction you desire and still work independently and productively. Easy-to-implement changes include peppering your schedule with several social encounters a week such as meeting friends for lunch, attending a professional association meeting, taking a lesson or class, exercising at a gym, volunteering, or going to a business support group. Once you identify some activities that provide the social contact you need, establish a regular schedule. Sign up for three months of classes or commit to assisting a group with a long-term project. This will make it more difficult for you to forgo your activity because of work.

One simple trick for dealing with isolation is to keep the radio on all day at a very low level so that it is almost like a murmur. This low-level sound simulates the background noise of an office and prevents you from having to work in complete silence. Silence can be stultifying. You may find that this noise helps keep your energy level up.

Whether you are an entrepreneur or a corporate telecommuter, you can deal with your isolation by recreating the camaraderie you had with office mates. I am part of a women's group that meets once every two weeks. There are five of us ranging in age from early thirties to mid-seventies, and we talk about our lives, our work, and whatever else comes to mind. It provides a community of people that I am in touch with on a regular basis, and fills in some of the gaps left by not having interaction at the office.

Entrepreneurs can also fight isolation by pursuing projects that require collaboration. This is becoming more common as people in different industries form "virtual corporations" to complete projects. Talk to other home-based business owners you know about how you might be able to work together, or join a business group and keep your eyes out for a project that could provide you with this opportunity. As the popularity of working at home grows, groups that provide support to home-based business owners have sprung up all over the country. These groups meet regularly to talk about business and provide an opportunity for social contact. Look in the calendar section of your local paper, or contact your professional association or small-business association to find out about meetings in your area. If you do not find one, start your own. You can ask home-based businesspeople you know, or put an ad in the local paper.

Corporate telecommuters can make contact with peers by establishing regular meetings with other virtual-office workers. Most mobile workers I've talked to still meet with their coworkers on a regular basis to socialize and talk about work. If this is not a ritual in your office, institute it. Your coworkers will be grateful. You should also talk to your manager and coworkers about your isolation. It is your manager's responsibility to insure that you are still involved in all office social activities and other gatherings. If your coworkers know about your isolation, they may make an effort to call you more regularly.

When I am wistful about having coworkers, I try to remember two things. First, I am probably remembering my office experiences as seen through rose-colored glasses. To be honest with myself, I did a lot of blab-bing in the office that was not necessarily enriching (but I also worked with great people who added a lot to my life). The second reminder is that nothing is perfect—including working in a virtual office. The downside of working on your own is that you will sometimes miss coworker interac-tion, but in my opinion, there are certainly enough benefits to justify putting up with occasional wistfulness.

BEING A GOOD BOSS TO YOURSELF

When you work on your own, whether you are an entrepreneur or a telecommuter working for a corporate boss, you depend more on yourself to be a manager, sounding board, coach, and provider of feedback. Even if you have a boss back in the office, your independent status will require you to be more self-sufficient. This increased self-reliance can be either positive or negative, depending on whether you choose to be a good boss or more like the worst ogre you ever worked for.

People perform better in every aspect of their lives from personal relationships to job performance when they receive feedback such as reminders of what needs to be done and praise of accomplishments. But in order for feedback to be effective, it has to be the right kind.

According to Esther Bogin, director of People Communication Skills, a Dix Hills, New York–based people-management consulting firm specializing in interpersonal dynamics, typically up to 75 percent of what you say to yourself is negative. You are most likely to tell yourself what you have not done, what you did wrong, and what you need to do. When something good happens, you are likely to take it for granted instead of basking in the achievement. This is problematic because consistent nega-tive feedback can lead to a loss of motivation and poor performance. Think about how you would feel if you had a boss who told you only what needed to be done, what you had not completed yet, and what you did wrong. Would you feel good? Chances are you would not do a very good job for this person.

Many of us got to be this way from our training in life. As kids we may have brought home a 95 on a test, only to be told to study harder so that next time we would get a 100! In some households, even a perfect score on a test is treated as "something to be expected" and therefore not a big accomplishment.

You may not be able to do away with all negative thoughts and statements you make to yourself, but you can reduce them and increase the positive feedback you give yourself. Bogin provides the following strategies for changing dialogue from negative to positive.

▶ **First identify *when* you use self-talk.** Do you talk to yourself to make lists, evaluate yourself, make excuses, criticize, or "all of the above"?

▶ **Talk about behavior.** When you talk to yourself, be specific so that you derive a benefit from the dialogue. Telling yourself that you are lazy or a fool invalidates you. Instead, identify what you believe you have done wrong. Did you speak when you shouldn't have or interrupt before listening to an entire statement? Did you talk yourself out of a sale by not believing you could do it? By being specific, you can figure out what you can do next time so you perform differently. It can even be beneficial to be specific with positive internal dialogue. Instead of just telling yourself you did a great job, describe why. It feels better to have someone enumerate the specifics of what you have done well, even if that someone is you.

▶ **Try Bogin's "two-to-one" exercise.** For every one time you tell yourself something you still have to do, or get down on yourself for making a mistake, make two positive statements about yourself.

▶ **Be a good friend to yourself.** Think about what kind of feedback you would give to someone else in your shoes and try to be a little nicer to yourself. Many of us are much more considerate, kind, and understanding when it comes to other people. Bogin coaches people to remember this adage when they talk to themselves: "If you have nothing nice to say, don't say anything at all."

▶ **Use active language to empower yourself.** Talk to yourself like a résumé with positive active language. Instead of saying "Hopefully I will," say "I will." This language is more persuasive when you are selling yourself to others. Use it to sell yourself to yourself.

See also "Acknowledging Your Accomplishments" in chapter 9.

AVOIDING HOME-OFFICE DEPRESSION

When we talk about working independently, in a home office or anywhere else, we think of words like *independence*, *freedom*, and *fulfillment*. But based on my interviews and the mail I receive from my readers and listeners, I believe there is another word that should be added to this list: *depression*.

The isolation of working alone, combined with the pressure of running a business or managing your workload more independently, can lead you to feel overwhelmed. Feeling out of control can trigger depression. This phenomenon is not surprising, given that nationally, depression is the most common complaint among people who see medical professionals. According to Harold H. Bloomfield, M.D., and Peter McWilliams in their book *How to Heal Depression*, one in twenty Americans experiences depression severe enough to seek medical treatment.

So, how do you know if your distributed work is depressing you? According to Katherine Crowley, the New York City–based psychotherapist who works with entrepreneurs, you may first notice that you do not feel like yourself. This can include an inability to complete tasks, a reluctance to start working on a project, and indecisiveness. Setbacks may appear to ruin a whole project, and small obstacles may appear as huge barriers.

Other signs are sadness accompanied by anxiety or irritability, diminished appetite for food or sex, or a loss of pleasure from things you usually enjoy doing. Sleep problems such as insomnia, restless sleep, trouble falling asleep, or sleeping more than you normally do may also be warning signs.

To stave off or cope with home-office depression, try the following suggestions.

▷ **Break your isolation.** Even if you don't want to go out, force yourself. Put yourself into a situation where you can interact with people you know. Call a friend, set up a business lunch, even go to a health club—just to be around people.

▷ **Take time off and do something you enjoy.** Working without breaks may cause depression because it creates a feeling that work is draining you, which may actually be true. Continued stress depletes your immune system by overworking your adrenal glands. When your body is depleted, you can become depressed.

In order to relax during your time off, you need to develop and maintain interests outside of work, something overworked entrepreneurs often neglect. Without outside interests, it will be difficult to enjoy the breaks you do take.

▷ **Attempt to trace the origin of the depression.** Common triggers are a disappointment, a loss, or a sudden change. Even the change of seasons can cause depression. Other people feel depressed even when they experience great success because they've gotten the things they wanted and realize they still do not feel good.

▷ **Try to gain perspective.** If you're depressed about a failure, remind yourself of past successes.

Crowley stresses the importance of regarding depression as a signal. "Depression has a purpose; it's a sign that something is off balance and needs your attention," she says. "That can mean too much work or it may mean you're not doing what you enjoy."

Of course, most people feel depressed from time to time. Depression is a part of life just like happiness, anger, and sadness. You may experience the feelings I've described for a few days before they pass. But if your feelings persist and you want some help, look under "Psychologists" in your yellow pages for a counseling referral service, or in the front of the white pages under "Community Resources." You can also call the National Mental Health Association's 24-hour referral number, (800) 228-1114, and obtain a referral to a local mental health association.

If you feel suicidal, call 911, go immediately to a hospital emergency room, or call a community crisis service that you will find listed in front of the white pages in your phone book.

DEALING WITH REJECTION

I have become very familiar with rejection over the years. I've had editors tell me my writing is boring, voice coaches tell me my voice is all wrong, and TV news directors tell me I am not good-looking enough to be on TV.

When you work by yourself, rejection can really take a toll on you if you're not careful, because there is no one around to laugh about it with you. After a while, it can stop being funny. I have learned some tricks over time for coping with rejection. The advice that follows may save you some anguish.

1. Expect some rejection. If you expect every pitch to be a sale, every person to be nice to you, and every proposal to win you business, you are going to take rejection really hard. Rejection is part of life; you have to accept that and expect to be rejected.

2. Celebrate rejection. When I first moved to New York City, my aunt Nan told me to think of every rejection as bringing me one step closer to success. She was talking about odds. If you have a failure or setback, it means you've gotten one setback out of the way and you are therefore closer to getting what you want.

3. Do not be upset by rejection. Rejection is a fact, but how you feel about being rejected is not a fact. People automatically assume that because you are rejected, you have to feel terrible. But rejection is just rejection—nothing more, nothing less. People have all kinds of reasons for rejecting you. Sometimes it has to do with you; many times it does not.

4. Do not be at other people's mercy. If you are always looking to other people for approval or to verify that you are worthy, your life will be a roller coaster. When you get a lot of acceptance, you'll feel great; when you get a lot of rejection, you'll feel terrible. When someone rejects you in a work situation, it doesn't mean you are no good; it means you got rejected. Period.

5. Share your rejection. You may not have coworkers nearby with whom you can commiserate, but find *someone* to tell. This will remind you that everyone experiences rejection, not just you.

6. Do not globalize. It is important to make sure rejection does not wreak havoc on your psyche. My mother is a therapist and she calls this *globalizing*. It means that when you fail at one thing, you think everything is terrible; she always reminds me not to do it.

To avoid globalizing, give yourself a reality check when you suffer a rejection. Make a list, mentally or on paper, of what is going well in your business or your life, to remind you of your successes and failures.

7. Read the following passage. I kept it above my desk for two years.

He failed in business in '31. He was defeated when he ran for the legislature in '32. He failed once again in business in '34. His sweetheart, his fiancée, died in '35. He had a nervous breakdown in '36. He went back into politics and was defeated in the election of '38.

He decided to run for Congress and was defeated in '43. He was defeated for Congress in '46. He was defeated for Congress in '48. He was defeated for the Senate in '55. He was defeated for vice president in '56. He was defeated for the Senate in '58.

After that, you'd say he was through, wouldn't you? He was, as they say, "all washed up," wasn't he? He had had it, had he not? No, he hadn't at all. He went on to be elected President in 1860! The man, of course, was Abraham Lincoln. Invincible!

What to Say to Naysayers

I once sat next to a man on a plane who was in the process of starting a home-based business, and he told me about a problem that I get lots of mail about: *naysayers*. Naysayers are people who say you won't be able to do what you're setting out to do, and they're the nemesis of people who work on their own. Naysayers are bad for everyone, but they're particularly toxic for those of us working on our own because we are isolated and can be profoundly affected by comments from one or two people. Some naysaying comes from genuine concern, some from fear, and a good chunk from jealousy. But whatever the source, there are a few ways to deal with it.

First of all, anticipate it. If you expect to encounter naysayers periodically, they'll do less damage to your enthusiasm. When you're planning to work at home you'll hear a lot of "How will you ever manage it in the house?" naysaying. People who say this are voicing their own fears, not your reality.

My other rule is that I heed advice only from people I would like to emulate. In other words, if you would like your professional life to be like that of the person who is giving you her two cents, you may want to listen. Otherwise, forget it.

Another good way to deal with naysayers is not to share your ideas with people who regularly shoot you down. This may take some readjustment if you're in the habit of sharing your plans with certain people. But if you don't change your ways, you'll waste a lot of energy building yourself back up all the time.

If the naysayers in your life are in your close circle of family or friends, it's a more serious problem. In this case I suggest two things. First, find another source of support immediately. Establish regular contact with people who support your endeavors. If you are an entrepreneur, join a group for entrepreneurs or home-based businesses (you can find notices of meetings in local papers or through business associations). If you are a telecommuter, meet up with other telecommuting coworkers or make time to go into the office where you can find the support you need. Second, confront the objections of naysayers who are close to you head-on. If you need to, write down their objections and prepare your strong rebuttals ahead of time.

And keep one more thing in mind. A friend of mine entered "naysayer" into one of those electronic thesauruses, and the word it spat out is an unprintable body part!

Troubleshooting Emotional Roadblocks

The quick reference guide that follows is designed to help you troubleshoot the psychological roadblocks you may encounter when you are working independently. The problems are listed in bold and are followed by a list of solutions. You may not find all of the solutions for a given problem applicable to your personality or your situation. Choose the solution that fits you best from among the list.

Problem: I allow roadblocks to make me question my goals.

(Continued)

Solutions:

1. Remind yourself that all successful people encounter roadblocks. It's how they cope with them that determines their success.

2. Remember that you are in control of how you interpret a roadblock. You can look at it as an indication that your goal is unattainable, or you can look at it as a test of your conviction. Resolve to pass the test!

3. Keep in mind that many things that are worth attaining will be difficult to attain.

4. Surround yourself with people who believe in your goals, and talk to them if you start to doubt where you are headed.

5. Have a piece of paper or a computer file that contains your business goals, along with a list of the skills and attributes you possess that will enable you to attain these goals. Use this list for encouragement when you encounter a roadblock.

6. Make a list of three things that are running smoothly and give yourself some perspective.

7. Before you begin to work toward your goals, identify the kind of obstacles (technical mishaps, delays in business deals, foul-ups with suppliers) that are likely to occur and factor them into your plans.

Problem: I do not see mistakes as part of any work situation.

Solutions:

1. Read a profile of any successful businessperson and find solace in the long list of mistakes he made.

2. Talk to other business owners about the mistakes they've made.

3. Figure out what you can learn from the situation, and consider the mistake part of your business training.

4. Think about three ways it could have been worse.

5. Share the mistake with a few people. Keeping it to yourself often magnifies a mistake.

6. Remember that if you're not making mistakes, you're probably not pushing yourself.

Problem: I have a difficult time forgiving myself quickly for making a mistake.

Solutions:

1. Think about the amount of time you spent fretting over your last mistake and evaluate whether it enhanced your business or your life at all.

2. Put aside a certain time every day to feel bad about your mistake. The rest of the day, push it out of your mind.

3. Evaluate whether you will still be feeling the effects of this mistake in three months or a year. If not, it is not something to spend a lot of time fretting about.

DEALING WITH COWORKER RESENTMENT

There is ongoing debate about how much resentment coworkers feel toward their telecommuting counterparts. Many of the telecommuters I have spoken to have said resentment is not an issue. I have also spoken to telecommuters whose coworkers resented their ability to work outside of the office.

Management should present the program as something that is available to anyone who has appropriate job responsibilities and meets a specific set of criteria. If someone is not eligible for telecommuting at a certain point, it should be made clear that if the employee's status changes, the situation can be reevaluated.

Following is some advice for coping with resentment if it does arise.

▲ **Talk to your manager.** Your manager or supervisor can help to stave off resentment by making it clear to office-bound employees that although you may not have to take part in some meetings or other tasks that are associated with being in the office all of the time, you are picking up work in other areas. Your manager can also do things for your office-bound counterparts such as occasionally giving them an afternoon off or some other perk, if the manager feels that the office-bound employee in a particular case has been picking up the slack for you. However, as a matter of policy, nontelecommuters should not be picking up work for telecommuters.

▲ **Police your manager.** Your manager should not create resentment by expecting nontelecommuting employees to pick up some of your workload while maintaining their own responsibilities. Be sure that everyone knows how to reach you when something arises in the office that needs your immediate attention. This will reduce the likelihood of a coworker having to pick up the slack.

▲ **Keep in touch with coworkers.** Sharing information via the phone or e-mail is a good way to subtly let people know that you are working. The few telecommuters who had experienced resentment said they share "FYI" information with people that will help them personally and professionally. An article from an industry publication, a note containing a piece of information you picked up during a client phone call, or a fact from a company report forwarded to a colleague sends a clear message that you are concentrating on work at home.

▲ **Tell them the reality.** One woman I spoke to said she shares some war stories about the struggles she faces working outside of the office with coworkers from whom she senses resentment. She talks about the isolation and other problems she faces with any employee whom she senses is resenting her telecommuting arrangement. She does this subtly by working it into a conversation about other things.

▲ **Spread the word.** In some cases, other employees may not realize they have the option of telecommuting. A telecommuting center employee at NYNEX told me that she encourages other employees in her neighborhood to ask about working at the center. She said sometimes they do not know it's an option available to them.

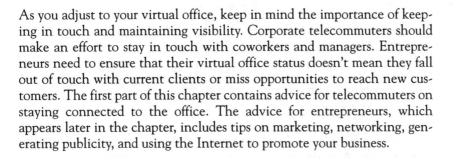

MAINTAINING VISIBILITY

As you adjust to your virtual office, keep in mind the importance of keeping in touch and maintaining visibility. Corporate telecommuters should make an effort to stay in touch with coworkers and managers. Entrepreneurs need to ensure that their virtual office status doesn't mean they fall out of touch with current clients or miss opportunities to reach new customers. The first part of this chapter contains advice for telecommuters on staying connected to the office. The advice for entrepreneurs, which appears later in the chapter, includes tips on marketing, networking, generating publicity, and using the Internet to promote your business.

PLANNING YOUR TELECOMMUTING DAYS

If you are a telecommuter working in a virtual office for your corporate boss, planning for days outside of the office will begin before you leave the corporate office. Part of your planning should be devoted to determining how you will communicate and provide information for people when you are no longer in the office. Think about who you communicate with, how often and by what means, what kind of information you will need to provide them with, and how they will contact you. Plan for this communication from your remote location, including a strategy for how you will insure that people can find you.

However, your primary concern should be making sure you have all the papers, files, and other materials you'll need to work at home, in the car, or wherever else you'll be. The simplest way to do this is to prepare a list in the afternoon before a telecommuting day. To compose a comprehensive list, get in the habit of writing down everything you plan to accomplish when you're telecommuting and what you'll need for each project. To make sure you don't miss anything, break your goals down into tasks (a task is each of the steps it will take to complete a goal).

Some people have a "telecommuting day" file in which they place appropriate telecommuting work as they encounter it during the week. This may include reviewing documents, writing, reading, phone calls, and project development.

Sample Telecommuting List

Goals	Tasks
1. Complete Ferguson report	Notes from meeting Ferguson file Computer disk Law firm number Extra company stationery
2. Draft July memos	Copies of June memos E-mail directory Karen's notes
3. Proof report	Report Red marker Report with Tom's comments

Elham Shirazi, a telecommuting and transportation planning consultant in Los Angeles, recommends a dry run before you telecommute for the first time. This involves going back through your last week of work and reconstructing it so that you are working outside of the office for a few days. When you are doing this, consider that you may not have all of the resources outside of the office and plan for what work will be best suited to completion outside of the office. Following is some advice from seasoned telecommuters about what you can do to insure that your telecommuting goes smoothly.

△ **Check the office schedule before you leave.** Make sure that there are no meetings or important events taking place on your telecommuting day. This should be easy enough to ascertain, and you will probably know without asking, but it's important to get into the habit of asking around just in case. Most telecommuting agreements stipulate that employees will make themselves available when needed. Sometimes this will mean postponing a telecommuting day if a meeting is scheduled or if you are needed in the office for some other reason.

△ **Be flexible and willing to go into the office,** if possible, if you are needed for a meeting or because of a technology foul-up that makes your telecommuting difficult.

△ **Realize how much you will accomplish** when you are away from the office and all of its interruptions, and bring enough work to keep you busy. Initially, bring more work than you think you can accomplish.

△ **If you count on a network** or access to other technology to complete your work outside of the office, bring other work with you in case there is a technical problem on your telecommuting day.

△ **Establish hours and stick to them.** You now have more freedom to create your schedule, but if you are too free-wheeling, coworkers and customers won't know when to reach you. If you work from 5 A.M. until 1 P.M., that's fine; just be sure you are consistently available during those times and let those hours be known. See "Avoiding Overwork" in chapter 9 for more information.

△ **Make sure to have a stock of basic forms and paperwork** you will need to work outside of the office and replenish them regularly. These include things such as status or inventory evaluations, special requisitions, quotas, and contracts. When you are making your list of things to take with you, be sure you have enough of these forms as well.

△ **Make critical information accessible to others.** Part of being productive outside of the office is making sure that life in the office can continue without you. One way to ensure this is to keep all files on current projects neatly organized and clearly labeled in your corporate office. You don't want a coworker, or worse yet, your manager, to have to gather together papers strewn all over your office. You also don't want to send them looking in three or four different places because you can't remember what you called a file or where you put it.

△ **Think of everything that could go wrong** while you are away, and try to plan for it.

△ **Do not be afraid to ask for help.** Sometimes telecommuters are afraid to ask for help with problems they encounter because they fear the telecommuting arrangement will be terminated if it has any glitches. But some adjustment difficulties are to be expected and you should seek help in resolving them.

△ **Don't take too much stuff with you.** You may not need to take the entire folder for a project to work on one piece of it. Carefully evaluate what pieces of information you will really need at home and leave as much as possible in the office. This is important because people in the office may need access to the material, and you will want to minimize the amount you must carry to and from the office. Some seasoned telecommuters advise against removing anything from the office if you can avoid it. Make copies or type pertinent facts into a file on a computer disk, and leave all originals in your office.

△ **Bring copies of materials you have mailed out recently** in case you receive calls about those items.

△ **Ship products like supplies to your home office** or telecommuting center so you do not have to carry them.

Life in the Virtual Office

KEEPING IN TOUCH WITH THE OFFICE

Visibility applies to issues as simple as making sure that people in the office know you are telecommuting, as well as to the more thorny issues of keeping in touch with coworkers and making sure your accomplishments in the virtual office are recognized. To make sure everyone knows you are telecommuting:

1. Regularly remind the receptionist or other person who has a finger on the pulse of the office. Type up a note, send an e-mail message, or issue a verbal reminder the day before you leave the office. Don't just give your number to the "pulse-person" once and assume it will always be available. Include it in e-mail or in a note you send each week or whenever you'll be out of the office. If you will be out of the main office all the time, check periodically to make sure information on where to contact you is readily available to anyone who needs it.

2. Post a note near your desk on your telecommuting days reminding people that you are telecommuting. Obviously this would be cumbersome if you telecommute frequently, so you may want to bother with this only in the initial stages of your telecommuting.

3. Encourage people to contact you at home or wherever you are. Alex Dickinson, a research scientist at AT&T Bell Laboratories, periodically works from his apartment in Manhattan, and when he does, he encourages his coworkers to use his office and video conferencing equipment to dial him up and visit him in his home office. "It is like popping their head into my office when I am at Bell Labs," Dickinson says. Suggesting that coworkers contact you is important because people are often leery about calling telecommuters. If you work at home or in a telecommuting center, people may worry that they will be bothering you if they call. If you are in a mobile office, they may assume you'll be difficult to reach. You and your manager will most likely have a designated time to speak during the day, and I also suggest placing a call to a coworker or two throughout the day. This will encourage people to contact you and give you an opportunity to get an unofficial update of what is happening in the office.

4. Make sure you receive your memos and magazines. Establish a system for receiving memos and magazines when you're out of the office. If you don't, you'll waste time chasing these things down when you get back to the office. The best way to do this is to set up a basket in your office and label it clearly. Make sure it's visible from outside your office. If this doesn't work, ask a coworker to get two of whatever is being given out and save one for you. Some people have industry publications delivered to their home office or telecommuting center as well as to the traditional office to make sure they do not miss anything.

5. Develop a buddy system. This is good for things such as receiving your mail and dealing with time-sensitive tasks that must be completed in the office. In the buddy system, another virtual-office worker who lives near you and is in the office on your days out brings your mail to you. You return the favor on that person's telecommuting day. The buddy system also works if you have job responsibilities similar to another telecommuter's. If you do, make an arrangement to fill in for each other if time-sensitive matters that must be handled in the office arise when you aren't there.

6. Also use the buddy system for designating someone in the office who will keep you informed of happenings there. This can be a peer, your manager, or an administrative support person. This is a way to make sure you do not miss out on important information, printed materials, or meetings. This person can also help you if you need something faxed to you or sent some other way. If this person has to send you a lot of materials, it may be a sign that you are not planning well for your days away from the office.

7. Schedule meetings with coworkers. Mobile workers I spoke to who spend lots of time outside of the office have regularly scheduled meetings with coworkers. One group meets weekly or biweekly in hotel lobbies or diners to talk. Another group has round-robins for meeting at each other's homes.

8. Use technology to keep in touch with coworkers and other people in the office by sharing information, humorous stories, or grapevine information through e-mail or voice mail.

9. Always attend social functions, meetings, and other work-related gatherings.

KEEPING IN TOUCH WITH YOUR MANAGER

Maintaining contact with your manager will be a juggling act of staying in touch without burdening your manager or yourself with too many updates on your work progress. Contact with your manager is essential for your peace of mind that you are prioritizing your work properly and being recognized for your accomplishments. It is also crucial for your manager's sense that you are accomplishing a sufficient amount of work outside of the office.

Generally, you will probably provide your managers with more updates in the beginning stages of your telecommuting. Once your manager is comfortable with the situation, meetings and communication will most likely be on an as-needed basis. Following are some guidelines.

Create structure for feeding information to your manager, and for your manager to feed information to you. Creating a structure for communicating with your manager may be part of your company's or supervisor's policy for telecommuting. If it is not, you should create one. This can be anything from meeting the day before and day after your telecommuting day to organize work and measure progress, to submitting monthly progress reports to your manager.

I've heard of weekly progress meetings, weekly phone calls, and expectations and accomplishments communicated by memo. What you choose to do will depend on you, your boss, and how long you have been telecommuting. This structure should be used for assigning and prioritizing upcoming projects, as well as for reviewing work that has already been begun or completed.

In order to insure that you are meeting your manager's standards and that your manager is comfortable with the work you are completing, you must clearly outline what is expected of you. This will also help you feel comfortable that you are focusing on the most important tasks. For your progress to be measurable, your manager must give you a clear idea of what she wants, the quality level she expects, and the timeframe within which you must complete it.

KEEPING IN TOUCH WITH YOUR CUSTOMERS

When you are making a case for telecommuting, your management will be worried about how customers will reach you when you are not in the office. When IBM rolled out its mobility program, 600 strong at the writing of this book, it created a one-day seminar and a series of follow-up seminars to train the company's salespeople in what they would need in order to stay in touch with the office and customers.

A significant portion of that day is devoted to technology—training in how to connect to the office via modem and how to use the IBM ThinkPad (its portable computer) features. IBM found through its research that people are less likely to use technology if they are not trained in it; the company determined that a one-day training course was all the sales force had time for, and designed a curriculum that covered care and feeding of a computer, how to connect via computer from anywhere outside of the office, how to contact the technical help desk, and how to use IBM's operating system. None of the employees were given portable computers until they completed the training.

All of this technical training was important because what makes IBM salespeople accessible, according to Debbie Zilai, Workforce Mobility Consultant at IBM is the ability to keep in touch with the office. This is done in two major ways. One is by updating a calendar kept on an IBM database that includes a schedule of where all salespeople are and how they can be reached. "We have had to learn to be disciplined about updating these schedules," says Zilai.

The second way is making sure callers can find you. When a customer calls into an IBM mobile worker's voice mail and chooses the option of speaking to a live person rather than leaving a message, the operator who takes the call can access the database and provide information on where the person can be reached. Even if you work for a company that does not have IBM's electronic calendaring system, you should have an option on your voice mail for reaching a receptionist or another person who has your information in front of him.

A few years before IBM rolled out its mobility program and gave its one-day training, the company had instituted a program for improving the voice-mail recordings that employees left on their machines. Messages now must include certain details including the name of a backup person who can take calls in the office and the option of reaching an operator or someone else if the caller chooses not to leave a message. Employees were also instructed to get back to people within the time frame they committed to in their message.

While it is not mandated by IBM, many of the mobile workers choose to customize their messages each day, including details of where they are and when they will be available to return calls. "It lets people know what to expect and tells them that you are checking your voice mail," says Zilai.

IBM now does monthly "Skill College" training on any issues that arise with mobility. This training is optional and topics have included work/life balance, time management, and technology.

USING THE PHONE TO STAY IN TOUCH

When you work outside of the office, the phone will be one of the primary tools you use to stay in touch with your customers and other people who need to reach you. But to be sure that you are reachable if someone needs you immediately, it is important for at least one person in the office to have information on how to reach you. In order for your telecommuting to be seamless, you must be vigilant about keeping this information updated and in the hands of the people who need it. This can be handled formally or informally. At IBM, all callers can press "0" and be forwarded to someone with access to a database that has information on all mobile workers.

This can also be handled in a less high-tech manner by making sure that whoever answers that phone at your office knows where you are and how you can be reached.

Making the phone work effectively for you requires some careful planning. Following is a list of some major considerations and recommendations.

Voice Mail   One of the primary considerations with voice mail is how often you will check it. You and your manager or company may have an agreement about this. If not, I suggest you check once an hour. If you will not be available to check your messages frequently, indicate that in your outgoing voice-mail message.

There is also the question of how much information you should include in your outgoing message. I think a good standard, and one that IBM has in place for all of its mobile workers, is that an outgoing voice-mail message must include the name of a backup person to take calls in the office, the option of reaching an operator or someone else if the caller chooses not to leave a message, and a time frame within which calls will be returned. While it is not mandated by IBM, many of the mobile workers choose to customize messages each day, including details of where they are and when they will be available to return calls.

One of the biggest questions when it comes to the phone and telecommuting is whether to tell people you are telecommuting. The answer to this can be answered only by you and your employer. My opinion is that there is no reason to tell anyone you are telecommuting if you check your messages frequently. In many cases, your telecommuting is irrelevant, because chances are that even if you were working in the office full-time, you would miss many calls when you were not at your desk.

Forwarding Calls   If you have the capability to forward calls outside of the office and you will be reachable, this will relieve you of having to check messages and will prevent you from missing any calls. However, because many telecommuters value the uninterrupted time they have outside of the office, many of them choose not to. If you do choose to use call forwarding, be sure you have a reliable, professional-sounding answering device in all of your workplaces, including the car.

Giving Out Multiple Numbers   It is becoming more standard now to have a variety of numbers listed on outgoing voice-mail messages, including beepers, home offices, and cellular phones. For some people this is unavoidable. However, in general I do not think it is a good idea. Providing a variety of numbers, whether in your outgoing voice-mail message or through other means, can create frustration for people who are trying to reach you. They may not know which number to call when, and they run the risk of leaving a message at a number that you are not checking regularly, thinking they have left word where you will get it. The preferable approach is to provide your contacts with one phone number that they can count on you checking regularly. As a backup, include an option in your outgoing message for your caller to reach an operator, receptionist, or assistant who can reach you in an emergency. Provide this person with your various phone numbers, and instruct this person either to give these numbers out sparingly to certain people, or to contact you if a call needs to be returned immediately.

Keeping the Receptionist Informed

If your company does not have voice mail, you need to be sure that anyone who answers the phone knows what to tell callers. Again, it is up to you whether you want people who call in to know that you are telecommuting. If you work at home, I do not recommend having a receptionist say that you are "at home"; this will discourage callers who are not comfortable with the home-office phenomenon from contacting you, for fear of bothering you. Instead, advise the receptionist to say you are working at another site or are not available. Be explicit in a note that you provide for the person who will be answering your calls as to how you would like them to be handled.

Sample Receptionist Reminder Note

Dear _____,

This is just a note to remind you that I'm telecommuting on Wednesday. I'll be checking my voice mail frequently so you don't have to worry about messages, but if you need me I'll be at:

Don't give my number out to clients. I don't want to confuse them with different numbers. Please tell them I'll get right back to them, and then call me. Thank you.

phone: (212) 555-1212
fax: (212) 555-1234
e-mail: 3516a

KEEPING A VIRTUAL COMPANY INTACT

I have business partners scattered all over the country and there are two major challenges to working this way: (1) keeping in touch without spending a whole day on the phone, and (2) maintaining cohesiveness and vision.

The following techniques are what we have used or what I've seen work in other virtual offices:

▶ **Maintain vision and priorities, companywide.** We indoctrinate everyone who joins our company in our standards and vision. To maintain this vision, we have quarterly conference calls in which we review where the company is and reiterate that vision. On an ongoing basis, we keep each other on track with e-mail. If I have a discussion with someone about company policy, vision, or performance standards, everyone gets e-mail on it as a reminder.

▶ **Establish a central clearinghouse.** One person—full or part time—coordinates schedules and takes care of company administrative work. Our administrative person keeps track of weekly schedules, keeps all important phone numbers on file, completes administrative work for all of us, and maintains important company files.

▶ **Share information.** Our newest company policy is to briefly summarize all magazine and newspaper articles in e-mail. Other ways to make the sharing of company information more efficient include joining a commercial online service or obtaining Internet access and attaching files to e-mail; linking all computers using a modem and communication software; or creating a central server, similar to network servers at large companies, that houses all company files.

▶ **Use voice mail to ask and answer quesitons.** Because we cannot always connect with each other to talk on the phone, we have learned to leave complete questions and answers on each other's voice mail and answering machines.

▶ **Take good notes.** Each participant in conference calls, and all phone calls, needs to take good notes to cut down on call-backs to clarify.

▶ **Plans to get together regularly.** Long-term strategizing is best done while at least some of you are in the same room. Spending time together is also important for maintaining relationships.

DEFINING A MARKETING PLAN FOR YOUR HOME-BASED BUSINESS

In order to help you make decisions about how best to market and publicize yourself, you need to take a leaf from the book of corporate America. When a large business decides to embark on a marketing campaign or seek some kind of promotion, the company usually spends some time figuring out exactly what it wants to accomplish.

This is often solidified through a *defining document*. This is a document which includes a series of questions about your place in the market, your challenges, and where you want your business to go. A defining document will help you strategize and will keep you on track when you make marketing and publicity decisions. You can, and probably will, redefine this document periodically.

The recommended structure of a defining document is listed below. Provide as much detail as you possibly can when answering each question. It is helpful to work on this document with someone else, or at least show it to someone else to be sure that what you are expressing is clear.

Background

Background encompasses what your business is and where your business fits in the marketplace. This section should also include your business challenges.

Vision for Business

Your *vision* is what you want your business to be. This includes exactly whom you want to sell to, what you will provide to this market, how you want your customers and competition to regard you, how you will differentiate yourself from your competition, and how large your company will be. For example, do you plan a high-volume, low-margin approach, or will you price yourself high and sell fewer items?

Target Market

Your *target market* is a very specific description of to whom you want to sell. This section should include details such as location, title, concerns, age, income, and company size (if applicable) of your target market. It is helpful to describe who you are *not* targeting as a way to hone your target market description.

Objective

Your *objective* is what you want to attain. It should be a specific, measurable goal that includes a time frame for attainment. An example objective would be to make $150,000 in revenues in 1996.

Strategy

Strategy is how you will attain your objective. A strategy for the preceding objective might be to land five new accounts.

MARKETING YOUR HOME-BASED BUSINESS

This section covers three ways to market your home-based business: word of mouth, networking, and mailings.

Word of Mouth The majority of home-based businesses use word of mouth and networking to find customers. Word-of-mouth advertising comes from two sources: customers who are happy with your service, and people who understand your business even though they've never bought from you.

Keeping this in mind, it's crucial to make sure that you satisfy your customers. This may sound elementary, but considering how much poor service I come across, I think a reminder is justified. Good service is one of the ways that those of us working at home can compete with our larger competitors, so it's crucial that we deliver.

The other way to generate word-of-mouth business is to make sure that people understand what you do. Most people you know probably couldn't refer customers to you because they don't understand your business. You can help them understand what you do by developing a one- or two-sentence description of your business that is easy to understand. To create a good business description, take out all the jargon and words that make people's eyes glaze over. Examples of glaze-inducing words are *strategic objective*, *reposition*, and *custom-designed*.

Think simple when you are describing your business. If you help companies figure out what computers to buy, say it. No one is going to ask your friends if they know someone who "helps Fortune 500 companies evaluate and determine what their technical decisions should be as they reposition themselves strategically." But they might ask if your friends know anyone who knows about buying (or upgrading) computers.

Networking

Networking is similar to word of mouth. It is simply a way of getting your name out to clients and people who can lead you to clients. A traditional way to do this is to join industry organizations or associations. Once you join a group like this, volunteer to help organize an upcoming event. This will let people get to know you and your business. You can get names of these groups from *The Gale Encyclopedia of Business and Professional Associations* at your library reference desk.

Professional groups are an excellent resource, but they aren't the only option. You can network on the tennis court, at weddings, at a Little League game—anywhere. The important thing is to be involved in a variety of activities where you'll meet people. The person behind you in the grocery line, someone you sit next to on a train, your neighbors, your accountant, and your barber can all help you expand your business. If they don't need your services, maybe their sister-in-law or their neighbor does.

I'm not suggesting you accost strangers with a sales pitch, but I do suggest that you casually work some mention of your business into your conversations—even when you don't think there's anything to be gained from it. A lot of people make the mistake of networking only at official networking events or only when they feel they are in the presence of "a prospect." But a conventional approach is not what it takes to succeed in your own business. When you're isolated, working in a home office, this is particularly true.

Mailings

Aside from networking and word of mouth, one other way of developing a client base is to do a mailing. A good way to put together a mailing list is to use a member directory from the industry association your prospects belong to. Sometimes you have to buy the directory; other times you must join to get the list. Either way, it will be well worth the investment.

If it's large companies you want, the library has a book called *The Dun & Bradstreet Million-Dollar Directory*, which lists the 50,000 largest companies in the country. The book organizes the listings by geographic location, alphabetically, and by category of business. There are also services that collect state and city information and provide it to you for a fee. This is information that you can find yourself for free at your city hall or the county clerk's office, but if you are too busy, these services will gather the information for you. To find these services, look under "Information Services" in your local yellow pages. A word of warning, though: People on public information lists tend to be bombarded with promotional material, so make sure your mailing is targeted to people who will really be interested in what you are selling. Otherwise, you'll be wasting your money.

You can also buy mailing lists through one of the many mailing-list vendors. Look in the yellow pages and start calling around. Most of these companies will give you price quotes over the phone.

I recommend two other low-cost ways of finding business. One is to make contact with people who can put you in touch with your customers. For a résumé writer, this would be a career consultant or a career counseling office at a university. For a desktop publisher, this might be a printer. The concept is to make contacts, each one of which has the potential to lead to multiple sales.

The other idea is to reach your customers by writing for a community newspaper or teaching a class at a local adult education center. This establishes you as an expert and gets your name out to customers. For example, if you have a cake decorating business, you could give a "Cake Decorating for the Holidays" class or write a similar article.

A Boston-based consultant I know also does something unconventional to market herself. She goes beyond the usual methods like accepting speaking engagements and writing articles. Once a quarter, she and seven other consultants produce a newsletter they mail to all their clients. The newsletter has practical articles about running a small business, and it does two things that bring in business. It reminds her clients that she's around, and establishes her as an expert in the field.

COMMON MARKETING MISTAKES

A man wrote to me one time asking for marketing advice. He had put flyers under the doors of 1,500 Long Island houses promoting his home-based business selling vacuum cleaners. He got no response. He even offered a slew of retailers a cut of any business they sent his way. Still nothing.

What was he doing wrong? After all, he asked, aren't you supposed to distribute promotional material to put out the word about a home-based business? Isn't enlisting the help of other businesses for referrals a good technique, especially for people who work at home?

The answer to his questions is "yes." But he was making a common marketing mistake: spreading himself too thin by believing that the more potential customers he approached, the more business he would have.

What he should have been doing was researching which households were the most likely to need a vacuum. Maybe it would be people with new children, newlyweds, or anyone who had recently bought wall-to-wall carpeting. You can buy this information from list brokers or collect it yourself. In the case of newlyweds, he could go to the city or town hall to look at a list of recent marriage licenses.

To get some more ideas on how to find your customers, you can hire someone who is excelling in the business you are in as a consultant.

How One Man Found His First Customers

Up until 1988 Robert Leuze had worked as an opera singer, a word processor, a book editor, a high school physics teacher, and a trade magazine reporter. He had never considered running a home-based business, but he was looking for work that would provide him with a steady income that his opera career never would.

It was at this point that Leuze's friend suggested he combine all of the skills and connections he'd developed through the years and start a desktop publishing business in his Manhattan apartment. Leuze took the advice, and for the last six years has been running Super-Script, a home-based business desktop publishing company that does editing, layout, design, and typesetting of long documents.

His first step was to register the name SuperScript with the county clerk's office in Manhattan. This helped him open a corporate bank account and protected his name so that no one else could use it. Leuze owned a computer, so his next step was to buy a printer and the desktop publishing software he would need to do his publishing.

One of Leuze's first publishing projects was a newsletter announcing his business and describing the process of desktop publishing. He also made a brochure for SuperScript and mailed it along with the newsletter to a database of 200 friends and colleagues he had gathered through his years of mailing out announcements for his opera performances. "I wanted to let people know what I was doing and tell them about desktop publishing in case they might be interested," he said.

This was a start, but what Leuze really needed was a sample of his desktop publishing work to show to potential clients. To get this, he volunteered to create newsletters and books for an association he is a member of. The pay was minimal, but he came away from it with a published book to his credit.

The first few years of SuperScript were lean, and Leuze had to fill in the income gaps with temporary work as a word processor. In retrospect, he said his start-up was slow because he didn't do enough of the right type of marketing.

His only marketing efforts during the first two years were mailings of brochures and newsletters to people he considered potential clients. This brought in some business, but never enough. Leuze says he has since learned that he needs to market to people who can put him in touch with his customers.

"If you go to the person who has the need for your service, that's only one need, and you always have to look for another," Leuze said. "But if you make a strategic contact who is always in touch with people who need referrals for your business, you will get a lot of business from that one contact." He learned this trick from talking to other business owners at an entrepreneurial support group and by attending a seminar put on by the Service Corps of Retired Executives (SCORE).

One of the best ways he's found to keep business brisk is to work as the managing editor of the newsletter put out by the publisher of the software he uses. This newsletter goes to approximately 150 people who use the software, and provides him with referrals from users of the software and other desktop publishers.

Business is good now, but Leuze said if he had it to do over again he would

(Continued)

have gotten more up-front help in how to run his business. His advice for anyone embarking on a home-based business is to look for marketing advice and help in setting prices high enough. "I wish I'd gone to someone earlier who could have told me how to market, instead of learning the hard way," Leuze said. "Also, people need to get advice on how to set prices and make sure they don't set them too low."

Choose someone who is not a direct competitor, but who can give you advice on the best way to drum up business. Pay them for a few hours of their time to tell you what has worked for them.

The other way to be sure you do not spread yourself too thin is to choose a few venues for networking and then become a regular at these events. This is preferable to attending many events only once or twice. By becoming a regular somewhere, people will get to know you and your business and will therefore be more likely to refer customers to you or buy from you themselves. When you are at an event, do not feel that you always have to work the room. You may be better off talking to people you know to solidify those relationships.

GETTING PUBLICITY FOR YOUR BUSINESS

The following are ideas and advice on how to get your business noticed.

Proven Publicity Ideas*

Caught up in ardor for your own product or service, you probably find it hard to step into the shoes of outsiders and objectively evaluate what about it might deserve public attention. But you don't need a PR firm on retainer to do that kind of thinking for you. Here's a method to come up with proven publicity ideas that's as cheap and close as your public library or your not-yet-recycled stack of newspapers.

As you look through any stack of magazines or newspapers, notice articles that highlight particular businesses, products, and service providers. Articulate what seems to be touted most about that publicity recipient, then ask yourself whether that's an angle you could use. For example, these twelve ideas emerged from articles in a pile of *Entrepreneur* magazines.

*The sections on publicity and press releases are excerpted from *Six Steps to Free Publicity*, by Marcia Yudkin, Ph.D. (New York: Plume/Penguin, 1995). The book is available in bookstores or by calling (800) 898-3546.

1. Two young men publishing original short stories—on T-shirts. (Can you use an unusual medium to deliver the goods?)

2. A reference-checking firm spotlighted in an article on the rising tide of résumé fraud. (Has the problem your business solves been getting better or worse?)

3. A profile of Jim Bouton, star baseball player-turned-entrepreneur. (Is there a story in what you used to do?)

4. A photo and quotes from a real estate developer audited thirty-two times in one year. (Have you gone through and survived a horrific business ordeal?)

5. A company placing Russian business owners in one-month internships in American businesses. (Do you have noteworthy customers or suppliers?)

6. Amidst a cover story on the best locations for small business, a mini-profile of an environmental consultant in Amarillo, Texas. (Is there an interesting reason why you're located where you are?)

7. Courtesy of McDonald's, a California coffeehouse called McCoffee had to change its name and staged a mock funeral to mark the loss of the "Mc." (Can you publicly celebrate what appears to be a problem?)

8. A restaurant owner who delivers free gourmet meals to hospice patients. (Why not gain community goodwill for your business's acts of charity?)

9. A hair salon owner who gets steady business during the normally slow winter months. (Might others benefit from learning about your seasonal promotions?)

10. In Santa Cruz, California, Pizza Hut is experimentally taking orders through e-mail. (Could you test an innovative customer outreach program?)

11. A New Hampshire builder became interested in post-Newtonian physics and implemented chaos theory in his business. (Has your reading or hobby had a significant impact on your firm?)

12. A consultant/author gives employee-of-the-month programs a severe drubbing. (What sacred cow have you or could you take on?)

Instead of copying the proven publicity idea, adapt it, especially if it originated in a field very different from yours. Freshness counts! The first inn that changed owners through a $100-per-entry essay contest is still benefiting from the national publicity that included the first owner's appearance on *Donahue*, while the second innkeeper to try a contest got no media attention at all.

Press Releases

While consulting with clients peddling everything from high-tech products to everyday services, I've noticed certain errors cropping up again and again. Beginning do-it-yourself publicists easily get the format right, but if they commit any of these four blunders, their work will end up in the newsroom's trash can.

1. Any hint of advertising. When the media publicize your product or service at no cost to you, they are practicing journalism, not advertising. So your release gets trashed if you leave in any clues of being insensitive to the difference. The most telltale difference between journalism and advertising is that grammatically, ads address themselves directly to the reader while journalism usually employs third-person writing. Especially avoid the words *you* and *your* in the headline or main text of a release.

Instead of "Now you can shop for worms without leaving home," for example, write, "Now fishing enthusiasts can shop for worms without leaving home." In place of "Call (888) 777-7788 for the store nearest you," write, "Interested parties can call (888) 777-7788 for further information."

2. The merest smidgen of hype. Avoid the rushed, overenthusiastic tone of an infomercial. In print, this means staying away from exclamation marks and from any self-praise that is not factual. Attribute any subjective comments, accolades, or predictions about the success of your offering to named individuals within quotation marks—preferably to third parties not connected with you company, like customers or industry experts. (Of course, you need those third parties' permission to do this.)

For instance, "A Garage-for-You franchise offers an ideal way for handy men and women to earn an impressive income in their spare time" represents an unsupported opinion. You can fix it by explaining what makes it ideal, as in, "Because of its low buy-in fee and easy-to-follow marketing methods, a Garage-for-You franchise. . . ." Or you can fix it by saying *who* says the franchise is ideal—a satisfied franchisee, named and located, or some sort of uninvolved business leader.

3. Lack of focus. You'll be tempted to toss in everything that makes you mediaworthy. Don't. Make sure you have one central point in each

---

Getting Your Press Release Read and Used

✔ Don't ever address the reader/prospect directly in a release. Stick rigorously to a third-person approach.

✔ Stay away from signs of hype, like exclamation points and unsupported adjectives. Focus on the facts, and attribute any opinions to named individuals.

✔ Concentrate on one media message per press release. If you have a lot to tell, issue a series of releases.

✔ Be specific. Give as much detail as you can to whet the media's appetite for more.

release, and that you include only the background and commentary that supports that point. Diffuse copy gets confusing and dilutes the impact of your primary message.

4. Vague characterizations. If someone can read your release and respond, "Yes, but what *is* it?" you have failed. I have seen press releases for new products that I could not visualize from the verbiage, or for services that I didn't have a clue as to how they would work. You're always better off including too many details about your offering than too few. If in doubt, have someone unfamiliar with your product or service read the release and ask her to describe what you are trying to publicize.

The key word to remember is *detail*. Instead of "Jackson's new book contains information designed to benefit any stock-market investor," write, "Jackson's new book contains seven principles of market analysis that enable even casual investors to choose profitable stocks." Even better, describe two of the seven principles right in the release.

ONLINE MARKETING

Online marketing is perfect for people working at home because it lets you market cheaply without leaving the house. Online marketing also gives you a chance to make your company look bigger than it is because in cyberspace no one knows your office is in your basement. There are lots of ways to spread the word online about your home-based business and you don't have to be a computer wiz to do them.

First you have to get online. If you're not hooked up yet you need to get software from one of the commercial services (names you may have heard are America Online, CompuServe, and the Microsoft Network), or get access to the noncommercial area of the Internet called the World Wide Web through an access provider. An *access provider* is the "on ramp" you may have heard referred to when people talk about the information superhighway. The difference between commercial services and access providers is that commercial services have content (bulletin boards, chat sessions, magazines on line, etc.) and access to the World Wide Web. In most cases, access providers just enable you to get onto the Web. Once you are online, either on a commercial service or the Web, search around by subject until you find a place where the people you want to sell to or network with spend time.

The first component of successful online marketing is to behave properly when you are online. Online etiquette rules, or *netiquette*, have been widely publicized, but many people still don't seem to know them because they are consistently broken. The basic rules for when you are posting a message or sending e-mail are: Use punctuation and don't use all caps. Punctuation will make your notes easier to read; posting a note in capital letters is the online equivalent of shouting at someone.

There are also rules about what you can post on bulletin boards. At all costs, avoid notes that are blatant advertising on a bulletin board. The preferred method of interaction is to make a noncommercial posting in which you share information. Sharing information enables you to generate interest in your business by demonstrating what you know instead of saying how great you are. Ads belong in the classified section of commercial online services or on a home page.

Once you know the rules of the online world, you can begin to market your small business. Following are some tips.

1. Get involved. The first thing you should do is participate in the online forums related to your business. Locate several potential forums and explore them to find out if the people you want to reach spend time there. If you determine that a particular forum is a good place for you to be, get involved. Answer questions on a bulletin board that demonstrate your expertise and then attach your *signature file* (who you are, what you do, and where people can reach you) at the end of your posting. You can also take part in a chat session about a topic related to your area of expertise. As people in a subject area get to know you and your business, your presence may generate customers.

What you should not do is post an ad on a bulletin board or be too pushy with a sales pitch during a chat session. People will see right through that, and it is more likely to get you "flames" (nasty messages) than customers.

2. Write something. You can also share information by writing an article or posting free files to a forum. An article doesn't have to be long or difficult to write. It can be about 500 words (two pages, double-spaced) and can consist of ten bulleted items and a short introduction. For example, if you are a wedding planner, you could write an article about ten questions to ask a caterer before you hire, or how to save money on a wedding. If your business is travel, you could write about how to plan a family trip or ten unspoiled getaway spots.

At the bottom of the file, include a paragraph about yourself and what you do. Daniel Janal, author of *The Online Marketing Handbook* (Van Nostrand Reinhold, 1995), recommends including the following in your file to encourage its distribution and to protect your copyright and mention of yourself at the bottom of the file: "Reproduction of this file on bulletin boards is permitted as long as it is not changed or abbreviated."

To find places online for your files, go to the directory of an online service, find relevant forums, and then send a note to the *sysop* (system *op*erator) briefly stating who you are and what is in your article, and attach the file. Before you do this, make sure you research the forum to determine if it really reaches your target customers.

3. Place a classified ad. Most commercial services have a place for classified ads. Some individual forums also have an area devoted to classifieds related to the forum's topic. But if you place an online classified ad, do not assume that the traditional classified ad form will do. Use the following tips from Janal's *Online Marketing Handbook* to make the most of your online ad.

Longer is better. It is important to include as much information as possible in your ad. The online consumer is an information seeker by nature, and the traditional marketing strategy of selling an image doesn't usually work with online promotion. Give enough detail in your ad so that your reader has a clear understanding of what you offer.

Test to see what works. Because online classifieds are easy to create, you should experiment with various formats to determine what works best.

Free is a good word. Give away a free information file, a copy of your newsletter, or a fact sheet. This creates dialogue and a relationship that can lead to a sale.

Make your headline catchy and use the word *free.* "Free information on. . . ." is a good way to start.

4. Volunteer. Offer to host an online conference in your area of expertise. When you host a conference, the person who runs the bulletin board will promote you and the conference ahead of time. A promotion will usually include a short biography on you and will establish you as an expert in your field.

Marketing on the Internet

If you believe everything you hear about the Internet, it is the ultimate vehicle for marketing a small or home-based business. For some companies, it is. High-tech vendors are drumming up business for their computers and accessories, and companies selling everything from flowers to coffee beans are seeing some payoff. The Internet can also make you appear larger and more sophisticated than you are. However, as with any business opportunity, you need to approach marketing on the Internet carefully and review your objectives for your business and who your target customers are, to determine what, if anything, you should be doing on the Internet.

One easy way to market on the Internet is to mirror the activity you engage in on commercial online services. Research newsgroups (the Internet version of bulletin boards) and participate in discussions in groups your target customers frequent. See the preceding section on commercial online services for details on netiquette and how to market your business on a bulletin board. To access newsgroups you need to have what is called *newsgroup* or *newsreader* software. This is built into most commercial online services, and access providers also incorporate it into their packages in most cases. To get a listing of newsgroups type news.lists, news.groups, or news.answers in your newsgroup software. This will provide you with a list.

The other way to market your small business on the Internet is to create a *web site*. A web site is like retail space on the Internet in which you can post information about your company, sell products or services, and solicit feedback from your customers. The storefront of this web site is your home page.

A web site can be a great way to publicize your business, create dialogue with potential customers from all over the world, and increase your sales, or it can be a waste of time and money. The differentiating factor is a plan for how you will get your web site and your small business noticed in the vastness of the Internet. Following is a list of ideas for marketing your web site and for establishing a web site that will keep people coming back.

1. Register with directories. "www.yahoo.com" is the Internet address for a list of directories; you can list your home page there for free. Some Internet search engines will also automatically register you in other directories.

2. Create a link with other web sites. There may be other web sites that have complementary products. To create a link, send a note to the site's web master (the address is usually listed at the bottom of each home page) along with a note suggesting that you link your pages and list each other's addresses and businesses.

3. Write a press release about your home page and send it to reporters. Trade publications, newsletters, and *USA Today* (Tuesdays and Thursdays) list new home pages.

4. Print your Internet address on all of your marketing materials.

5. Run surveys and contests. Run a contest to attract attention and offer a prize to encourage participation.

6. Make sure your web site has enough information. According to *Doing More Business on the Internet*, by Mary Cronin (Van Nostrand Reinhold, 1995), it is also important to your marketing. The quality of the information in your site is the single greatest determinant of the site's long-term success as a marketing vehicle. Whatever is posted there must be accurate, current, and clear. It should also include details of what distinguishes your products as well as what customers have been able to achieve using your products and services.

7. Create a web site that encourages comments and discussions. This can be created as a feature of any web site. Some possibilities are suggestion boxes and prompts for comments and questions. Dialogue between you and the people who come to your web site will help generate sales.

8. Make sure mechanisms are in place for responding to feedback you get from your site. If you ask for feedback in your web site, you should respond to all suggestions, questions, and comments; otherwise you will not be conducting yourself in the spirit of the Internet. You cannot just put up a home page and wait for orders to come in. The Internet is all about communication. To cut down on the resources needed to provide information to visitors to your web site, create a list of Frequently Asked Questions (FAQs) and post them in your site.

COMMUNICATING EFFECTIVELY THROUGH TECHNOLOGY

13

Most of us use technology for important communications from our virtual offices every day and are judged on how we present ourselves. Given this, it is ironic that very few people are trained in how to communicate effectively on the phone, in conference calls, in a fax, through e-mail, and in newer technologies such as groupware. This chapter will tell you how to make a good impression and use technology as effectively as possible to stay in touch when you work outside of the office.

SOUNDING YOUR BEST ON THE PHONE

When you are working in a virtual office, you will undoubtedly spend more time communicating on the phone. If you want to operate effectively in this mode, you may need to improve your phone skills.

One of the first steps toward good phone communication is realizing that most people are not really comfortable on the phone. Part of the problem is that everyone is worried that the person on the other end of the line isn't really listening. This fear is exacerbated by our tendency to be colder and less enthusiastic on the phone than in person. To counteract this, step up your responses when you're on the phone by laughing out loud instead of just smiling, responding verbally instead of nodding, and putting warmth in your voice.

Good phone communication also includes monitoring how loudly you speak. People will be frustrated if they have to strain to hear you because you speak softly, or pull the phone away from their ear because you shout. To gauge the volume of your voice, ask your friends or colleagues for a critique. If you want to evaluate yourself, tape a few business

More Telephone Tips

✔ **Get calls off to a good start** by asking the people you call if it's a good time to talk. This gives them some breathing room and lets them know you are interested in what's going on with them.

✔ **Minimize interruptions.** They can indicate a lack of respect for the other person. Some interruptions are unavoidable, of course, but do everything in your power to keep them to a minimum. If you are calling from a car phone, try to call people when you think you will have a clear stretch for a while. If you think you may be cut off, reassure the person that you will call her back. If you are calling from your home, turn call waiting off during the call.

✔ **Establish rapport.** You do not have to discuss a person's life history before getting down to business, but some small comment, such as "How are you today?" or "Thanks for calling me back—I know how busy you are," gets the call off to a pleasant start and does not require much time.

✔ **End the conversation on a positive note.** Thank people for their time and effort.

✔ **One other tip from phone veterans:** Treat a phone appointment the way you would any other. If you say you'll call at 9:30, don't call at 9:40. It's inconsiderate and will start the call off on a bad note.

calls with one of those inexpensive suction-cup devices that attach to the phone receiver.

But no matter how good you sound on the phone, you won't be effective unless you know the purpose of your call before you dial. Before you pick up the phone, know whether you want to set up an appointment, make a sale, or just get some information. When you are actually on the phone gathering information, don't be afraid to ask people to slow down, spell names, or repeat what you didn't catch the first time around. If you don't, you'll have to call back or make a guess, and neither of these is a great option.

It's also important to make sure the person you're talking to understands what you are saying. It's easy to determine if people get your point face-to-face, but when you're on the phone you have to monitor recognition levels other ways. If you sense that someone isn't following what you're saying, ask if you're making yourself clear, or suggest going over the information again. People may not want to admit that they do not understand you, so eliminate their discomfort by saying, "Let's go over it again," or "Am I going too fast?"

Good phone communication is easier if you're in a good mood, so postpone a call if you're harried or stressed. It's crucial to be polite and courteous on the phone; if you can't be pleasant, use an excuse like an impending meeting and offer to call the person back. If you take the call, you run the risk of appearing disagreeable, difficult to work with, or incapable of resolving a situation.

Leaving Effective Phone Messages

We all leave and receive countless messages every day without thinking much about them. But the impression you make on someone's voice mail or answering machine can determine when they return your call, or whether or not they ever do.

A message can exhibit enthusiasm and competency or a lack of both. The information in your message also speaks for you. Following are some tips for leaving messages:

▲ Do not turn into a machine when you are speaking into one. When you leave a message for someone, put some enthusiasm into your voice. Try to sound as though you are looking forward to the person returning your call.

▲ Leave your phone number, even for people you call frequently. They may be out of the office or not be able to get their hands on your number for any number of reasons. People often check messages from outside the office and, thanks to speed dial, don't even know their mother's number by heart. The exception is internal calls within a phone system which automatically supplies a phone extension with your message.

▲ When you leave your phone number, especially for someone whom you are calling for the first time, say it slowly and repeat it.

▲ Tell people when they will be able to reach you. If all you require is a returned message on your voice mail, say so in your message, or tell them that no response is necessary.

▲ Include your company name along with your name. We are all the centers of our own universes, but you may not play a central role in the life of the person you are calling and he may need a reminder of who you are.

▲ Say "please" and "thank you." You are more likely to get a quick response if you are courteous.

▲ Be concise. Do not ramble on and on. If it is crucial that you make a good impression in a particular message, draw up an outline before calling.

▲ Use the machine to advance the conversation. If you leave a message that just says, "I'm returning your call," you haven't furthered the project. Instead, give the person something to work with. Leave your request for information, ask her to figure out when she can meet before calling you back, or pose a question so she has time to think it over.

▲ Always request specific action. Ask for something, even if it is just a returned call.

▲ Speak clearly. You may want to tape yourself at some point to see if you are intelligible on the phone; you may be surprised at the result.

▲ Listen carefully to the outgoing message before leaving your voice-mail message. I cannot tell you how often people leave messages requesting an immediate call back when my voice-mail tape says, for example, "I will be out of the office all week and will return calls when I come back." Judging by the increasing frequency with which I encounter outgoing messages saying, "Please listen to this entire message," I am not the only one who has callers who do not listen. If you do not listen to a message, you may leave one that gives the impression that you are not paying attention.

▲ Listen to how the person pronounces his name on his recorded message if you are not sure how to pronounce it. I recently received three calls in a row from a prospective consultant who kept calling me "Ms. Gredin." I went back and listened to my voice mail to see if my name is intelligible. It sounded clear to me, and no one else has had a problem understanding it, so his message led me to believe he was not paying attention. Since I was hiring a researcher, I didn't choose him.

Constructing an Outgoing Message

I have a close friend who enjoys taking potshots at my outgoing message on my office voice mail. He tells me when it's too long, too short, or not energetic enough, or when I've gone overboard with verve. Even though it sometimes hurts my feelings, his critiques of my recordings have taught me a lot about what works on an outgoing message and what does not. Considering that an outgoing message may be a person's first opportunity to make an impression, I am often amazed at the poor quality. It is not uncommon for me to meet an energetic and interesting person face-to-face, and then find an uncompelling, rambling message greeting me when I call her in the office. The best messages can usually be found within companies that have provided guidelines for recording an outgoing message properly. If you've never had the benefit of any training, use the following tips to make sure you're on track with your message.

△ Keep it short. Be considerate and realize that people do not want to listen to a long phone message. Assume that people realize you are not available to take their call if you do not pick up the phone, and do not bother saying it.

△ Do not say the "b" word. By now, most people know that they should leave a message after the beep; again, do not bother saying it.

△ Do not say your number. Saying your name and your company name is sufficient; your number is superfluous, unless there is some special reason for it.

△ Do not apologize for missing someone's call. If you want to let people know that their calls are important, the subtext of apologizing for missing their calls, say that instead. It is more positive.

△ Make specific requests. Ask your callers to tell you when you can reach them. If you want people to leave their numbers, request that too.

△ Tell where you are. If you travel a lot or are frequently unavailable for long stretches, update your message frequently. I like the "It is the week of March 1 and I will be in the office all week. . . ." approach.

△ Reassure your callers. If you are out of the office or traveling, let them know that you are checking messages and will return calls.

△ Create an escape hatch. To keep callers from falling into the black hole of voice mail, give them the option of pressing "0" or another extension if possible.

△ If pressing a key to skip your message is possible, state that at the beginning of your message.

△ Listen to your message to be sure it has some energy in it. People who call you want to be greeted with some enthusiasm and feel as though you are glad they called.

△ Get rid of "ums" and "ahs" in your message.

△ Don't make a promise about a time frame within which you will return calls, unless you know you can consistently follow through.

RUNNING A CONFERENCE CALL

Telephone conference calls are increasingly common because of distributed work, and important issues are now being handled over the phone that might formerly have only been handled face-to-face. A conference call is like any other meeting and requires the person in charge of the call to facilitate. If you are in charge of the call, you should state the agenda, how long the conference call will last, what you hope to accomplish during the meeting, and how long you will devote to each issue. If the participants do not know each other, give them a chance to introduce themselves and briefly state how they are involved in the meeting or project being discussed. This establishes rapport and sets the stage for effective communication. If the group is large and everyone doesn't know each other, you may want to fax a list of short bios and project roles to everyone beforehand. Faxing an agenda ahead of time to everyone who will be part of the call provides them with an opportunity to air their grievances before the call begins, thereby minimizing the chance that the call will be sidetracked by people who do not agree with the agenda.

Once the conversation begins, everyone should say his name before speaking and say the name of the person he is speaking to. If you are lead-ing the meeting, acknowledge input from others so that people are encouraged to participate. It is easy to tune out during a conference call. Periodically ask if there are any questions, and bring out people who have not contributed by asking for their opinions. Set the tone for the meeting by speaking slowly so that none of what you say is lost.

Making a Conference Call the Best It Can Be

✔ Request that people keep their comments as brief as possible.

✔ Insure that everyone is looking at the same document or computer screen during a meeting.

✔ Make sure it is known that the conference call is not the time for expressing disagreement with a project agenda; that should be handled separately. Obviously, use your judgment to determine when an issue is important enough to supersede the agenda. If someone raises an issue that threatens to sidetrack the call, let her know that it can be handled some other time.

✔ Acknowledge the learning curve involved in using technology such as conference calls. Over time you will discover the best techniques for facilitating communication among your group.

✔ Don't get the call off to a bad start by bombarding people with data; this will cause people to tune out. If you must refer to numbers, include them in the fax you send before the meeting begins.

✔ Let people in the meeting know they will be called on. This keeps them listening and prevents them from doing other things while they are on the phone, which is a natural tendency for all of us. At the top of the meeting, remind people that you will be asking for their input; otherwise the call turns into a passive event.

✔ If you are working at home, turn off your call waiting and make sure you will not have any other interruptions on your phone line. Some people use their fax line for conference calls for this reason.

✔ Take steps to eliminate other potential interruptions and distractions. If you are in an office with other people, ask them not to interrupt you, or put up a note near your desk explaining that you are on a conference call and should not be disturbed. If you work at home, put up a note for delivery people, notify your doorman, or take any other steps to ensure that you will not be interrupted.

✔ No matter where you are, do not do anything else while you are on a conference call. Give the conversation all of your attention, even though it is tempting to do other things while you are on the phone. People can tell when you are not paying attention by the sound of your voice. If you do not pay attention, you also run the risk of asking a question that has already been answered or making some other embarrassing mistake.

✔ Let participants know if the system is voice-activated (allowing only one person to speak at a time) or full duplex (like a normal telephone call).

✔ Some systems do not pick up female voices as well as male ones. If you find that female voices are not coming through well, ask women to speak louder or move closer to the microphone.

✔ If you have participants who speak foreign languages, make an extra effort to draw them into the conversation.

✔ If possible, plan to have fax machines accessible to all participants in case material generated in the meeting needs to be reviewed.

✔ Get dressed; do not conduct important conference calls in sweatpants. According to Joyce Newman (see footnote), "You are not in your executive head in your sweats."

✔ If you are facilitating the call, bring people into the discussion by asking them what they think about a certain point. If someone has not spoken up during the call, ask for her opinion specifically: "What do you think, Joan?"

✔ If you are using a speakerphone so that other people can listen in, tell everyone on the conference call.

✔ Occasionally tape-record yourself so you can evaluate how you performed during the call.

✔ Line lower-level participants up for a conference call before going to the higher-level participants. Make sure the operator who is setting up the call tells the participants there will be a wait while they are linked in with the rest of the callers. This delay can be as long as two minutes; people often believe they have been cut off if the operator doesn't explain.

✔ Anticipate and plan for how long it will take to link everyone together on the call. If you have thirty people participating in a 10 A.M. conference call, you may need to begin calling people at 9:30 A.M.

✔ If you are alone in the office, stand up so that your voice will be bigger.

✔ As with any meeting, thank people for their participation and reiterate action plans, responsibilities, and the time frame for completion of each item. Be sure everyone is clear on these items.

Source: Some of the tips above came from Joyce Newman, president of the Newman Group, a New York City–based company specializing in coaching high-level executives in leadership, speaking, and media relations. She is also the co-author of *Selling Yourself: Be the Competent, Confident Person You Really Are!* (MasterMedia Ltd, 1994), (800) 334-8232.

RUNNING A VIDEO CONFERENCE

Many of the guidelines for facilitating a conference call apply to video conferencing, but video meetings are more complex. A camera in the room can make participants uncomfortable and therefore stiff. Many people do not know where to look during a video conference or how to address someone who is not in the room. Here are a few tips:

▷ Your video conference may be restricted by time, so be sure to stick to the agenda.

▷ Make reference to the camera and explain briefly where the image it's recording is being sent.

▷ Advise participants to treat the camera like someone in the room. Joyce Newman says she makes light of the camera and gives it a name, referring to it as a "guest."

▷ Participants should look at the camera only when they are addressing someone in another location; otherwise, they should look at the person who is talking. This is important because people often think they should look at the camera the whole time.

▷ It is also important to encourage participants or attendees (if applicable) to relax and react naturally to what is being said. Many people will freeze up around a camera, and it is your job as a facilitator to encourage people to relax. This is standard operating procedure before television talk shows, when the audience should be relaxed on camera.

▷ As with any meeting, discuss the time allotted for each component of the agenda. As with a face-to-face conference, you can establish signals for letting participants know when they need to wind up what they are saying. This can be pointing at your watch, raising your hand, or any other signal you choose.

▷ Build time into your schedule for getting everyone online. If you want a meeting to begin at 2:00, you will want everyone to be online at least five minutes before you want to start.

▷ Be aware of what your body language is communicating. Do not slouch, play with a pen, or fidget the way you might on a phone call.

▷ If you are in charge of the meeting, arrive early to make sure everything is running smoothly. This includes having water for attendees (without ice—it makes noise).

▷ If an outside vendor will be handling the technical end of the call, you may want to sit in on another call the vendor is facilitating, or use a vendor recommended by someone you trust. A good technical facilitator can make the difference between a meeting that goes smoothly and one that is problematic.

▷ Make sure you have one person in each location who understands the equipment. This should be someone who has used the equipment before, and who can perform basics such as setting a data line needed for video conferencing.

▷ If possible, position participants at equal distances from the camera.

▷ Make sure that you know how to operate the control panel before the conference begins. You want to avoid fiddling with the device after the conference begins.

▷ Be sure that attendees have the phone number for the person convening the meeting, in case any problems arise.

▷ If the system has memory positions for the camera, program these for where participants are sitting, or for the positions of chairs in the room, and remind participants not to move chairs when they arrive.

▷ A dedicated video room will have neutral colors and lighting. Otherwise, try to avoid rooms that are light blue, beige, or white. These can create a stark-looking background. Turn lights all the way up and try to have participants' faces lighted. Natural lighting is good for a short conference during which lighting is not likely to change much, but be sure the sun is not shining directly on the camera.

▷ It is a good idea to identify the location with a tag line at the bottom of the screen or a tent card on the table.

▷ Let participants know if the mechanism is voice-switched or continuous-presence (where a controller directs who gets to be heard).

▷ If people involved in the video conference do not know each other, tent cards at each person's place are helpful. Keep in mind that the letters on these name cards need to be two or three inches high for them to be legible.

▷ Avoid white clothing; it reflects too much light.

▷ Make sure microphones are set out close enough to pick up participants' voices.

Video Conferencing Do's and Don't's

✔ **Do** be camera-conscious. Make sure that all meeting participants are within view of one of the cameras in the room. It is frustrating for people at the remote site to hear from people they cannot see.

✔ **Do** maintain a reasonable distance from the camera. Remember that the concept of "personal space" applies to video conferences just as it does to face-to-face meetings. A comfort-able view is usually from the desktop or conference table up, rather than close-ups of faces only.

✔ **Do** use "mute" selectively. Muting your microphone is the equivalent of whispering during a meeting, and it usually makes people uncomfortable. If you must mute for a private conversation, ask the remote site's permission.

(Continued)

✔ **Don't** shout. Be sure that all meeting participants are within microphone range so they can speak normally. Use the same voice you use to communicate across a large conference table.

✔ **Don't** confuse video conferencing with Hollywood. Remember that the important part of your meeting is the content. Avoid getting hung up on adjusting cameras, directing action, and framing shots.

Source: These tips are from Compressions Labs, Inc. (CLI), a manufacturer of video conferencing equipment in San Jose, California.

DESKTOP VIDEO CONFERENCING

Desktop video conferencing enables you to conduct a video conference through your computer. It works through a camera attached to your computer that transmits a video image to other sites. You see the person you are speaking to if the conference is one-to-one. If your desktop video conference involves many people, the computer screen shows an image of the person who is speaking. The person who is speaking sees the person who last spoke. Here are a few tips for using this technology.

△ You will be looking at the computer screen and having your image transmitted to other computer screens. Position your camera so that it projects your face and not just your ear. Many cameras have a "local feed" function that lets you check the image of you the camera is projecting.

△ Do not rock back and forth in your chair.

△ Resist the tendency to look at the screen image of the person you are talking to. Instead, look at the camera because otherwise the image your camera picks will be of someone looking away from the camera.

△ Resist the natural tendency to move closer to the image of the person you are talking to when a conversation becomes intense. This may move you out of view of the camera.

△ Large arm movements and other movements will blur the image.

△ Remember that your image will be picked up when you speak and remain on the next speaker's screen after you speak. This means you cannot look bored, shuffle through papers, or file things the way you would on a telephone conference call.

△ People who use this technology recommend that you do not make any noises you don't intend to broadcast, such as blowing your nose during a desktop video conference.

△ If you are doing a desktop video conference, dismantle your call waiting, turn down the ringer on your fax, and otherwise eliminate the possibility of distractions. Treat the conference as you would a meeting with someone in the room.

△ Talk at a normal volume level; you do not need to shout.

GETTING THE MOST OUT OF YOUR CELLULAR PHONE

Cellular phones are gaining on computers as the most crucial tool of the virtual office. They make it possible for people to keep in touch almost no matter where they are. But sometimes this technology works better than at other times. I've had important discussions terminated three times in a row. I've tried to communicate crucial details over crackly lines, and I have experienced frustration and confusion when, after being cut off, phone calls were delayed further as both parties tried to return calls only to get a busy signal. Following are some basic tips for making sure you get the most from your cellular phone and save money. See the section on security later in this chapter for tips on how to avoid cellular phone fraud.

▶ If possible, make important calls during the least busy time of the day. If you need to make an important call, avoid drive time. 6 A.M. to 10 A.M. and 3 P.M. to 6 P.M. are the busiest times for cellular calls, and therefore the times of day when you are most likely to run into problems making a connection or securing a clear line for an extended time.

▶ Know that cloudy or drizzly weather can affect call clarity as well as accessibility.

▶ Have voice mail that picks up if you are outside of a cell site and cannot be reached.

▶ Find out when your carrier's rates go down and return calls or leave messages during off-peak times. Some carriers even offer free weekend calling, time you can use to leave messages for people.

▶ Give out your number selectively, because you will pay for all calls you receive as well as the ones you make. You can buy a phone that is also a pager, which lets you see who is calling before you pick up the phone.

▶ When you are leaving a phone number as part of a message from a cellular phone, always repeat it because the phone may cut out just as you are saying one of the digits.

▶ Always tell someone what you will do if you get cut off—if you want them to call you back or if you will call them back. It cuts down on confusion.

▶ Get to know "dead spots." Some federal land and even things like pine trees can cause problems with your cellular connection. Learn the dead spots (spots with no cells) or the variables that will cause you problems, and avoid making important calls when you are near them. Crossing state lines may mean you are entering a new cell site; this can make it more likely that you will lose a call.

▶ If you use your phone frequently in rural areas, you might want to consider a fixed mobile or a transportable rather than a pocket phone. Fixed mobile and transportable phones have more wattage, which may be necessary in rural areas where cell sites are farther apart.

▶ Know that your phone may or may not work in other parts of the world; other countries may have different standards that your phone may not be compatible with. Check with your carrier before planning to use your phone abroad. For example, the United Kingdom and Japan do not have standards that are compatible with U.S. standards. Compatible areas include: Australia, Brazil, Canada, Chile, Costa Rica, Hong Kong, Indonesia, Israel, most of Mexico, New Zealand, the Philippines, Singapore, South Korea, Thailand, Taiwan, and the Virgin Islands.

▶ Have your cellular phone calls forwarded to your destination. If you want to save money, offer to call people back from a phone in the office.

FAXING WITH FINESSE

Faxing is old hat to most of us, but that doesn't mean we are doing it as well as we can. Following are some helpful tips.

▷ Call to check before faxing anything over two or three pages. Long faxes tie up phone lines and use lots of paper and ink. Many people prefer messengers or overnight delivery for long correspondence.

▷ Written communication runs the risk of being misunderstood. You may want to make a phone call to accompany your fax, to minimize the chance of a misunderstanding.

▷ If you are faxing documents to a hotel desk, the recipient will be charged a per-page fee. This may not matter to the recipient. On the other hand, some people will not appreciate a long fax at a dollar or two a page.

▷ If you are sending a fax to a home-based business owner, verify that it is okay to send it late at night. I have my fax machine ringer turned all the way down, but not all machines have that function and a late-night call can be disruptive.

▷ Do not send a cover page unless necessary. Home-business owners usually do not want or need a cover page on a document; it wastes paper and ink.

▷ People have a tendency to want to fax things as a way to get off the phone. But it's important to make sure that the person you are talking to understands what information you need and doesn't just send you a "reflex fax."

▷ Double-check the fax number you have typed in before pressing the "send" button.

▷ Do not write in the margins. Most fax machines will cut off what you wrote when they print out your text.

WRITING AND SENDING GOOD E-MAIL

If you are working in a virtual office, you may send more e-mail than you used to. How you present yourself in e-mail will impact how you are perceived. Every communication you have with people is judged. A typo, poor grammar or punctuation, and an inability to express yourself succinctly will reflect negatively on you. "I have never seen a senior manager look at a typo and say, 'Gee, she must just not have had enough time,' " says Joy VanSkiver, president of The Writing Exchange, a Chatham, New Jersey– based training and consulting firm specializing in business writing. "They see carelessness."

Despite this reality, people still believe that e-mail with typos and stream-of-consciousness text is acceptable. Part of the reason for this may be that when e-mail was first introduced, it offered limited editing capabilities. Many of the initial trainers in e-mail usage also encouraged this belief by promoting e-mail as an efficient way to send a message that would be held to a lower standard. Keeping these tendencies in mind, apply the following techniques to make sure your e-mail writing is up to snuff.

▲ Proofread before you send. Since you are saving time by writing e-mail, take a few minutes to proofread your correspondence. Don't think that because you are done writing, you are done. Get your thoughts down and then return to the e-mail and look for misspellings.

▲ Use the inverted pyramid. This is one of the first rules journalists learn: Put the most important details at the top of a story, in case an editor needs to cut your story to fit it in the paper. Your reader may not read your entire e-mail, so put important information up front. Because many people find it difficult to organize their thoughts before they write, write e-mail in whatever order it comes to you, and then move the information around into a logical format before sending it.

▲ Make your messages easy on your readers. Don't write e-mail that is a big blob of text with no paragraph breaks or headings. This is difficult for people to read, which means they may not read it. Be sure to follow all the rules of structure that you would follow if you were writing a letter. Collect recommendations under a heading called "Recommendations," have a "Requested Actions" section, or summarize your points in a conclusion. More people will understand your message this way.

▲ Do not send "knee-jerk" e-mail. Just because you receive an e-mail message does not mean you must respond in e-mail format. For example, if your manager asks you how one of your accounts is faring, you can send a bottom-line e-mail and follow up with a hard-copy detailed report. Long e-mails can be difficult to read; use your judgment about the best way to respond to an e-mail message.

▲ Avoid wordiness. Just about everyone needs to edit their work. After you write something, go back and evaluate whether you can take words out or substitute words for long phrases.

▲ Do not type in all caps. This is the equivalent of screaming at your recipient and it is hard on the eyes.

▲ Indicate what you want the recipient to do after reading your e-mail. If no response is necessary, say so.

▲ Do not use e-mail as a steam valve. As with the telephone, many people are braver in e-mail than face-to-face. If you shoot off an angry e-mail without thinking about how it will be received, you will hurt only yourself.

▲ It is easy for e-mail messages to be misunderstood. If you are sending an important message that could be misunderstood, make a phone call to go with it.

▲ Be discriminating about who you cc e-mail to. If you frequently send irrelevant e-mail to people, they may stop reading your messages.

▲ Be sparing with graphics; they take a long time to download.

▲ Request a time frame within which you would like your recipient to respond.

▲ Keep your e-mail messages short, ideally no more than two or three paragraphs. If you choose to distribute a lengthy document electronically, attach it as a separate document and provide a short cover note. This is so people can review the note quickly and save the longer document for later.

▲ Do not daisy-chain (forward your message attached to a number of other ones). It's okay to attach your note to one other and send it to someone else, but sending a number of notes makes for a confusing message. Instead of forwarding a note and attaching your own that says, "I agree with Fredricka," write your own note saying, "I just received a note from Fredricka that said. . . . and I agree."

▲ Be aware that all e-mail is company property (look for more on this in the security section later in this chapter). It is not difficult for other people in the company to see your e-mail. This is true even if you delete your e-mail because it is often backed up on system files.

▲ Limit a message to one topic. People who file messages in work folders for reference or action will appreciate this.

▲ Always include a descriptive subject line. Some people receive 150 e-mail messages a day. An interesting and accurate subject line will increase the likelihood of your note being read.

▲ Do not send your message again and again. If you have communicated your message through a fax, voice-mail message, or other medium, do not replicate the data in an e-mail message.

▲ Do not expect an immediate response. Just because e-mail enables you to communicate instantly does not mean you should expect an immediate response to your message. It is important to show respect for other people's schedules.

If you need more information on communicating through the written word in the workplace, look in *The Writing Exchange Business Style Guide* by Joy VanSkiver (Wrex Press, 1995), available at (201) 822-8400, 466 Southern Blvd., Chatham, NJ 07928.

LEARNING TO SHARE WITH DOCUMENT SHARING

As fewer and fewer workers sit in the same room sharing documents, and more work is done in groups over computers, document sharing is becoming increasingly important. Document sharing means that a variety of people can look at or edit an electronic document and then return it to where they found it.

There is a certain level of control that the software and hardware you use will exert over how you access and work on documents. Other decisions will be made by *you* about how you want to structure your group's or company's access.

1. You can download files from a network, change them, and return them. This can be risky, however, because the software contains no checks and balances for the changing of work. For example, the software may not tell you who made a change or when it was made. It also may not keep each version so that changes can be reconstructed or deleted.

2. Some document-sharing software knows that someone is using a document and will not let two people make simultaneous changes.

3. Document management programs will manage access to documents even more. These make accessing a program similar to going to the library. Users can see when a document has been checked out and by whom. When it has been returned, someone else can access it. This software also lets you choose whether or not to copy over old versions of the document.

The document manager also determines how many people get *write*, as opposed to *read-only*, access and whether or not they want to keep previous versions of a file.

When a document is shared *real-time*, two or more people are working on it from different locations simultaneously during a telephone or video conference. The person running the meeting starts out with control over the document. During the meeting, this control is relinquished as other people become involved in the discussion and work on the document. Following are some tips for keeping real-time document sharing running smoothly.

△ As with any other meeting, establish ground rules for participation in the meeting, which in this case means working on the document.

△ Taking turns working on the document is imperative because the technology takes text in the order it receives it and will print nonsensical text if two people are typing at once.

△ Remind people not to hold onto the mouse during the meeting—a nervous habit—because in share mode, mouse movements are the sum of everyone's activity.

△ When a group is sharing an application or document, each person needs to announce when he is going to work on it.

△ Remind yourself to use white-board capabilities. This function enables you to sketch something while you are talking about it and greatly enhances the effectiveness of communication.

USING GROUPWARE EFFECTIVELY

As you might guess by its name, *groupware* is a category of software tools that enables individuals to work in groups sharing information and moving work processes forward via computer. The term is used to describe software products such as Lotus Notes and others that allow you to build applications based on your needs for sharing files, uploading and downloading information from databases, and tracking processes. Groupware also includes e-mail and discussion databases.

Working in a group is never easy; online communication has the potential for even more problems if it's not handled carefully. Take the following steps to get the most out of groupware if you work outside of the office.

1. Find out what your company has created. Ken Lownie, president of Connexus, an Andover, Massachusetts–based consulting firm specializing in helping companies implement groupware, suggests conducting an inventory of the applications your company has in place that could provide you with access to the information and people you need to reach when you work outside of the office. Take inventory by talking to the groupware administrator or groupware project manager at your company.

2. If you are using the groupware from Lotus Development called Lotus Notes, or another program that has this feature, learn about *replication*. Replication is the transfer of data from a computer at your central work site to your desktop computer. By bringing documents to your desktop computer rather than working while connected to the central computer via modem, you save time and money. Phone costs will drop because you are connected only during download and upload, and you save time because response from files on your desktop is better than that from data traveling over a modem.

3. Think about possibilities. Ask yourself what applications could be put in place to enhance your remote access. Take action toward having these applications built by talking to the groupware project manager. Ask what processes could be enabled in groupware that could tie you into the flow.

4. The discussion database component of groupware can contribute to information overload if it is not handled properly. To keep discussion databases from being used for venting or as a means for generating simply more information to wade through, use the tool to address a process. This means focusing a discussion database on something specific such as improving turnaround time for customer orders, gathering consensus on marketing strategy, or collecting feedback from customers on a proposed price increase.

5. Make your subject line in a discussion database catchy, but also descriptive. Do not make it too difficult to understand or people will not be enticed to read your message.

USING A MATRIX TO CHOOSE THE RIGHT REMOTE COMMUNICATION TOOL

The material in this section is developed from work done by research director Andrea Saveri and Tomi Nagai-Rothe of the Institute for the Future, a think tank in Menlo Park, California.

More Groupware Tips

✔ Agree as a team how often members should check databases.

✔ Limit the length of entries in groupware and encourage use of e-mail for one-to-one communication, to cut down on clutter in the system.

✔ Assign someone the role of database manager. This person is responsible for the editing, filtering, and categorizing of comments in the database. This person keeps the discussion on track and makes sure it is logical and easy to follow.

✔ Provide shared address books, either electronic or on paper, so that participants in a discussion know whom they are talking to.

✔ Do not use a discussion database as e-mail. It has many more capabilities. It should be used to make general comments, post responses to issues in the database, and provide information to the discussion at large. Information that would be useful to many should be posted once in the database, as opposed to sending e-mail to multiple recipients.

✔ As a remote user, be sure to replicate databases both just before and just after using. Pull down changes before you start working and send any of your updates to the server right away. If you do not replicate after use, your changes will not make it to the server until the next time you dial in.

✔ If you need to download a large, widely-used database, do so when people are not likely to be using it—for example, on weekends. Your download slows things down considerably for other users.

✔ Find ways to consolidate what you plan to download. If there is a long memo you want to read, highlight the entire document, choose Copy from the Edit menu, and then go to Compose Mail. You are actually posting your document to your local mail database. Now you can read your mail off-line.

These matrixes will assist you in choosing the appropriate tools for each mode of communication. We all have forms of communication we use most frequently, either because we are comfortable with them, or because they are easiest for us to use. But using technology effectively requires more than choosing a medium based on habit. It requires you to put careful thought into what you want to accomplish, the circumstances of the communication, and the information being communicated. The matrixes below take into account work relationships, culture, the number and distance of people, the nature of interaction, the frequency and duration of your communication, and the purpose of your communication. Keep in mind when you are using the matrixes that they contain suggestions of what works well. The best solution for your communication may differ if one variable carries significantly more weight than others in a given situation.

Matching the Medium to the Message

Each matrix can be used in two ways:

1. Look across the top of the matrix for the communication tool you want to use and check it against the circumstances of your communication.

2. Identify the circumstances of your communication and check the technology you intend to use for it. Then check the appropriateness of the technology you have in mind.

Definitions of Matrix Categories

Work Relationships

It is important to take a close look at the people you are communicating with when choosing a technology. Their relationship to you, how long you have known them, the project stage, and their commitment level to the project will all affect what technology is best for your communication. Paying careful attention to the subtleties of work relationships will enable you to avoid being insensitive, rude, or overly familiar by choosing the wrong communication tool.

1. **Relative Power.** What is the nature of the power relationship between you and the people you are communicating with? Are you all on equal footing in a grassroots effort to move a project forward? Are you part of a hierarchical team with varying degrees of power and influence among people who are part of the communication?

2. **Personal Relationship.** How you communicate with someone you know well is different from how you relate to someone you just met.

The same kind of sensitivity is appropriate when you are choosing a communication tool.

3. **Stage of Work.** The way you interact when you are starting a project is different from the interaction that occurs when you are in the midst of a long project in which decisions have been made and roles are clear. Some tools are more appropriate for one stage than for another.

4. **Relative Work Priorities.** Communicating with someone who shares your priorities is very different from trying to get the attention of someone who is ignoring your request. For this reason it is important to understand how each participant in a communication ranks a particular communication.

Culture

Cultural differences can relate to ethnic or national background, function or professional discipline, company or department, gender, age, or other social and technical factors. Recognizing when differences exist and factoring that knowledge into your communication decision will make for more clear communication.

Number and Distance of People/Nature of Interaction

Some tools are better than others at bridging distances, time zones, and large numbers of people. If you are communicating with one other person, chances are you will choose a different tool than if you are addressing a group of more than ten.

Frequency and Duration

When you are involved in a long-term project, your communication with coworkers is very different from how you would contact someone with whom you communicate irregularly. The tools you use will vary with these changes.

Purpose of Communication

Are you brainstorming, looking for feedback, coordinating schedules, or do you have other goals for your communication? Knowing the activities that will take place during a communication and the purpose of a meeting will clarify which tool you should use.

Key to Ratings:
● Supports need very well
◗ Highly dependent on other factors
○ Does not support need very well

Communication Tools Matrix: Separated by Place/Same Time

	Audio Conference	Video Conference	Remote Screen Sharing
WORK RELATIONSHIPS			
Relative Power			
Communication among colleagues, equal in power	●	●	●
Communication across levels of power, seniority, hierarchy	◗	◗	◗
Personal Relationship			
Never met	◗	◗	○
Recently met/familiar with person(s)	●	●	◗
Know person(s) very well	●	●	●
State of Work			
Initial stages of orientation and trust building	◗	◗	○
Setting goals, roles, responsibilities, and commitment to action	◗	●	●
Implementation of work and high performance	●	●	●
Renewal, transition, reflection	◗	◗	○
Relative Work Priorities			
Communication involves shared priorities	●	●	●
Communication does not involve shared priorities	◗	◗	○
CULTURE			
Communication crosses cultural boundaries	◗	◗	○
Communication involves multiple languages	○	○	◗

(Continued)

	Audio Conference	Video Conference	Remote Screen Sharing
NUMBER AND DISTANCE OF PEOPLE			
Communication is with one other person	●	○	●
Communication involves two to ten people	●	●	◗
Communication involves more than ten people	◗	◗	○
Communication crosses one time zone	●	●	●
Communication crosses many time zones	◗	◗	○
NATURE OF INTERACTION			
Communication is from one to many people	○	●	●
Communication is from many to one person	○	●	○
Communication is from many to many people	●	◗	◗
FREQUENCY AND DURATION			
Communication is a regular, frequent pattern or drumbeat	●	●	●
Communication is irregular and unpredictable	●	◗	○
Communication is ongoing, a permanent activity	●	◗	●
Communication is temporary, short duration that will end	●	◗	○
PURPOSE OF COMMUNICATION			
Encourage collaboration of groups	●	●	●
Support individual work	○	○	○
Make decision(s)	●	●	◗
Brainstorm	◗	●	●
Manipulate/process information	○	◗	●
View documents, plans, designs with others	○	●	●
Distribute, disseminate information	○	○	●
Obtain feedback from others	●	●	●

	Audio Conference	Video Conference	Remote Screen Sharing
PURPOSE OF COMMUNICATION (Continued)			
Coordinate people, work, or schedules	●	●	●
Support teams or processes in between events or meetings	●	●	●
Serve as the main event	●	●	◗

Source: This matrix is adapted from research conducted at the Institute for the Future, Menlo Park, California, 1994.

Key to Ratings:
● Supports need very well
◗ Highly dependent on other factors
○ Does not support need very well

Communication Tools Matrix: Separated by Place and Time

	E-Mail	Voice Mail	Computer Conferencing	Fax	Lotus Notes
WORK RELATIONSHIPS					
Relative Power					
Communication among colleagues, equal in power	●	●	●	●	●
Communication across levels of power, seniority, hierarchy	◗	●	◗	◗	◗
Personal Relationship					
Never met	○	◗	○	○	◗
Recently met/familiar with person(s)	○	●	○	○	○
Know person(s) very well	●	●	●	●	●
Stage of Work					
Initial stages of orientation and trust building	○	◗	○	○	○
Setting goals, roles, responsibilities, and commitment to action	○	◗	●	◗	◗
Implementation of work and high performance	●	●	●	●	●
Renewal, transition, reflection	○	◗	◗	○	◗
Relative Work Priorities					
Communication involves shared priorities	●	●	●	●	●
Communication does not involve shared priorities	◗	●	○	◗	○

	E-Mail	Voice Mail	Computer Conferencing	Fax	Lotus Notes
CULTURE					
Communication crosses cultural boundaries	○	◐	○	◐	○
Communication involves multiple languages	○	○	○	◐	○
NUMBER AND DISTANCE OF PEOPLE					
Communication is with one other person	●	●	○	●	○
Communication involves two to ten people	●	●	●	◐	●
Communication involves more than ten people	●	●	●	○	●
Communication crosses one time zone	●	●	●	●	●
Communication crosses many time zones	●	●	●	●	●
NATURE OF INTERACTION					
Communication is from one to many people	●	●	●	●	●
Communication is from many to one person	◐	◐	●	◐	○
Communication is from many to many people	◐	○	●	○	●
FREQUENCY AND DURATION					
Communication is a regular, frequent pattern or drumbeat	●	●	●	●	●
Communication is irregular and unpredictable	◐	●	○	●	○
Communication is ongoing, a permanent activity	●	●	●	●	●
Communication is temporary, short duration that will end	◐	●	○	●	○

(Continued)

	E-Mail	Voice Mail	Computer Conferencing	Fax	Lotus Notes
PURPOSE OF COMMUNICATION					
Encourage collaboration of groups	○	○	●	○	●
Support individual work					
Make decision(s)	○	○	◗	○	●
Brainstorm	○	○	●	◗	●
Manipulate/process information	◗	○	◗	○	◗
View documents, plans, designs with others	○	○	●	◗	●
Distribute, disseminate information	●	◗	●	●	●
Obtain feedback from others	●	●	●	●	●
Coordinate people, work, or schedules	◗	●	●	◗	●
Support teams or processes in between events or meetings	●	●	○	◗	●
Communication serves as the activity itself	○	○	●	○	○

Source: This matrix is adapted from research conducted at the Institute for the Future, Menlo Park, California, 1994.

SECURING YOUR INFORMATION

Security of information is a major concern for many employers, and it stops some of them from instituting telecommuting programs. There is no denying that information is easier to protect when it is concentrated in a central work site; as soon as portable computers are sent into the field, the chance of proprietary information falling into the wrong hands increases. People also tend to be more lax about security measures in a home office because they do not think about security.

However, the security of a traditional office is sometimes overestimated. After all, the IRS has employees working at home, and they are sticklers for everything. Some offices have locking filing cabinets, combination locks, and surveillance cameras, but the vast majority of the time, information is readily available for the taking if someone wants to steal it. An office provides an illusion of tight security, but not always much more. Gil Gordon, editor of *Telecommuting Review* and president of Gil Gordon Associates, a telecommuting consulting firm based in Monmouth Junction, New Jersey, points out that most people can walk out of their offices unchallenged about what secrets or proprietary information they are taking with them.

Your obligation as an employee is to follow the same security rules when you are telecommuting that you follow when you are in the office. Some employers will stipulate the security measures you must take if you access the computer network from home. AT&T requires that when home-based computers access the company network, a software lock must be placed on the system whenever it is left unattended. Other employers do not spell out the security measures that must be taken at home,

Protecting Portable Data

Even if the loss of your computer does not result in a major security breach it will be a major inconvenience to lose your computer with all of your data on it. The chances of getting a stolen system back are slim. By the time you realize what you're missing, the thief will have erased your hard drive and resold your system.

There are a few ways you can guard against this.

✔ Back up your information frequently. This will minimize your loss. You can obtain a mobile tape drive for backup in case you do lose your system. This will also protect you in case you simply drop your computer.

✔ Use removable hard disks that allow information to be kept separate from the computer.

✔ Because I live in New York City, I like this last one. Get a computer bag that does not look like a computer bag. If you are carrying a traditional computer carrying case in New York City, I have always believed you may as well wear a sign that says, "Expensive equipment inside, please steal." Newer-designed carrying cases that look more like backpacks are a good solution.

but require that you maintain a level of security equal to what exists in the office. This can include things such as storing proprietary information in a locked file cabinet or desk when it is left unattended. Disposal of proprietary information will also be handled carefully. You will most likely be asked to return the information to the corporate location for shredding or recycling.

If you work in a telecommuting center, you will need to be vigilant about security because there may be employees from many different companies sharing your work area. Mobile workers run the greatest risk of security breaches, because they work outside of the office more than most other employees. Below are a few options for stepping up security.

▶ Have servers not connected directly to the mainframe or LAN.

▶ Use a call-back system for reaching a central computer in which the central computer dials a telecommuter's home or other prearranged number.

▶ For data security from people who want to steal what you have on your system, you have a few choices. Most new laptops have password protection, but this can be bypassed easily if someone steals your system, brings it to a dealer, and says he forgot the password. So if you want to protect your data, you should obtain security software that makes it impossible to access your files.

▶ Encryption is the best form of data security. When you finish working on a file or files, you can request that the system encrypt that file or a directory of files.

▶ Request a clause in your contract about who is responsible if there is a security breach because you are working outside of the office.

▶ If you work at home, train your family to respect your work area. Tell your kids that when the computer is on, it is off-limits, for example.

Protecting E-Mail When you work outside of the office you will probably send more e-mail messages, leave more voice mail, use cellular phones and calling cards more often, and transmit more data through faxes and modems. Research from Telecommunications Advisor, Inc., a Portland, Oregon, consulting firm, says that in 1993 there was $3.3 billion worth of fraud just through calling cards,.voice mail, cellular phone, and regular phone systems.

Following are some of the facts about how insecure your data is and some ideas for protecting yourself.

E-mail messages can be intercepted during transmission or read on your computer in the office without your knowledge. Lots of companies now have warning banners on their e-mail systems that say the system is company property and your company may monitor what is sent. This is considered good legal protection for any company heads or managers who want to snoop around in e-mail. At the writing of this book, there was no law protecting e-mail similar to the one that protects regular mail until it is received. For this reason, you should not consider e-mail private.

When you send e-mail through the Internet, it is even easier to intercept than when you send e-mail inside the office. The reason is that computer hackers can, and do, tap into phone lines and intercept e-mail easily. Hackers watch phone lines for unencrypted transmissions and grab them. Not only does this mean that they can read what you are sending, they also find out your address and your recipient's address, which they can use to break into your computer system. A trusted address enables a hacker to gain access to a computer system by posing as a person who is allowed into the computer system. Hackers may be interested in what is in your file, but they may also just want your e-mail address as a vehicle to gain access to a system.

If you are sending e-mail only within a company-wide e-mail system, the security of your e-mail will depend on what kind of passwords the system allows you to establish and how those passwords are managed. Following are some precautions you and/or your company should take to protect your transmission of information. They are from Dave Powell, editor of *Infosecurity News*, a Framingham, Massachusetts–based bimonthly magazine for people who are in charge of voice and data security in business, education, and government.

▷ Set up your company-wide computer system so that a user is knocked off the system if a password is entered incorrectly three times. This will stop people from entering a variety of words to try to figure out your password.

▷ Do not have a system that uses default passwords like "manager"; they are too easily guessed and will enable people to break into your system.

▷ Change your password frequently—at least once a month.

▷ When you choose a password, do not use something obvious like your name or the name of someone in your family, unless you mix it with a number, hyphen, asterisk, or some other variable. Powell says that any word out of the dictionary is dangerous, because people can easily obtain a computer tool that will try every word in the dictionary on your computer system until it hits on your ID. "Do not use anything that people can guess easily," Powell says. "If you collect Corvettes, "vette" is easy."

▷ Watch out for voice mail systems with factory default passwords.

▷ Do not keep your password on a piece of paper near your terminal or anywhere else someone might look for it. This includes making it part of your system "boot." Powell says lots of people make their password part of their BAT file, the file that DOS computers use to boot up each time you switch them on, in order to save themselves a step when they are turning their computers on. This is a mistake, he says, because anyone can easily look in your BAT file and find your password.

▷ Realize that sending data through a modem may not be any more secure than sending it through one of the computer online services.

▷ Faxes are not safe either. There were rumors in 1994 that Japan was capturing faxes coming into the country and distributing information to competitors. Whether or not this particular fraud occurred, the risk exists.

▷ Cellular phones are risky from two standpoints. The first is that someone can obtain your ID and number and make unauthorized calls. It's almost impossible to fight this because whenever you make a call, this information is transmitted by the phone and easily picked up by other people who have whole computer setups to capture those numbers, program them into their computers, and "become" you. The only way to fight them is to watch your bills and make sure that *you* made all the calls you were charged for. The other risk with cellular phones is that anyone using a radio scanner, which can be purchased at any electronics store, can listen to what you are saying. So save private conversations for another time.

Products to Help You Secure Your Data

The answer to security of voice and other data is encryption. You can buy all kinds of add-on devices and software, as well as products that come with encryption capability. *Infosecurity News* publishes an annual *Buyers Guide*, which lists over 900 security products. The *Buyers Guide* comes out every year with the November-December issue and is available for $35. A disk version is also available for DOS or Windows for $80. For more information, call (508) 879-9792.

You can also get a simple encryption software package called ViaCrypt PGP, which is based on the freeware program Pretty Good Privacy (PGP) by Phil Zimmerman at MIT. PGP encrypts e-mail, spreadsheets, graphics, and anything else you can put on a disk. PGP is so effective in protecting data that its export is banned by the United States. PGP is available at Internet address http://www.viacrypt.com.

Cellular Phone Fraud

If you use a cellular phone, you are at risk of having your conversations listened to, your phone number commandeered by thieves, and your equipment stolen. The technology lends itself to theft and fraud because of its nature, but there are a few things you can do to reduce the likelihood of fraud.

▲ Keep any paperwork which contains your electronic serial number for your cellular phone outside of the car, not in the glove compartment. This will prevent crooks from breaking into your car and using your phone.

▲ Wait a few minutes after leaving a tunnel or walking out of an airport before turning on your phone. Crooks know that people turn on their phones after leaving tunnels or getting off planes or trains. For this reason they position themselves outside of these places with equipment that can pick up your electronic serial number and mobile identification number, which are sent to a central site whenever you switch on your phone. If you wait until you are five minutes away from these places, you may be out of their reach.

▲ Check your bills carefully and make sure that you made all the calls you are being charged for. Look for calls to unfamiliar, out-of-state, or international locations.

▲ If someone calls you and hangs up or asks for someone you don't know, report it immediately to your carrier. This could be a sign of cellular fraud.

▲ Do not tempt valets or anyone else who will be in your car. Lock your phone.

▲ Do not publish your number on a company-wide list.

▲ Ask your service provider to shut off your international service if you don't need it. Many fraudulent calls are made to foreign countries.

RESOURCES

Chapter 2: Is the Virtual Office Right for You?

"Alice Bredin's Home Office Advisor." A software package that tests your strengths and weaknesses as a home-based entrepreneur and offers a customized solution based on your responses. For more information, call The Potomac Group at (617) 577-1067.

Chapter 3: Working for a Corporation

Making Telecommuting Happen: A Guide for Telemanagers and Telecommuters, by Jack Nilles. Van Nostrand Reinhold, 1994.

Telecommuting: How to Make it Work for You and Your Company, by Gil Gordon and Marcia Kelley. Prentice Hall, 1986.

Chapter 4: Working for Yourself: Evaluating the Options

Making a Living Without a Job: Winning Ways for Creating Work that You Love, by Barbara J. Winter. Bantam, 1993.

Business Opportunities

The Business Opportunities Handbook. This quarterly publication, sold on newsstands or through the mail from Enterprise Magazines, lists franchises, business opportunities, and trade shows. (414) 272-9977.

Call for Action. A nonprofit group that provides free mediation services to people who have been defrauded and general consumer advice for small businesses on debit cards, phone service, and potential business opportunities. Volunteers across the country work hotlines at radio and television stations, providing free and confidential resolution. To find one of Call for Action's affiliates near you, contact the Washington, D.C., office at 3400 Idaho Avenue NW, Suite 101, Washington, DC 20016, or look in your local phone book. TTY/TDD services are available for the deaf, hard-of-hearing, or speech-impaired.

The Detective Information Network. A company made up of former FBI, Secret Service, and military investigators will advise you on how to search public records, or will conduct the search for you. (800) 419-4194.

National Fraud Information Center. Provides information to consumers about how to avoid consumer fraud. Will take information on fraud and enter it into the Federal Trade Commission fraud database; the FTC then takes action as it sees fit. The NFIC does not give reports on companies, but will give generic counseling to people who believe they have been defrauded. (800) 876-7060.

Franchising Resources

Bond's Franchise Guide, by Robert Bond. Irwin Publishing, Burr Ridge, IL. To order a copy, call (510) 839-5471.

Entrepreneur, Success, and *Inc.* magazines all have annual franchise and business opportunity issues. Beginning in March 1996, you can get *Franchise Buyer* magazine, a new Crain Communication publication.

Frandata Franchise Fax Service. Provides a summary of a franchisor's initial investment, fees, royalties, agreement structure, financing offers, and other information before you obtain a UFOC. The service charges $10 for a three-page "snapshot" of a franchisor. The company also sells UFOCs for approximately $100. (800) 535-9399.

The Franchise Hotline. Provides free information to help you investigate a franchise or determine your suitability for franchising. (800) 794-6722.

Franchise Opportunities Guide. A list of franchises and their total investment figures, available from the International Franchise Association. To order a copy, or for membership and trade show information, call (202) 628-8000.

The Franchise Opportunities Handbook. This government publication has a checklist of twenty-five questions you should consider before purchasing a franchise, as well as 1,200 franchise opportunities. Send a check or money order for $21, along with your request for stock number 003-009-00649-0, to the Superintendent of Documents, P.O. Box 371954, Pittsburgh, PA 15250-7954, or call (202) 512-1800.

Multilevel Marketing Resources

Direct Selling Association. For written guidelines on how to evaluate an MLM organization, send an SASE and a written request to the DSA at 1666 K Street, NW, Suite 1010, Washington, DC 20006, or call (202) 293-5760. If you have a problem with an MLM company that is a member of the DSA, you can contact the DSA's Code Administrator at the preceding address, or by fax at (202) 463-4569. The independent administrator will attempt to resolve the situation to the satisfaction of both you and the company.

Chapter 6: Customizing Your Workplace for Efficiency and Comfort

Organizing Your Home Office for Success, by Lisa Kanarek. Plume, 1993.

To get rid of junk mail, send letters to these organizations asking to have your name and address deleted from direct-mail lists.

The Direct Marketing Association
Mail Preference Service
P.O. Box 9008
Farmingdale, NY 11735

TRW Target Marketing Division
Mail Preference Service
901 North International Parkway, Suite 191
Richardson, TX 74081

Chapter 7: Technology: How to Evaluate, Buy, and Maintain Electronic Office Equipment

Computer Shopper and *PC Magazine,* Ziff-Davis Publishing, One Park Avenue, New York, NY 10016.

Home Office Computing magazine, Scholastic, Inc., 411 Lafayette Street, New York, NY 10003. (800) 228-7812.

The Internet Business Book, by Joe H. Ellsworth and Matthew V. Ellsworth. John Wiley & Sons, 1994.

Mobile Office magazine, Cowles Business Media, P.O. Box 5727, Boulder, CO 80322. (800) 271-1218.

NetGuide. A monthly magazine featuring reviews of more than 100 Internet sites or areas each month. (800) 829-0421.

900 Know-How: How to Succeed with Your Own 900-Number Business, by Robert Mastin. Aegis Publishing Group, Ltd., 1994. Newport, RI (800) 828-6961.

Telecom Made Easy: Money-Saving, Profit-Building Solutions for Home Businesses, Telecommuters, and Small Organizations, by June Langhoff. Newport, RI: Aegis Publishing Group, Ltd., 1995. (800) 828-6961.

World Wide Web Sites

How to put your business on the WWW:
http://pass.wayne.edu/business.html

Internet Business Center:
www.tig.com/IBC/index.html

Online Services

AT&T Worldnet—(800) 809-1103
America Online—(800) 827-3338
CompuServe—(800) 524-3388
Delphi—(800) 694-4005
eWorld—(800) 775-4556
Genie—(800) 638-9636
The Microsoft Network—(800) 386-5550
Prodigy—(800) 776-3449

Chapter 8: Nuts and Bolts

Financing Your Small Business, by Jeffrey Seglin.
McGraw-Hill, 1990.

The Home Office and Small Business Answer Book, by
Janet Attard. Henry Holt, 1993.

*It's Not What You Make—It's What You Keep! How to
Keep as Much After-Tax Money as the Law Allows*, by
Julian Block. Prima Publishing, 1995. (916) 632-
4400.

101 Home Office Secrets, by Lisa Kanarek. Career
Press, 1993. (800) CAREER-1.

*Why Entrepreneurs Fail: Avoid the 20 Pitfalls of Run-
ning Your Own Business*, by James W. Halloran.
Liberty Hall Press, 1991.

Insurance Resources

Free consumer booklets on insurance are available
from the Health Insurance Association of America,
1025 Connecticut Avenue NW, Suite 1200, Washington, DC 20036. (202) 223-7780.

Insurance Rating Service. A division of the Robert
S. Warner Insurance Agency; provides financial
analysis of life insurance companies for $15 each

(limit of three companies). Analysis is based on data
from A. M. Best, Standard & Poors, Moody's, and
Duff & Phelps. (800) 497-6561.

*Insuring Your Business: What You Need to Know to
Get the Best Insurance Coverage for Your Business*, by
Sean Mooney. Insurance Information Institute, 110
William Street, New York, NY 10038. (212) 669-
9250.

National Insurance Consumer Helpline. Provides
information on many types of insurance, handles
complaints, and provides advice on a recommended
course of action for dealing with grievances. (800)
942-4242.

Health Insurance Resources

Co-op America. This nonprofit organization offers
members a directory of socially and ecologically
responsible companies that also includes some
health and life insurance providers. A $20 annual
membership gets you a copy of the directory and
access to group insurance. (202) 872-5307.

Quotesmith. A company that provides free print-
outs of health insurance options, based on your
requirements, from its database of more than 400
HMOs and private insurance providers. (800) 556-
9393.

Support Services Alliance. A group of approximately 10,000 small-business owners and sole proprietors
that provides group dental, health, and life insurance. (800) 322-3920.

Wilkinson Benefit Consultants. Unlike Quotesmith, Wilkinson does not sell any insurance, but
provides a similar service from a larger database.
The price is $270 for companies of three or fewer
employees, and varies for larger companies based on
their size. (800) 296-3030.

Credit Card Merchant Status

How to Achieve Credit Card Merchant Status, by Paul
Mladjenovic. Available for $29.95 at (201) 714-
4953 or (800) 98-SUCCESS.

Chapter 12: Maintaining Visibility

Doing More Business on the Internet, by Mary Cronin. Van Nostrand Reinhold, 1995.

Making Marketing Manageable: A Painless and Practical Guide to Self-Promotion, by marketing expert Ilise Benun. This booklet tells you how to generate word-of-mouth business, create a mailing list, make cold calls, and develop a marketing plan. (201) 653-0783.

The Online Marketing Handbook: How to Sell, Advertise, Publicize, and Promote Your Products and Services on the Internet and Commercial Online Systems, by Daniel Janal. Van Nostrand Reinhold, 1995.

Six Steps to Free Publicity, by Marcia Yudkin. Plume, 1994.

State-of-the-Art Selling, by Barry Farber. Career Press, 1994. (800) CAREER-1.

Chapter 13: Communicating Effectively through Technology

Infosecurity News Buyers Guide. Lists over 900 security products. Available on disk for DOS or Windows for $80, or in a hard-copy version which comes out annually in the November-December issue for $35. (508) 879-9792.

Marketing Online by Marcia Yudkin. Plume, 1995.

Selling Yourself: Be the Competent, Confident Person You Really Are! by Joyce Newman. MasterMedia, Ltd., 1994. (800) 334-8232.

The Writing Exchange Business Style Guide, by Joy VanSkiver. Wrex Press, 1995. 466 Southern Boulevard, Chatham, NJ 07928. (201) 822-8400.

Free Services for the Virtual Office

Art Marketing Hotline. Free marketing advice for artists and other creative business owners. The service is underwritten by Color Q, a printing company in Dayton, Ohio, and is staffed by an artist with 25 years of marketing experience. (800) 999-7013.

Bootstrappin' Entrepreneur. Some of the services I've written about came from this quarterly 12-page newsletter that helps people "learn more, earn more, and bring in more business, fast—using a lot less cash." For more information, send an SASE to *Bootstrappin' Entrepreneur*, Suite B261, 8726 South Sepulveda Boulevard, Los Angeles, CA 90045-4082.

The Credit Process: A Guide for Small Business Owners. If you're looking for funding for the first time, this free 26-page booklet contains resources, a glossary of terms, and funding sources. Write to the Federal Reserve Bank of New York, Public Information Department, 33 Liberty Street, New York, NY 10045.

The Grammar Hotline. Provides free answers to short questions about writing, grammar, punctuation, spelling, diction, and syntax. To get a directory of hotline numbers, send a business-size SASE to Tidewater Community College Writing Center, 1700 College Crescent, Virginia Beach, VA 23456.

The Mail Flow Planning System. Free from the U.S. Postal Service, this IBM-compatible disk helps you evaluate the most cost-effective way to send your mail. (800) 238-3150.

The National Institute of Occupational Safety and Health. If you have physical strain from running your home business, this organization can help. It publishes newsletters and tip sheets on how to avoid on-the-job injuries, including common home-based business ailments like eye strain and repetitive stress syndrome. (800) 356-4674.

The Small Business Guide to Advertising with Direct Mail: Smart Solutions for Today's Entrepreneur. An 88-page guide containing money-saving tips and instructions for planning a direct-mail marketing campaign. Write to the U.S. Postal Service, Sales/Account Management Department, Room 5540, 475 L'Enfant Plaza SW, Washington, DC 20260-6300. (800) 238-3150.

Taking Care of Business: A Guide to Census Bureau Data for Small Business. A free 26-page booklet of demographics and business data gathered by the Census Bureau. Write to Customer Service Branch, Bureau of the Census, Washington, DC 20233. (301) 763-4100.

Web Sites

Many of these sites have links to other sites you may find valuable. The name of each web site is followed by the web site address.

AT&T Home Business Resources Web Site
http://www.att.com/hbr
If you have AT&T as your long distance residential carrier this Web site lets you join the Home Business Resources program for free and receive a quarterly magazine focused on running a home-based business; access to a 24-hour 800 number to help you determine what phone technology you need for your business; and deals on AT&T products and services. The site has articles, resources, and links to other home business web sites. If you don't have AT&T service you can still access some articles and links.

Small Business Administration Home Page
http://www.sbaonline.sba.gov/
The home page of the SBA has information on SBA loans and a listing of local SBA offices and programs

SOHO Central
http://www.hoaa.com
The home page of the Home Office Association of America.

Mobile Office Resources
http://virtual.office.com/tech/home.html/
A list of mobile office resources and web sites, sponsored by a company called Virtual Office. The site includes a list of cell phone companies and other suppliers of products for working in a virtual office.

Business Resources Center
http://www.kcilink.com/brc/
This site has articles about starting and running a small business. Its strength is in computer-related businesses or businesses selling to the government.

Entrepreneur's Law Center
http://www.axxs.com/lawctr/lawctr.html
The Entrepreneur's Law Center provides legal resources relating to capital formation and business enterprise. Its primary focus is on understanding and using some of the mechanisms available under the federal (and in some cases, state) securities laws to raise money for business development. Materials available range from a complete private placement memorandum to the SEC release on the 1992 Small Business Initiative to interesting excerpts from law review and magazine articles. It also contains links to material at other legal resource sites.

MCI Small Business Center
http://www.mci.com/SmallBiz/
The MCI Small Business Center provides a variety of resources for small businesses, from how to find an accountant to the latest small business news. Separate sections cover business financing, hiring, professional services and associations, government agencies, and news and information services.

Intersoft Solutions
http://www.catalog.com/intersof/commerce/entre-pre.html/
A list of resources for entrepreneurs, including web resources; entrepreneurs' support; businesses catering to entrepreneurs; and legal issues and resources.

Gil Gordon's Web Page
http://www.gilgordon.com
Gil Gordon is an internationally-known expert on telecommuting and his web site is a good place to check for a variety of information on telecommuting.

INDEX

ABOUT THE AUTHOR

Alice Bredin is the country's most sought after virtual office expert. Bredin writes the nationally syndicated newspaper column "Working At Home" and broadcasts her home office and virtual office tips on 200 radio stations nationwide on public radio's Marketplace program. Her virtual office expertise has been quoted by media including *Fortune* magazine, Reuters, *The New York Times*, and CNN. Bredin's popular online forums—The ExpressNet Small Business Forum and The Home Business & Telecommuting Forum—can be found on AOL and the Microsoft Network.

Bredin is also a successful entrepreneur. Her home-based business, WorkAnywhere, Inc., conducts research and advises companies interested in reaching the small business, home office, or telecommuting market. WorkAnywhere's virtual office covers the Northeast corridor. It has staff in home offfices in New York, Connecticut, New Jersey, and Maine.